KENT

A POCKET GUIDE

**Other books in the Helm
Pocket County Guide Series:**

Oxfordshire
Carole Chester

Gloucestershire
Carole Chester

KENT

A POCKET GUIDE

Frank Victor Dawes

Additional research: Kate Dawes

CHRISTOPHER HELM
LONDON

© 1990 Frank Victor Dawes

Line illustrations by Richard Allen
Maps by Graham Douglas

Christopher Helm (Publishers) Ltd,
Imperial House, 21–25 North Street,
Bromley, Kent BR1 1SD

ISBN 0-7470-0615-6

A CIP catalogue record for this book
is available from the British Library

Kent arms taken from an illustration from
G. Briggs. *Civic and Corporate Heraldry 1971*
(Heraldry Today, Ramsbury, Wiltshire)

Typeset by Florencetype Ltd,
Kewstoke, Avon
Printed and bound in Great Britain by
Billing and Sons Ltd, Worcester

CONTENTS

The County of Kent

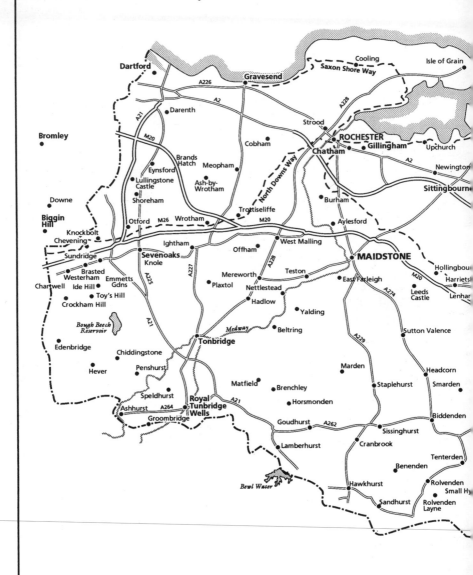

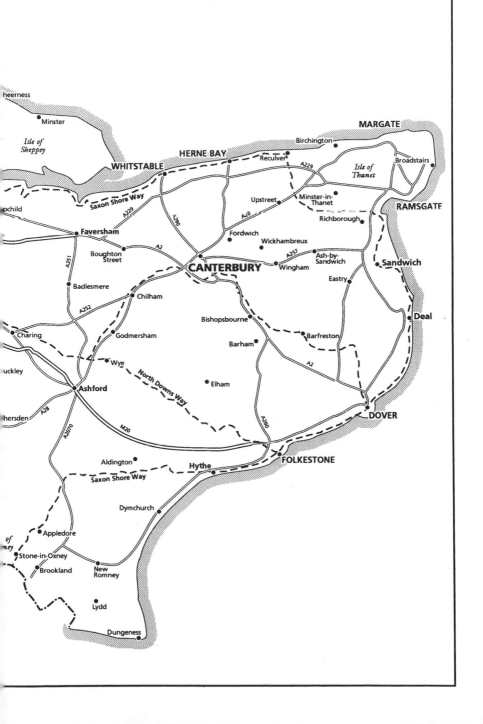

1

INTRODUCTION

'Kent, Sir—everybody knows Kent—
apples, cherries, hops, and women'

—Mr Jingle in *The Pickwick Papers*

Kent is not one of England's larger counties, but it is one of the better known, most beautiful and at the same time most ravaged. It is just over 60 miles from the celebrated white cliffs of Dover to Westerham on the Surrey border, where Sir Winston Churchill made his home, and less than 40 miles from the 'Saxon shores' of Sheppey and Thanet to Dungeness Point. This area of no more than 1,500 square miles houses over one and a half million people. As Mr Jingle suggests, everyone has heard of Kent's orchards, hopgardens and distinctive white-cowled oast houses (not to mention its women) – 'Garden of England' is the cliché almost always used. Rarely does anyone mention in the same breath Kent's cement works and papermills, gravel pits and quarries, and (up to 1989) coalmines. In other words, its belching chimneys and towering electricity pylons. The picture postcard charm of thatched and timbered villages and coaching inns clustered round Norman churches shaded by ancient yews is offset in many places by the drab terraces built for the Victorian working classes and the even more frightful 'high-rise' apartment blocks of the 1960s.

These sometimes stark contrasts make Kent a constant source of surprise to the visitor and are, for this writer at least, part of its attraction. Suddenly, in the midst of a seedy housing estate or in the grim shadow of a factory, you stumble upon the remains of a Roman villa or a Norman castle or discover some abstruse piece of myth or legend lost in the roar of a motorway. Was Wat Tyler, who led the revolt against the first poll tax, a Maidstone man or did he come from Dartford? Or Brenchley? Daniel Defoe is said to have written *Robinson Crusoe* in a backroom over a wash-house in Hartley when he was in hiding from the government – but was it the Hartley near Gravesend or the one near Cran-

Oast houses, traditional hallmark of Kent

brook? William Caxton printed the first book in English and was born in the Weald of Kent. But where? At Tenterden, or near Sevenoaks? Kent abounds in these minor mysteries to which there is no definitive answer and in villages with half-forgotten associations with the great, the good – and the bad.

The Gazetteer which forms the main part of this book includes not just Canterbury, Maidstone and Royal Tunbridge Wells, Rochester and Chatham, Leeds Castle, Hever, Penshurst, Knole and Chartwell, the Cinque Ports and the coastal holiday resorts (although all these places are covered in depth), but also the little out-of-the-way villages with fascinating stories to tell and things to see and do. To make the best use of this research, read a section in conjunction with other places marked with *. Travel Information Centres in the main towns and villages, which can provide free maps and leaflets as well as the latest information on accommodation, are listed with their addresses and telephone numbers. A brief selection of hotels and restaurants of all grades, pubs,

guest houses, youth hostels and camping sites is given, where appropriate. Museums are listed too, and there are plenty of them, from the traditional archives and archaeological collections in local public libraries, to high-technology 'time walks' like the one provided by Canterbury Heritage.

Kent is rich not just in history but in folklore, myth and legend, too. It is said that the Saxons who set up the first settlements in England around AD 450 invaded Kent under the banner of a prancing white horse, and this is the county's emblem to this day. When William of Normandy invaded in 1066, the chieftains of the 'Kentings' persuaded him to confirm the independent status of their little kingdom and this is why the word *Invicta*, or unconquered, appears on the county arms. Place names throughout Kent illustrate the Saxon heritage. Nearly 500 villages in the county end in 'den', meaning a clearing or swine pasture in the 'wold', or wood, which once covered the greater part of it. The next most common suffix 'hurst' means simply wood or forest. The time-honoured division between those living west of the River Medway and those east of it probably has its origin in the period when the earliest Saxon invaders were driven across that river by successive waves of Jutes and settled along the shores of the Thames to become 'Kentish Men' rather than 'Men of Kent' east of the Medway. The distinction still holds.

The Medway rises in the High Weald of Sussex not far from Gatwick Airport, and dallies among the orchards and hopfields of the Low Weald while being fed by a host of tributaries: the Eden, Shode, Teise, Beult (pronounced 'Belt'), Loose and Len, before carving its way north through ragstone and chalk to meet the Thames at its estuary. It is the chief river of Kent, although a mere 70 miles in length. Its little brother, the Darent, flows in an arc from the Thames at Dartford round to the Surrey border just beyond Westerham, shadowed by the M25 Orbital Motorway just outside the expanded boundary of Greater London. The rivers in the east and south of the county, the Great and Lesser Stour and the Rother along the East Sussex border, are but shadows of their former selves after centuries of silting and changing course. So, too, are the 'Islands of Kent', three out of four of which are landlocked: Grain in the north, Thanet in the east and Oxney in the south are still marked as 'islands' on the map, but in name only. They are, however, intriguing places to visit. Grain, at the tip of the Hoo peninsula, is on the doorstep of the ever-expanding

Medway towns and not much more than 40 miles from central London, yet the estuary with its container ships and tankers is busier than the few roads of this lonely shore and herons fly undisturbed over the dykes and marshes. The churchyard at *Cooling is much as it was when young Pip disturbed the escaped convict Magwitch among the gravestones in the opening scene of *Great Expectations*. Sheppey (the 'Isle of Sheep'), just across the mouth of the Medway from Grain, is the only one of the four islands still completely surrounded by water, the Swale girdling it to the south with the old towns of *Sittingbourne and *Faversham nursing their memories of the days when ochre-sailed and tarred barges carried crops of cherries and hops from their creeks. Although Sheppey is mostly marshlands, bird reserves and abbey ruins, its main port of *Sheerness has found new life as a ferry and container port since the departure of the Royal Navy. The remaining coastline of Thanet is one almost continuous conurbation from *Margate round to Pegwell Bay but behind the bucket-and-spade resorts lay mile after mile of empty fields and marshland. There is no sign of the 3-mile channel which had to be crossed by ferry at Sarre in ancient times but some of the old island rituals like the 'Hooden Horse', a mock horse's head with a flapping jaw into which coins are dropped, still appear. It may well be linked with the Jutish god Woden from whom we derive our Wednesday ('Woden's Day').

The geology of Kent is a series of belts. South of the Thames and Thanet marshlands, the North Downs (thousands of feet thick and studded with flints) run northwest-to-southeast across the county and meet the Channel in a sheer wall. Overland routes from London to the ports for the Continent of Europe beyond run parallel to this great backbone of Kent while the main rivers of the county cut through it heading for the Thames and the North Sea. Behind the coastal cliffs, 2,000ft down, are deposits of coal, around which grew the colliery villages of Betteshanger and Tilmanstone, Snowdown and Aylesham on Acol Down. To the south of the chalk, the Weald, part clay, part sand, and formerly covered by dense forest, is like a molar worn down from its former dome-like height into a broad valley between the North and South Downs, the latter entirely outside the borders of Kent. The counties of Kent, Sussex and Surrey merge imperceptibly at their landward meeting places. Substantial stretches of the ancient forest of Anderida survive, as one can see from a jetplane circling overhead in the 'queue' waiting to land at Gatwick. The Forestry Commission looks after many thousands of acres of Kentish woodland and has laid out 'forest walks', picnic sites and car parks but much of it is still privately owned. The sweet chestnut coppices are typical of Kent, cropped every twelve or 15 years for fence posts and hop poles. Some of the oak trees are a thousand years old and mentioned in the Domesday Book (an old Kent tradition is that anyone cutting down an oak will die within a year). A freak hurricane in October 1987 tore up and knocked down 15 million trees. There had been nothing like it since the Great Storm of 1703 when Daniel Defoe counted 17,000 uprooted trees in Kent before he gave up the self-imposed task. But nature renewed it all in time and will again. A range of hills with strata of ragstone runs roughly parallel to the Downs from *Westerham to *Hythe, climbing to the county's highest point, around 800ft, at *Brasted Chart. Great outcrops of ironstone are seen in and around *Tunbridge Wells. South of the Weald, bordering East Sussex to the sea, lie the wetlands of the River Rother and Romney Marsh famed for its sheep and much of it reclaimed from the sea. Inland, new expanses of fresh water have been created. In 1976 the largest lake in southern England appeared at *Bewl Water, which straddles the county borders near *Lamberhurst, and in the High Weald a valley of 280 acres was flooded to create *Bough Beech reservoir. Apart from their utilitarian purpose of supplying water to the most heavily populated county in England, these lakes provide sport and leisure facilities and a natural habitat for migratory and wading birds. Despite the fears of traditionalists, they have blended into the scenery, thanks to the enlightened policies of the water authorities.

For all the suburban expansion

of towns like Ashford and Maidstone (there remains only a narrow corridor of green between the county town and the voracious Medway Towns conurbation) Kent is still largely a county of farms and villages. Hops grow well in the fertile soil of the Low Weald. Barley grown between the Medway and Canterbury is very suitable for brewing. Wheat is a maincrop. William Lambarde, who wrote of his 'perambulation' of Kent in Tudor times described this area neatly as 'the cherry garden and apple orchard of Kent' and in time the orchards spread to the other side of the North Downs. Half the country's apples and hops and nearly all its cherries still come from Kent. The closing decades of the 20th century have seen the revival of a branch of agriculture introduced into Britain by the Romans nearly 2,000 years ago. Vineyards and wineries are flourishing at *Lamberhurst and *Tenterden, at *Ash and *Penshurst and various other places.

But Kent is more than just the Garden of England, for many centuries it has been London's nearest provider of raw materials. The Kentish ragstone quarried round Maidstone and shipped down the Medway by barge went into the building of the Tower of London by the Normans and the building of St Paul's Cathedral by Christopher Wren after the Great Fire. The iron railings and gates that provided the setting of his jewel were forged in a Wealden furnace at Lamberhurst, as were guns used by Drake and French corsairs alike. Flemish weavers, settled in towns like *Cranbrook, *Biddenden, *Goudhurst, *Tenterden, *Headcorn and *Smarden, used some of their profits to embellish their fine churches with the marble quarried from the clay between Marden and Frittenden, especially at *Bethersden. Their handsome half-timbered houses and Cloth Halls are a splendid heritage. *Dartford, in the early 1600s, was the first town in England to make paper, an industry that spread along the waterways of northwest Kent, and survives to this day. Cement manufacture followed, coating the whole area in fine grey dust.

This unacceptable face of Kent (as far as tourists are concerned) has abetted the uninformed opinion of many that it's a place of crowded and inadequate roads leading to overloaded cross-Channel ferry ports such as *Dover, *Folkestone and *Ramsgate, better driven through as quickly as possible, without stopping. Leave the motorways and trunk roads (which, as I have said, follow the same east–west direction of the first major road ever built in these islands, the Roman Watling Street), and a different prospect opens up. It takes longer, because the north–south routes across the county follow Chesterton's famous lines 'Before the Romans came to Rye or out to Severn strode, the rolling English drunkard made the rolling English road.' But these meandering lanes take us through bluebell woods, orchards and hopgardens to villages that have remained un-changed for centuries, where there are weatherboarded and tile-hung inns and oast houses, thatched cottages, Norman churches, black and white Tudor manor houses. Where cricket is still played on the green at weekends and the general stores sells everything from a bag of nails to a box of hand-made Belgian chocolates. Narrow coun-try roads lead to stately homes like Penshurst Place and moated houses such as Ightham Mote, to the well-preserved castles of *Hever, *Allington and loveliest of all, *Leeds, rising from a lake where black swans glide. Along the way there are narrow medieval bridges spanning rivers, slumber-ing abbey ruins, megalithic stones, Roman pavements, romantic gar-dens like *Sissinghurst and Great Maytham Hall at *Rolvenden, the inspiration for Frances Hodgson Burnett's *The Secret Garden*.

Kent has the two oldest cathe-drals and bishoprics in England – Canterbury and Rochester – and the glory of each is reproduced in miniature in literally hundreds of parish churches throughout the county. Each one is a treasure house of local history, telling the stories of generations since the Conquest in stone, glass, lead and brass, not just the great families like the Culpepers, Cobhams and Wyatts but old servants, soldiers and labourers who would other-wise be forgotten. Even in this destructive age, the doors of most village churches in Kent are left open for visitors. The inns have their stories, too, of ghosts and

smugglers and visiting monarchs. Down the ages writers, from Chaucer and Marlowe, through Dickens, H.G. Wells and Conrad, to Noel Coward, Ian Fleming and H.E. Bates, have lived and worked in Kent, drawing inspiration from its people and places. The Reverend R.H. Barham, born in Canterbury, set down folklore and fable hilariously in his *Ingoldsby Legends* and another man of the cloth, Russell Thorndike, captures the eeriness of Romney Marsh and its smugglers in his stories of Dr Syn, Vicar of Dymchurch.

The beauty of Kent, where it hasn't been 'developed' or other-wise ravaged, needs no advertise-ment. It is nothing short of magnificent and embellished by great architects and landscape gardeners such as Benjamin Latrobe, who also built the White House and the Capitol in Washing-ton, Edwin Lutyens and Herbert Baker, knights who built the sym-bols of the British Empire around the world, Humphrey Repton, Decimus Burton, creator of Royal Tunbridge Wells, George Devey, Norman Shaw and the Tradescants, father and son, who came from Meopham and launched a thousand 'Acacia Avenues'. Details of historic homes, parks and gardens, with opening times, are given in the Gazetteer. The open countryside in which they are set has never been more open to all, with thousands of acres turned over to 'country parks' with nature trails and picnic areas. Long-distance trails such as the North Downs Way and the Saxon

Shore Way are clearly marked and can be easily sampled in short sections.

Apart from the items mentioned by Mr Jingle, Kent is known for cricket, played from village green to county level. It is also a great place for golf courses (including three of the best along the coast at *Sandwich, where James Bond played in *Goldfinger*). Its fishing ranges from the undisturbed trout waters of Bough Beech to the 'cod mecca' of *Dungeness Point. Many of the larger towns have leisure centres with state of the art swimming pools and projectile ranges as well as courts and pitches for every conceivable type of indoor and outdoor pursuit. There are even artificial ski slopes – floodlit at Capstone Country Park and popularly known as the 'Chatham Alps'. All these facilities are listed, with details, under the relevant place names in the Gazetteer.

Always a corridor from the Channel ports to London, Kent was a favoured place from Roman times for a country estate for courtiers and civil servants and it still has a higher proportion of second homes than most other counties as well as a good many retired professional people. Since World War II it has accommodated a substantial amount of London's overspill population, and some of the new towns and villages which have been created in north Kent and around Ashford, not to mention some private housing estates encroaching on what were until recently country villages, are, frankly, a blot on the 'Garden of England'. Commuting to London and other major centres has grown into a daily major movement of population. The Channel Tunnel which is to open on 15 June 1993 is seen by many who live in Kent as a threat to their environment. Certainly, the open country crossed by the Pilgrims Way between Canterbury and the coast is being filled with new terminals, tracks and roads and Ashford, as the main terminus on the English side, with parking for 6,000 vehicles, is the scene of further development and expansion. But Kent has faced many threats to its environment in the past, from deforestation to feed the iron foundries and shipyards in the Middle Ages to indiscriminate building of tracks in all directions, some going nowhere, in the first Railway Age. It survived those threats and it will survive this one. Kent's closeness to the Continent, 22 miles away across the Straits of Dover, made it more European-minded than any other English county. Who knows, the Tunnel may renew the ancient social entity of Kent and Normandy. It was William of Poitiers, historian of the Conquest, who remarked 'Kent is situated nearer to France, wherefore it is inhabited by less ferocious men than the rest of England.' The poet Richard Church saw Kent as 'the daughter who lives next door ... has married into England'. He argued that Kent has the same sort of scenery as Normandy and should have her vineyards, too. The vineyards have been coming back, so perhaps the daughter really is going home to mother.

2

HISTORY

The first known human inhabitants of Kent were the wandering tribes of Neanderthal hunters who left their flint spears in caves at Oldbury near *Ightham. Traces of later Stone Age implements have been found among the fossilised bones of woolly rhinoceros and reindeer on the banks of the Medway at *Aylesford. An aeon before they came (and went) the Weald lay at the bottom of a great lake on whose waters giant diplodocus cruised while iguanodons grazed the shores. Bones of these creatures were found in a brickworks at Tunbridge Wells more than 55 years ago. Upheavals of the earth's crust turned valleys into hills, new rivers carved their way to seas which rose, then fell again, until some 5,000 years ago the Channel irrevocably divided Britain from the rest of the Continent. The Weald was an impenetrable forest and the nomads supported their brief lives along the river banks with fishing and hunting. In the New Stone Age, Neolithic peoples migrated from the continent, venturing up the Medway and other Kentish rivers, raising livestock, making pottery and burying the dead in the barrows and stone-lined chambers whose remains can be seen at Kit's Coty and *Trosley Country Park near Maidstone. Gradually, with the introduction of metal implements, tools and weapons, more permanent settlements formed – again at Ightham, there are the remains of an Iron Age hill fort. After three millenia of slow, painful progress the native Celts were ripe for invasion and it arrived, via the Medway, with the Belgae, an advanced people with wheel, plough and coinage. The famous bronze and wood Aylesford Bucket in the British Museum came from them, as did all kinds of smaller implements and ornaments found at All Hallows, Minster, Marden, Saltwood and Sittingbourne. They took over Canterbury, already established as a settlement at a crossing of the Stour, and made it their 'capital', and developed a thriving sea trade with the Greeks and the Phoenecians, exporting their hunting dogs and skins and buying, in return, brass, ivory and glass.

Dover Castle guards Britain's oldest gateway

THE ROMANS

In 55BC the first Roman forces waded ashore at *Deal under the bronze eagle of Julius Caesar, and returned again the following year in greater strength but it wasn't a case of *Veni, vidi, vici*, more an exploratory probe. The Romans came, saw and went and didn't return for nearly a hundred years. The key battle in AD43 was at Rochester, which they named Durobrivae. They fortified *Reculver (Regulbium) and *Richborough (Rutupiae) at either end of the Wantsum Channel, then a tidal strait between the Isle of Thanet and the rest of Kent. The remains of the latter fortress, an amphitheatre and the Triumphal Arch erected by the Emperor Claudius can be seen, together with the Pharos (lighthouse) at Dubris (Dover) which guided the galleys across the Channel from Gaul. It was from Sandwich that the Roman governor Agricola set out to map the boundaries of his domain, sailing around Caledonia and proving for the first time that Britain was an island. This was a remarkable period of civilisation which saw the founding of great cities such as London and York and the building of paved roads – the first being Watling Street, whose straight line is followed by the existing A2. The Romans introduced vines and, having recovered from their disappointment that there were no pearls in the native oysters, cultivated a taste for them. They greatly extended the Wealden iron industry begun by the Celtic people of the Iron Age, supplying the army and the fleet, or *Classis Britannica*, with vast amounts of hardware. Apart from the bloomeries where iron was extracted from ore and a few roads, the forest of Anderida remained largely impenetrable. Around the coast and in the lower Medway valley, however, the presence of the Roman Empire was visible everywhere. Civil servants built their villas here where they felt a little closer to Rome, with spacious rooms and baths, underfloor heating and immensely thick walls to keep out the cold. The area around *Upchurch on the estuary just above the Medway towns was one great potters' field keeping the *civitate* of Rochester supplied with ornaments and cooking ware. A bridge was built just downriver from the one that today carries the M2 motorway across. Canterbury (Durovernum) was another important Roman city but all that remains from three centuries of Roman occupation is a piece of tessellated pavement and under-floor heating (hypocaust) beneath the Longmarket shopping precinct. There are surprisingly few substantial Roman remains in Kent apart from about 60 villas, temples and burial places. The best example (indeed, one of the best to be found anywhere) is at *Lullingstone, south of Dartford.

THE ANGLO-SAXONS

Forty years after the last legion left Britain, recalled to Rome to guard the heart of a failing empire, the hordes of warriors in winged helmets fell upon the largely undefended island, arriving in a fleet of dragon-headed longboats at Ebbsfleet near Ramsgate in AD 449. This was the beginning of Saxon settlement of England and of the Dark Ages. The struggle to wrest power from Vortigern, the Romanised king of Kent, took some years. Hengist and Horsa, having established themselves on the Isle of Thanet, seized Richborough and Reculver and marched towards London, sacking Canterbury on the way. Unable to force their way across the Roman bridge at Rochester, they turned inland towards Aylesford (Aeglesford) where the decisive battle was fought and won. Aylesford can thus claim to be the cradle of the English nation. It was at this strategic river crossing that great battles with the Danes were fought twice in subsequent centuries, marked by repeated raids from the Continent and counter-attacks and an almost total breakdown of the law and order that Rome had maintained. Paradoxically, in the midst of the bloody turmoil that raged around the beaches and riverbanks of Kent as one wave of marauders followed another, the Christianity which had been introduced by the Romans and lapsed after their departure, was revived with the arrival of Augustine with 40 monks on a mission of conversion from Pope Gregory. Traditionally, the landing place is again Ebbsfleet and the year (very much guesswork) AD 587. As far as King Ethelbert and his wife were concerned they were literally 'preaching to the converted' and after only ten years Augustine was installed as the first Archbishop of Canterbury, primate of the Christian Church in England. The see of Rochester was established soon afterwards. Initially, Kent was supreme among Saxon kingdoms in the south but came under the domination of Wessex with its capital at Winchester. The ancient track of the Pilgrims Way from that great city to Canterbury and the

Channel coast traverses the whale-back of the North Downs. Settlement of the great forest which the Romans called Anderida and the Saxons Andresweald only began with the clearing of 'dens' or swine pastures. Settlements followed the rivers inland to places like Marden on the banks of the Teise and *Tonbridge which was part of the Saxon 'lathe' of Elsefort (Aylesford) extending along most of the Medway valley. To this day Saxon place names predominate in Kent. The roots of villages and towns that would last a thousand years were already laid when the greatest, and last, invasion of England took place in 1066.

THE NORMANS AND PLANTAGENETS

When William of Normandy landed with his invasion force on the coast of Sussex and won the Battle of Hastings, he didn't attempt to march on London through the dense forest which was crossed by only a few roads laid by the Romans and reduced to overgrown tracks during the Dark Ages. Instead, he moved around the Kent coast – then further inland than it is now – sacking Romney (*New Romney) and seizing Dover and Canterbury before heading towards London from the east, taking Rochester and crossing the Medway. At Swanscombe, near the next river crossing of the Darent at Dartford, he encountered fierce opposition from the Kentings, who managed to extract some concessions to 'the custom of Kent' from the Conqueror. The first priority of the Normans was to keep the population in check and other potential invaders out, so they built the White Tower of London and other castles up and down England and especially in Kent, with coastal fortresses like Dover Castle, others at strategic points such as Rochester and Canterbury and others inland at Allington, *Chilham, *Eynsford, Leeds, *Sutton Valence and Tonbridge.

Castles were accompanied by the building and rebuilding of cathedrals and churches because the arrival of the Norman invaders enhanced an already powerful Christian authority. William gave large tracts of Kent to his half brother Odo, Bishop of Bayeux. The first Norman-appointed Archbishop, Lanfranc, began the present Canterbury Cathedral and Bishop Gundulf, builder of the White Tower, was responsible for Rochester Cathedral and several other fine churches. As much as a third of the Kent countryside and its villages, painstakingly valued and listed in the Domesday survey of 1086, belonged to the archbishop and his ecclesiastical representatives and the monasteries and abbeys. The new lords of England, whose wealth was derived from the peasants who toiled in the fields and tended the stock, needed a ferry service to keep them in touch with their other domains in Normandy and this led to the founding of the Cinque Ports of

Dover, Hastings, Hythe, Romney and Sandwich to provide 57 ships for 15 days annually. Ships were also provided to carry knights from Kent to the Crusades in the Holy Land. When tyrannical King John lost Normandy to the King of France in 1204 (eleven years before he was obliged to sign the Magna Carta at the insistence of his barons) the Cinque Ports formed a rudimentary navy with the Constable of Dover Castle as Lord Warden. In 1278 they were granted a royal charter by Edward I, but a succession of terrible storms, one of which change the course of the River Rother, and a gradual silting process, led to the decline of them all, except Dover. The murder of Archbishop Becket in Canterbury Cathedral in 1170 by four knights who believed they were carrying out the unspoken orders of Henry II was followed by the building of a chapel and shrine in his name. For four centuries this was the destination of pilgrims. However, the ancient trackway across the North Downs wasn't the route followed by the characters in Chaucer's *Canterbury Tales* (published *c*. 1386): they travelled the old Roman road of Watling Street from London via Rochester. These were unhappy times, when Kent was ravaged by the Black Death and racked by the discontent which led to an uprising against the first poll tax led by Wat Tyler, who marched to London at the head of his peasant army and murdered the Archbishop of Canterbury and the Lord Treasurer. The coast was under constant attack by the French and, worried about the vulnerability of the Thames Estuary, Edward III built a castle on the Isle of Sheppey, which grew into a town named *Queenborough after his queen, Philippa. The same monarch brought Flemish weavers to Kent and East Anglia to train English workers instead of exporting the wool and this, alongside iron-working, became a great medieval Wealden industry. The son of Kent clothmakers, William Caxton printed the first book in English in Bruges before setting up the press in London that produced, among other books, the *Canterbury Tales*.

England and France were almost continuously at war for a hundred years in the late Middle Ages, the period of many of Shakespeare's most stirring dramas. The Black Prince, whose body lies in Canterbury Cathedral, fought the Battle of Poitiers in 1356 and more than half a century later Henry V rode through Kent on his way to meet 'brother France' and returned in triumph from the field of Agincourt. But foreign wars cost a great deal of money, and the taxation needed to pay for them resulted in more rebellion. In Kent not only peasants, but artisans and husbandmen, yeomen and gentlemen also rose up under the leadership of Jack Cade of Ashford to demand less tax and more justice. In those days it took five days to travel from Westerham to quarter sessions in Canterbury. The starting of sessions at Maidstone as well as the cathedral city led eventually to the former becoming the county town.

THE TUDORS

The ending of the Plantagenet era and the succession of the Tudors to the throne of England was to have marked repercussions on Kent in the 16th century. It was at Allington Castle near Maidstone that Henry VIII is said to have first set eyes on Anne Boleyn and he paid court to her at Hever and Leeds. The 'Holy Maid of Kent', a maid-servant from *Aldington who had visions, accurately predicted dire consequences from the affair and paid for it with her life. On breaking with Rome to secure his divorce and marry Anne, Henry tore apart the great Roman edifice of the Church and nowhere in England was the effect more strongly felt than in Kent, where vast landed estates and several archbishop's palaces were controlled from Canterbury and Rochester. As elsewhere, the monasteries were sacked and the abbeys left in ruins. Becket the Martyr was denounced for 'treason, contumacy and rebellion'. The gold and jewels removed from his shrine in Canterbury Cathedral on Henry VIII's orders filled 26 carts. Henry built up the defences of his sceptred isle against the Catholic monarchs of the Continent with a string of expensive castles around the coast of Kent (those at *Deal and *Walmer remain in an excellent state of preservation) and founded a proper navy. The proposed marriage of Mary Tudor to Philip II of Spain provoked another Kentish rebellion led by Sir Thomas Wyatt the Younger and the accession of 'Bloody Mary' to the throne in 1553 and her marriage to the Catholic king signalled monstrous persecution of Protestants. Churches throughout the county bear witness to martyrs who were burned at the stake at Ashford, Canterbury and Maidstone. Under Elizabeth I, however, the established church regained ascendancy and English Catholics and Puritan Dissenters became the martyrs.

Under the Tudors Kent, like the rest of England, prospered and played its part in the innovations of the age, the flourishing of art and architecture and the discovery of new lands across the sea. Sir Thomas Wyatt, father of the rebel who was executed on Tower Hill, wrote the first sonnets in the English language to Anne Boleyn in his chamber at Allington Castle before Shakespeare was born. Sir Philip Sidney, who when mortally wounded on a battlefield in Holland refused a drink of water and handed his flask to a wounded soldier with the words 'Thy necessity is yet greater than mine', was a distinguished poet as well as a statesman, courtier and soldier. Christopher Marlowe, whose drama ranks with that of Shakespeare, was born in Canterbury and murdered at Deptford in a brawl. In the latter part of the century Walloon refugees from Flanders flooded into Canterbury and Maidstone and country towns and villages such as Biddenden, Cranbrook, Headcorn and Smarden to play their part in the thriving wool trade. The Wealden iron industry was becoming almost too successful; in 1573 complaint was made to the Queen's Privy Council of 'the great spoil and consummation of Okes, Tymber and other wood within the counties of Surrey, Sussex and Kent by means of iron mylles and furnaces.'

THE STUART AND GEORGIAN ERAS

When Elizabeth I died in 1603, Kent was still a county of knights and gentlemen, yeomen and merchants, but a new aristocracy was rising with the Sidneys at *Penshurst and the Sackvilles at *Knole, the Finches, the Tuftons and the Culpepers, landed families whose profits from iron armaments and wool were developing the southeast fringes of London at Greenwich, Blackheath and Woolwich and colonies overseas in Virginia and New England. It was Dame Dorothy Selby of *Ightham who urged James I, the Stuart monarch who succeeded Elizabeth, to take seriously an anonymous warning of the Catholic Gunpowder Plot. In the Civil War some of the Kent gentry sided with Cromwell's Parliamentarians and a valiant attempt at resistance by the Royalists around Maidstone in 1648 was swiftly put down by General Fairfax after a famous advance over the bridge at *East Farleigh.

With the Restoration of the Stuart dynasty to the throne, the Kentish aristocracy by and large resumed its seats and continued to prosper. As already mentioned, the cast iron railings and gates of St Paul's Cathedral built by Wren after the Great Fire of London came from Lamberhurst foundry but with the introduction of coke as furnace fuel rather than charcoal and the increased demand for Wealden timber for other uses such as shipbuilding the iron industry eventually moved north. But Kent's reputation as the 'Garden of England' was established with the growing demands from the capital for its hops and fruit, cereals from Thanet and sheep from the marshlands. Its little farms with their small enclosed fields advertised peace and plenty, its woods abounded with game, its rivers with fish and its harbours bustled with activity.

Even the Dutch fleet sailing into the Medway under the very guns of Upnor Castle in 1667, pillaging and carrying off a flagship as their prize was no more than an embarrassing hiccough in an age of progress. *Chatham was the major supplier of 'men o' war' for the Royal Navy during a period spanning four centuries (including *Victory*, Nelson's flagship at the Battle of Trafalgar) and none other than Samuel Pepys surveyed the repair yards at Sheerness. The English Revolution of 1688 produced less of a ripple in Kent than its French counterpart a hundred years later when the Channel ports were a bolt-hole for aristocrats fleeing 'the Terror' and subsequent fears of an invasion by Napoleon prompted the building of Martello fortress towers around the coast and garrisons at Dover and Chatham. At the same time stately homes and parks were laid out and older houses and castles improved upon. Poets like William Blake and his protegé, Samuel Palmer, who founded the 'Ancients' group of artists at *Shoreham, left us a romantic rural idyll. Nowhere was the prosperity of Kent better reflected than at *Tunbridge Wells, the new spa town which mushroomed among the outcrops of sandstone in the woods south of Tonbridge following the discovery of a chalybeate spring by Lord North in 1606. In the sunset of the Georgian era, Decimus Burton remodelled Tunbridge Wells in Greek Revival style and it was during that spacious age of elegance that William Cobbett, on one of his *Rural Rides*, wrote 'From Maidstone to Merryworth is about 7 miles, and these are the finest seven miles that I have ever seen . . .' But the idyll was about to be trampled upon.

THE STEAM AGE

On 3 May 1830, when Victoria was still a child princess, the world's first passenger-carrying steam train, *Invicta*, passed through the first ever railway tunnel from Canterbury to *Whitstable to the ringing of cathedral bells and the booming of cannon. The Steam Age began in Georgian times but it came to maturity during Victoria's reign and inaugurated the erosion of the countryside which has been continuing ever since. Railway lines were built in all directions across Kent by competing companies on a scale that makes 20th-century motorways or the Channel Tunnel link seem no more than a modest interference with the landscape. Wherever the railway went, Steam Age industry grew, belching smoke and soot, together with street upon street of standardised terraced housing for the workers. By 1889 the Kentish villages of Deptford, Greenwich, Lewisham and Wool-wich disappeared into the maw of the newly formed London County Council and parts of the Garden of England along the Thames shore and around the lower reaches of the Medway had long since begun to look more like the Black Country. When Charles Dickens revisited Ordnance Terrace in Chatham where he spent the happiest years of his life he scarcely recognised it, since Chatham Station was built opposite. The railway brought some old Kent towns an importance they had never known before – Ashford found itself at the hub of lines converging from all points of the compass and the South Eastern Railway Company set up its workshops there. Tonbridge, another important staging post on the SER's long, straight and level Wealden route, suddenly found itself playing host to Napoleon III and the Sultan of Turkey *en route*

17

from Paris to London (via Redhill!). It also suffered three outbreaks of cholera and the deaths of hundreds of children before health controls were enforced. Kent was at the forefront of the Steam Age. Hall's engineering workshops at Dartford adapted the new power to ships both by paddle and screw and to agricultural machinery. The first steamship from England to Australia sailed from Whitstable in 1837. In 1883 the SER had actually started digging a Channel tunnel when they were obliged to stop because of a military scare.

The train introduced the concept of the seaside holiday to the crowded population of the Metropolis and the redbrick terraces crept round the coast from Herne Bay to Ramsgate as hitherto quiet fishing villages became desir-able watering places. Those unable to afford a 'proper holiday' in a seaside hotel or boarding house found consolation in the annual migration to the hopgardens to help harvest the crop and enjoy clean air while at the same time earning a little money. A single-track railway going apparently nowhere into the depths of the Weald beyond *Goudhurst relied on this invasion for its meagre profit. 'Hopping', with all its traditions of the tally man, stripping of the vines and the bitter-sweet smell of hops drying over fires in the round kilns, was very much a family affair involving all generations from toddlers to grandparents. It was finally killed off in the 20th century by the newer forms of mechanisation which succeeded steam.

THE TWENTIETH CENTURY

In 1909 the landing of a flimsy cloth-covered aeroplane on top of the white cliffs at Dover, like the maiden trip of the Invicta steam train 79 years previously, was a portent. Louis Bleriot was the first man to cross the Channel by air. A year later Charles Stewart Rolls of the Rolls-Royce partnership flew the Channel both ways in a single flight and soon afterwards was killed in a crash on the Isle of Sheppey. This isolated place was the site of the first aeroplane factory in England, set up by the Short Brothers, who in 1913 switched to building seaplanes at a works by the river at Rochester and later produced the Sunder-land flying boat which saw service over many oceans in World War II. It was on Sheppey that Winston Churchill learned to fly and Lord Brabazon achieved the first powered flight of one mile. World War I was looming and the early application of aviation was military. A field on Lord Radnor's estate at Hawkinge near Folkestone was used for ferrying Royal Flying Corps biplanes to the war zone across the Channel. Pilots took compass bearings for St Omer from two large white circles cut into the turf. The first air raids on English soil were carried out by Zeppelin airships and later Gotha bombers attacked Folkestone and

Chatham. A single 110lb bomb dropped on a naval barracks at Chatham killed 136 men. Kent was a supply base for the Western Front and the sound of gunfire across the Channel could be heard like distant thunder. Lord Kitchener, who had been War Minister from the outbreak of hostilities, left for a mission to Russia from Broome Park, his mansion on the downs at *Barham, in 1916. His ship HMS *Hampshire* was mined and he never returned. Nor did many millions of others who were shipped through the Kent ports in the four years of the war on their way to the Western Front, together with thousands of horses, vehicles, tanks, guns and supplies. There is no town or village in the county without some form of memorial to its own fallen.

Little more than 20 years later, World War II put Kent in the front line of mechanised combat. After the arrival of 337,131 troops evacuated from the beaches of Dunkirk (82,000 of them were landed at Ramsgate), Britain stood alone against Nazi-occupied Europe. From August to October 1940 the Battle of Britain raged in the skies over southeast England and fighters 'scrambled' from airfields dotted throughout Kent at *Biggin Hill, *West Malling, Hawkinge, Manston and Gravesend to shoot down nearly 2,000 Luftwaffe aircraft in dogfights in broad daylight above the wheatfields, orchards and hopgardens. Gravesend aerodrome has disappeared without trace beneath a housing estate but a plaque in the Cascade Leisure Centre remembers the 14 pilots who died in the summer of 1940 while flying from the local aerodrome. Kent Battle of Britain Museum has been established at the disused RAF station at Hawkinge near *Folkestone and a Spitfire and a Hurricane fighter are on display at Manston near *Ramsgate. A tablet set into a wall outside the village church at *Brenchley says simply 'To the undying fame of the gallant lads who fought the Battle of Britain over this corner of England'. A large part of Canterbury was devastated by a firebomb attack in 1942 but the Cathedral and much of the medieval city miraculously survived. Towards the end of the war, Maidstone came under fire from a German gun battery on the French coast – a parting shot from artillery as the new Rocket Age was ushered in by Hitler's last 'secret weapon', the V2.

In 1965 the Greater London Council extended its greedy fingers deeper into the green countryside of Kent to gather in towns such as Bromley, Beckenham and Bexley. Housing development at Biggin Hill – up to the 1960s still a rural retreat – shows how quickly the concrete jungle replaces green fields and woods. I have included Biggin Hill in this guide to Kent because, since the Battle of Britain, that is where its roots will always be, as will those of *Downe, where Darwin lived, and *Bromley whose most famous son, H.G. Wells, saw more clearly than most where the 20th century was taking us.

3

GAZETTEER

ALDINGTON

South of the River Stour, the M20 and the approach to the Channel Tunnel between *Ashford and *Folkestone, this village has two famous associations of the Tudor period. Erasmus, the Dutch priest and professor who brought the painter Holbein to the court of King Henry VIII and was a friend of Sir Thomas More, spent some time there as rector. It was an odd appointment, as he spoke very little English. The Saxon and Norman church where he preached to an uncomprehending congregation survives unaltered with its beautiful 16th-century tower. In a small Tudor house nearby, during the incumbency of Erasmus, there was a maidservant called Elizabeth Barton who became famous as the Holy Maid of Kent after claiming communication with the Virgin Mary in 1525. She entered a nunnery at Canterbury and was arrested on trumped-up charges of fraud after prophesying death for Henry VIII if he divorced Queen Catherine to marry Anne Boleyn. Like so many others who stood in that monarch's way she met an untimely end on the gallows. The ruined chapel at nearby Court-at-Street became her shrine.

APPLEDORE

The name means 'apple tree', apt enough for a Kent village, yet before the River Rother changed course during violent storms in the 12th century, Appledore was a medieval port on the Isle of Oxney. The sea is now 7 miles away across bleak Romney Marsh populated mostly by sheep but once the notorious haunt of smugglers. The Danes occupied Appledore in the 9th century and it was invaded again, this time by the French, 500 years later in 1380. They burned the church but it was rebuilt soon afterwards and restored in the 19th century. It has a battlemented tower with eight fine bells, one of them 500 years old. The roof of the church has 14th century beams and

The 14th-century bridge at Aylesford (see page 26)

there is some beautiful stained glass, including a window at the west end of the nave showing the good shepherd with a 'flock' of the wildfowl which inhabit the marshes. This, together with small painted coats-of-arms all round the church, was the work of a local artist, Godfrey Wood Humphry. Sir Philip Chute, Henry VIII's standard-bearer and a former curate of Appledore, is buried beneath the sanctuary floor in front of the alter in an unfastened coffin in accordance with his own wishes. Appledore has but one main street with Tudor houses of brick, timber and tile at either side, opening into a marketplace. It spans the Royal Military Canal, built across the marshes in 1804 to keep Napoleon's army at bay. Part of it has been taken over by the National Trust who have planted trees along its banks.

HORNE'S PLACE CHAPEL, a mile to the north of the village, is an English Heritage property, open to visitors. It was attached to a farmhouse dating from the Middle Ages and boasts a crypt, traceried windows and a barrel roof. The present farmhouse was built in the 17th century around the original timber frame. Its first owner, William Horne, was one of the commissioners sworn in to put down the revolt led by Wat Tyler in 1381 – just a year after the French attack – and found himself under siege by the peasant army.

ASH-BY-SANDWICH

Fine Tudor architecture, old inns and Brook House on the outskirts survive, but a centuries-old windmill fell into disrepair and was finally demolished in the 1950s. The 13th century church, whose copper spire can be spotted from boats out in the Channel, is more solidly constructed of huge blocks of stone. A chapel off the chancel is full of monuments to the Septvans, prominent local landowners: Sir John Septvans, who joined the rebellion of the men of Kent against King Henry VI in 1450 led by Jack Cade; from the 16th century,

Sir Thomas Septvans with his wife and seven daughters (the smaller ones carrying skulls) and Christopher Septvans in armour with his wife in an embroidered petticoat; from the 17th century Walter Septvans and his wife reading books with their six children.

VINEYARDS

SAINT NICHOLAS, Moat Farm, Moat Lane, Ash (0304 812670). Vineyard, winery and gardens with a pond clustered round a 16th-century farmhouse. Tastings and sales at the thatched shop. Picnic area. Open year round.

STAPLE ST JAMES, Church Farm, Staple (0304 812571). Self-guided tours of the 7-acre vineyard and winery and tastings are available. Open daily and Sunday afternoons from May to September.

ASH-BY-WROTHAM

Although only 25 miles from London, this village high on the hills between the valleys of the Medway and the Darent still seems isolated. During the exceptionally hard winter of 1963 it was cut off for days, ale froze in the bottle at the White Swan and foxes crazed with hunger killed and ate cats and pigs. A 13th-century church of grey stone (with some columns of chalk in the traditional Kent style) stands beside the red brick manor house built in 1637. On the south wall of the church is a memorial to James Fletcher, who retired to Ash after serving the colours at both Waterloo and Trafalgar. There is a eulogy in Latin to a rector of Stuart times Thomas Maxfield, who was 'shepherd to his flock, preacher and doctor as his purple gown shows'. It concludes: 'The tomb holds his ashes; his soul is in heaven'. Post World War II housing development has created less attractive 'villages' at NEW ASH GREEN and WEST KINGSDOWN nearby.

ASHFORD

Situated where the Great Stour River crosses the road to Canterbury from the south, Ashford has been for centuries a cattlemarket town and the crossroads of Kent. In the 19th century it became a railway junction, with lines converging on it from London, Canterbury, Tonbridge, Folkestone and Hastings. The South Eastern Railway Company set up its work there. As the 20th century draws to a close, Ashford has a pivotal role in the second Railway Age as the terminal on the English side of the Channel Tunnel, with parking for 6,000 vehicles. The local branch of the county library in Church Road (0233 20649) maintains a research room for railway enthusiasts and there is a local history room with exhibits of war and domestic and agricultural life.

Shakespeare wrote of 'John Cade of Ashford', a prosperous landowner who took the lead when the men of Kent rose in 1450 against the misgovernment of Henry VI, but most of ancient Ashford has been bulldozed to make room for office and industrial development since World War II except for a few of the narrow, winding streets (MIDDLE ROW has a house dating from 1659) and alleys leading into the church square. At one side of it stands WILK'S MEMORIAL HALL, formerly the 17th-century grammer school built by Sir Norton Knatchbull, its oak panelling crudely carved with the names of generations of boys. At the other end of the square, the vicarage incorporates the COLLEGE OF PRIESTS founded by Sir John Fogge in the 15th century. He is buried in St Mary the Virgin church which he refurbished and which contains a remarkable selection of tombs in the SMYTHE CHAPEL, thus named for the family which endowed it and whose various branches are immortalised with panels of heraldry in blue and gold and sculptures depicting armour and embroidery alike in scrupulous detail. Unfortunately, the church and the other historic buildings are kept locked most of the time for fear of vandalism.

With the arrival of large overspill populations from London since 1945, at KENNINGTON to the north and towards KINGSNORTH in the south, Ashford has become a new town with a vast modern shopping centre arranged around a pedestrian precinct. There isn't much here of appeal to tourists but there is a TOURIST INFORMATION CENTRE in Lower High Street (0233 37311) which can provide details of interesting places round about and availability of rooms.

MUSEUM
TEMPLER BARRACKS houses an interesting and unusual small museum, that of the Army Intelligence Corps, including documents as well as uniforms, medals and colours. It is open Monday to Friday all year.

SPORT AND LEISURE
THE STOUR CENTRE (0233 639966) A 4-acre park in Tannery Lane on the banks of the river providing facilities for badminton, squash, indoor bowls and swimming, with a sauna and solarium, and outdoor tennis. The centre is open daily year round from 9am to 11pm and charges are moderate, with reduced rates for children, pensioners and disabled.
ASHFORD GOLF CLUB (0233 620180) An 18-hole course in Sandyhurst Lane welcomes visitors on weekdays and at weekends after noon.

ENVIRONS
Although industrial and housing estates have been spreading outwards from Ashford into the surrounding countryside (a process that is expected to accelerate when the Channel Tunnel is opened) many outlying villages with broad greens where cricket is played at weekends and historic homes in stately parks and gardens have managed to survive thus far.

Bestride the A20 as it approaches from London is HOTHFIELD COMMON NATURE RESERVE – 140 acres of heathland where gorse and bracken flourish and many rare plants and birds can be seen. Aspodel thrives in the bogs at the lower end. To the west on the far side of the Great Stour river is LITTLE CHART where the author H.E. Bates made his home and where there is one of the largest Forstals where cattle were penned or 'forestalled' before being driven to the great markets of Ashford. Sir John Tufton played host to Queen Elizabeth I at HOTHFIELD PLACE and his ornate and colourful marble tomb can be seen in the ancient church of St Margaret at the edge of the park. Among the stones in the churchyard is that of a butler who died at the age of 79 having served three Earls of Thanet in his lifetime. A curious mound in the park is a primitive deep freeze – snow was shovelled into it during the winter and preserved through the summer by the earth and shading elms above it.

Swinford Manor, less than a mile away, was the home of the Victorian Poet Laureate Alfred Austin, who wrote of it in *The Garden That I Love*. Nearby is GODINTON PARK (0233 620773) whose formal gardens were laid out in the 18th century and embellished by topiary hedges of this century. The house dates from 1628 and has fine Jacobean wood panelling and carving as well as beautiful china, furniture and portraits. A unique frieze in the Great Parlour illustrates the arms drill of the Kent Halbardiers in 1630. At that time the squire who lived here was Nicholas Toke, who was married five times. He was on his way to London on foot at the age of 93 to find a sixth wife when he dropped dead.

The church at GREAT CHART, whose tower looks across the valley to its taller cousin at Ashford, includes many of the Toke family of Godinton Park among its impressive collection of brasses from the 15th to 17th centuries.

At KINGSNORTH just a mile south of Ashford on the A2070 is a collection of 20th-century memorabilia started by Joe Ripley as a child and lovingly maintained by his family. It includes a 1914 Harley Davidson motorbike with sidecar, a 1924 bullnose Morris motor car and a horsedrawn carriage (0233 621609). The Bethersden marble altar in Kingsnorth church is the tomb of Humphrey Clarke and his wife who were nearly at their gold wedding when he died in 1579. Their eleven children are depicted in brass and his helmet hangs on the wall.

Between Kingsnorth and Mersham, up a lane off the old Roman road to Aldington, is a working, restored mill in a 3-acre garden. SWANTON MILL (0233 72223) won an Architectural Heritage Year award in 1975 for its exhibition of mill workings. Flour ground on the site is sold to visitors.

Sir Norton Knatchbull, who built the grammar school at Ashford, lies in the village church at MERSHAM near the manor house which had been in the family since the reign of Henry VIII. Opposite the inn and another old mill is another of the Forstals peculiar to these parts.

Three miles to the north of Ashford the triangular green of BOUGHTON ALUPH stands at the gates of EASTWELL PARK with its 40-acre lake where herons nest among the cedars of Lebanon. It is claimed to be the resting place of the last member of the royal house of York. Legend has it that he was the illegitimate son of King Richard III, who summoned him to Bosworth field to acknowledge him as heir the day before he was defeated and slain by Henry Tudor. The young man fled and earned his living as a workman until his identity was discovered by Sir Thomas Moyle, who noticed him reading a book in Latin during rebuilding of the mansion at Eastwell Park in 1545. Both their tombs are in the ruins of the church in the park, which fell into disuse after World War II until 1980 when the great house (totally rebuilt in Jacobean style in 1926) was converted into a country house hotel.

ACCOMMODATION

EASTWELL MANOR, Eastwell Park, Ashford TN25 4HR (0233 35751). Possibly the most luxurious hotel in Kent set in 3,000 acres of parkland with views of the Stour Valley and the slopes of the North Downs. Oak panelling, huge bedrooms and bathrooms and gourmet food in baronial surroundings – at a price.
POST HOUSE, Canterbury Road, Ashford TN24 8QQ (0233 625790). A 15th-century manor house as hotel with a 17th-century barn converted to a restaurant. Expensive.
MASTER SPEARPOINT, Canterbury Road, Kennington, Ashford TN24 9QR (0233 36863). Comfortable country-house-style hotel in 5-acre garden. Moderately expensive.
CROFT, Canterbury Road, Ashford TN25 4DU (0233 622140). Family run, 28 bedrooms, most with private facilities. Two-acre garden. Moderate.

ASHURST

Traffic on the narrow, winding A264 road from East Grinstead to *Tunbridge Wells rushes endlessly through this little village where the River Medway crosses the border from Sussex into Kent as a little waterway between pretty wooded banks. There is just one pub, the BALD FACED STAG. The village church, St Martin of Tours, has two 17th-century sundials. One is on the gable of the south porch beneath the coat of arms of the Rivers family and the other is on a pillar among the gravestones with the inscription 'Elias Allen made this Diall and gave it to the parish of Ashurst AD1634'. In Tudor times pilgrims came here to see a rood or crucifix which hung inside an arched recess in the northeast corner of the chancel and was reputed to have miraculous powers. It hung above an altar to St Anne, patroness of the local ironstone miners. In 1609 one

Thomas Browne of Ashurst deposed that since 1591 he had delivered 463 tons of iron ordnance and shortly afterwards was granted a pension of 18 pence for life. The furnace was by the mill race in Pond Field a quarter of a mile northwest of the church. The church is left open for visitors and is worth seeing for its wooden belfry and old beams inside, despite the traffic noise.

AYLESFORD

On the M20 and A20 approaching *Maidstone from London, amidst industrial estates, paper mills and sand pits, this is the cradle of the English nation. In the mid-5th century the indigenous tribes fought the Battle of Aeglesford here against the invading armies of the Saxon warlords, Hengist and Horsa. It was here that Alfred the Great in 893 and Edmund Ironside in 1016 defeated the Danes in battle. The ford at Aylesford was an important crossing of the Medway as far back as the Bronze Age and evidence of pre-Roman settlement can be found in KIT'S COTY HOUSE and LITTLE KIT'S COTY HOUSE, the tombs of some unknown ancient Britons on the slopes of the North Downs above the village, just off the busy A229 Maidstone–Rochester road. The larger barrow consists of four standing stones and a capstone weighing at least 10 tons, reminiscent of the dolmens and menhirs found in profusion in Brittany. There is no documented evidence of its origin or of other megalithic remains such as the White Horse stone on the opposite side of the A229. They are known collectively as The Countless Stones and legend records that a local baker who tried to count them by placing a numbered loaf on each stone found when he came to collect them that the Devil had added an extra loaf. In May 1989 a coven of white witches performed a ritual intended to persuade British Rail not to take its high speed Channel Tunnel link through this area, which would involve moving some of the stones.

The graceful 14th-century Aylesford bridge (see p. 21) with a wide central arch flanked on either side by three smaller ones was for hundreds of years the only road across the Medway between Rochester and Maidstone. Mercifully, the river view from the bridge of banks shaded by willows and lined by black and white half-timbered houses, with the Norman church tower rising behind, hasn't been spoiled. The bridge takes only a single line of vehicles and is too narrow for lorries. Nearby are two pubs, the CHEQUERS, a 16th-century coaching inn, and Kent's smallest tavern, the LITTLE GEM, which dates from 1106. The ground floor bar is no bigger than an average family living room, with low beams and doorways. Just across the road is a delightful hillside garden with a lily pond and gazebo, created to mark the Silver Jubilee of Queen Elizabeth II in 1977.

On the outskirts of the village, beside the muddy Medway, is THE FRIARS (0622 717272), the first Carmelite house in England in 1242 on a site given by the lord of the manor Richard de Grey on his return from the Crusades. The cloister, refectory and Pilgrims' Hall survive, restored by the Carmelites who returned to Aylesford in 1949 four centuries after being expelled by King Henry VIII at the Reformation. In the meantime, the estate was owned by various families and changed hands between the Puritans and the Royalists during the Civil War. When Samuel Pepys visited The Friars in 1669 and recorded it in his diary it was the country seat of Sir John Banks. Today pilgrims come to picnic beside a lake where swans glide and ducks paddle and to visit the outdoor shrine of Our Lady of the Assumption, capable of accommodating 5,000 people, and several smaller chapels and shrines decorated with the ceramics of the Polish artist Adam Kossowski. The church is circuited by a quiet Rosary Walk through a landscaped garden. A wide range of pottery made by the friars in their own kiln (open to visitors) is sold at reasonable prices and there is a tearoom. Inexpensive accommodation is offered to groups and young people and two thatched Tudor barns are being restored and converted.

Despite its Norman tower, Aylesford's parish church of Kentish ragstone is mostly 15th century and sheltered by a yew tree planted by William Farncomb in 1708. It contains many interesting brasses, sculptures and tombs, including that of Thomas Culpepper, his wife, three sons and three daughters, surmounted by helmets, gauntlets and crossed swords. The ancestral home of the Culpeppers, Preston Hall, lay south of the river. The Victorian mansion which replaced it now houses the workshops at the heart of the ROYAL BRITISH LEGION VILLAGE, separated from the rest of Aylesford by the M20.

BADLESMERE

This small village on the A251 in the heart of the Weald south of *Faversham boasts one of the largest greens in Kent, edged with lime trees which give out a marvellous fragrance in summer. It is the birthplace of one of Queen Elizabeth I's favourite courtiers, Sir Thomas Randolph, with whom she loved to play cards. The church has a two-decker pulpit, 14th-century beams and box pews.

BAPCHILD

On the A2, the Roman Watling Street running straight as an arrow from *Sittingbourne to *Faversham, Bapchild has seen much traffic between Dover and London down the centuries and in the

8th century, before William the Conqueror invaded, it was the scene of a Council of Kent. The builders of the village church in the 12th century set into one of its pillars a tooth from a prehistoric mammal which they uncovered during their excavations. It was extracted and put on display in a glass case in more recent times.

BARFRESTON

High on a hill, 5 miles inland from the white cliffs of *Dover, this otherwise unremarkable village has one of the finest examples of Norman architecture and skill in stonemasonry and sculpture to be found anywhere. More than 100 figures adorn the exterior walls and doorways of St Nicholas Church, some bizarre – a dog playing a harp, a monkey riding on the back of a goat with a rabbit over its shoulder – some everyday. One of the figures carved over the inspired south door is believed to be Archbishop Thomas Becket.

After eight centuries of weathering by Channel winds, sun, rain and snow the sculptures still dance with imagination. Inside, there is yet more fine work captured by the light through a large Wheel Window with delicate tracery. It is on a miniature scale – the nave is less than 30ft in length – yet the effect is of a cathedral. Local legend has it that a 12th-century lord of the manor, Adam de Port, hired the best craftsmen available to decorate the church on his marriage. Not to be missed.

BARHAM

On the downs around this village southeast of *Canterbury Caesar's Seventh Legion camped 2,000 years ago. He was on his second visit from Gaul with a British general, 40,000 men and 3,000 horses and a little help from 20,000 defectors from the defending tribes. But it was not a case of *veni, vidi, vici* – he soon departed. Other armies came and went down the years. To the southeast of the village in lovely grounds bordered with beeches is Broome Park, now the home of a country and golf club (0227 831701) open to visiting golfers, provided they book in advance and are members of a golf club or have a handicap certificate. The ornate redbrick 17th-century mansion was the last home of Field Marshall Earl Kitchener of Khartoum whose moustachioed features glowered from 1914 recruiting posters with the slogan 'Your Country Needs *You*'. He came here when he wanted to get away from the battle in the trenches on the other side of the Channel and his signallers camped on the downs. The downs have known peace for nearly half a century now and have escaped invasion by developers so far. A black smock mill, restored in the 1980s, stands outside the village, catching the breezes across the Elham valley in its sails. And a delightful village it is, with a long street running down into the valley, dominated by the green copper spire of St John the Baptist church. Among the collection of brasses beneath the old beams and decorated kingposts of the nave is a headless man with a dog at his feet, dating from 1370. The stained glass window which shows St George slaying the dragon is in

memory of Kitchener's signallers. Many of the sturdy old timber-framed houses in Barham are reinforced and decorated with 18th-century brickwork, including BAR-HAM COURT, which stands in a garden behind a wall by the church and is said to have been the home of one of the knights who murdered Thomas Becket in Canterbury Cathedral.

BARMING

This hamlet amidst hopfields and orchards, just west of *Maidstone on the A26, has a wooden bridge that carries motor traffic across the Medway, but not enough to disturb the peace of walks along its banks, to the older bridges and locks at *East Farleigh or *Teston, or cruises in small boats. Fishing

rights are privately owned, however. The village church has a mounting stone for horse riders by the gate and a screen made from a brewer's vat. But its greatest treasure is its oak choir stalls from Flanders, 600 years old and carved with saints, devils, dragons and lions, Samson and St George.

BELTRING

In the heart of hop country by the Medway between EAST PECKHAM and PADDOCK WOOD on the B2015, this hamlet has one of the county's best days out for the whole family at the WHITBREAD HOP FARM (0622 872068), where the white cowls of no fewer than 25 Victorian oast houses gleam in the sun. Until hop-picking was mechanised, a railway called the Hop Pickers' Line used to run from nearby Paddock Wood to *Goudhurst and beyond but these oast houses are no longer in use for drying hops. They are a museum of hop-growing and other local agriculture and crafts such

as coopering. Beltring is also the home of the Whitbread Shire Horses which haul the brewers' drays and there is a pets' corner, play and picnic areas and a nature trail. It is open from 28 April to 22 October.

ACCOMMODATION
Inexpensive bed and breakfast in oast houses:
LITTLE FOWLE HALL OAST, Lucks Lane, Paddock Wood TN12 6PA (0892 832602).
MASCALLS OAST, Badsell Road, Paddock Wood TN12 6LR (0892 832747).

BENENDEN

Near *Hawkhurst on the East Sussex border, the black-and-white-fronted, red-roofed houses, an ancient timber barn and a little village school are grouped round an idyllic green where, in cricketing annals, a ball once went between the stumps without removing the bails. A bronze war memorial stands by the green and the church contains a mosaic reredos of the Nativity, donated by Lord and Lady Cranbrook in celebration of their golden wedding anniversary. Nearby Hemsted Park, covering 300 acres, is the home of BENENDEN SCHOOL where royal daughters are educated. Its majestic pines, grown from seed brought from Norway two centuries ago, suffered badly in the freak hurricane which hit Kent in October 1987.

BETHERSDEN

In medieval times this village west of *Ashford was famed for the marble quarried from the local strata in the heavy Wealden clay. Various shades of grey, blue and brown and glittering with tiny particles of fossil shells, Bethersden marble was used in ecclesiastical architecture and can be seen in the towers of churches at *Biddenden, *Headcorn, *Smarden and *Tenterden as well as the altar stairs at Canterbury Cathedral. From the 17th century it went into decline and Bethersden's own 15th-century church makes no great use of it. It is noted instead for its three-in-one 'oven grave', a type of burial mound.

ACCOMMODATION

LTTLE HODGEHAM, Bull Lane, Bethersden TN26 3HE (0233 82323). Idyllic restored medieval cottage in a garden with a duck-pond, rose beds, blossoming trees and a swimming pool. Three rooms. Meals provided. Moderate.

BEWL WATER

Off the A21 south of *Lamberhurst, a sign points to the largest expanse of inland water in the southeast. This reservoir fills the valley of the Bewl River, straddling Kent and Sussex, to provide water supplies to the Medway towns. Like most man-made lakes in Britain, its potential for leisure has been developed with the active encouragement of the Southern Water Authority. Sailing and angling clubs use it as a base and boats can be hired for trout fishing between April and October. Bewl Water also offers facilities for boating, canoeing, rowing, windsurfing, diving, riding or simply walking, as well as picnic sites, shelters and ample public conveniences. The VISITOR CENTRE (0892 890661) on site provides detailed information and there are passenger cruises round the lake from April to October.

BIDDENDEN

Although it is crowded with visitors' cars in summer, Biddenden has changed little in appearance since it was a centre of Kent cloth-making in the 16th century. A sign on the village green depicts the Biddenden Maids, Siamese twins Elisa and Mary Chulkhurst who were born in the village in the 12th century and survived for 34 years. Land left in trust by them provides to this day dole for the needy and on Easter Monday at the Old Workhouse wheaten biscuits in the shape of two women joined at the hips and shoulders are handed out.

A tithe barn, the vicar's pond, a gazebo and a lichened sundial in an old garden, the painted figurehead of a ship from the Spanish Armada – these are just some of the things which catch the eye on a stroll round. Many of the half-timbered cottages are antique shops or restaurants catering for tourists. The CLOTH HALL, with its black and white front beneath russet tiles and seven distinctive gables, has been converted into private homes and the weavers' houses and shops in the High Street are officially designated ancient monuments.

*Bethersden marble can be seen in the pavements and in the church tower, which commands a view over the Sussex Downs to the sea. The church contains portraits in brass of 70 of its inhabitants of earlier times and in the churchyard a gravestone records how Thomas Collings, 96, went out into the cornfields to reap on the eve of Waterloo with his 74-year-old son and daughter aged 66. A recent addition to the local farming scene is BIDDENDEN VINEYARDS south of the village, started by the Barnes family in 1969 with just one-third of an acre of vines imported from Germany. The Ortega and Muller Thurgau vines now extend over several acres off the A262 on the road to Benenden. The vineyards (0580 291726) are open to casual visitors and there is a shop. Tours by appointment.

MUSEUM
A mile west of Biddenden off the A262 at the 15th-century Bettenham Manor is the BABY CARRIAGE COLLECTION (0580 291343) whose owner Jack Hampshire conducts personal tours by appointment only. A converted oast house in the 15-acre garden contains an assortment of Victorian and 20th-century prams and Edwardian bassinettes.

FOOD AND DRINK
WEST HOUSE, 28 High Street, Biddenden (0580 291341). Italian restaurant, good service.
YE MAYDES, 13–15 High Street, Biddenden (0580 291306). An eye

to tourists, but good value.

THREE CHIMNEYS, rustic setting 2½ miles west of Biddenden on the A262. Serves good food, hot and cold, in the bar and in a separate restaurant, as well as a selection of Kent and Sussex draught ales and Biddenden cider. Open fires warm the beams and bare brick interior.

BIGGIN HILL

This unprepossessing village, straggling along the A233 to *Westerham at the edge of the North Downs, has become a part of Greater London outer suburbia over the past 25 years. But its name will be forever famous as the Kentish aerodrome from which Churchill's 'Few' fighter pilots flew their Spitfires and Hurricanes during the Battle of Britain. The aerodrome came into existence 23 years earlier during World War I when the Royal Flying Corps was looking for an alternative to a camp near Woolwich. A large meadow 1½ miles north of the village proved ideal because the long deep valley to the west of it put it above local mist or fog. In the summer of 1940 it controlled 'C' Sector of the air defences and managed to continue operations despite heavy attack by the Luftwaffe. There were many deaths and casualties and three members of the Women's Auxiliary Air Force (WAAF) were among those decorated for valour during the raids. Later in the war an American Eagle squadron joined those based at 'Biggin'. Today a lone Spitfire stands guard at the gates of the non-operational North Camp behind which is ST GEORGE'S CHAPEL OF REMEMBRANCE. It replaced the temporary wood and asbestos structure which burned down in 1946. Superstitious people have reported hearing the distinctive drone of a Merlin engine overhead, but what was formerly South Camp is now busy with civilian light aircraft coming and going and is the scene of an annual AIR FAIR in June.

BIRCHINGTON

The white cliffs which begin here on the Thames shore of Thanet, west of *Margate, and march around North Foreland to *Ramsgate, are less celebrated than those of Dover and the South Foreland but the chalk's the same. Birchington's mostly 13th-century church is the last resting place of Dante Gabriel Rossetti, poet and artist son of an Italian patriot who settled in London in 1824. The cross over Rossetti's tomb by the door was carved by Ford Madox Brown, under whom he studied at the Royal Academy before forming the pre-Raphaelite brotherhood with Millais and Hunt. Panels depict scenes from his life and work and a window reproduces one of his lesser-known paintings 'Preparation for the Passover'. Many of the other tombs, memorials and brasses here are associated with the Crispe family, whose estate at QUEX PARK nearby is dominated by a piece of early 19th-century braggadocio – a gleaming metal campanile designed to carry the biggest peal of bells in Kent, twelve in all. Canterbury Cathedral subsequently added another two bells to its peal to match it.

MUSEUM
The collection of Major Horace POWELL-COTTON during a lifetime's travelling is in an extension of Quex House (0843 42168). His trophies from Africa and Asia are displayed in amazingly realistic natural settings – white rhinoceros, a giant elephant, nyala and kudu – together with tribal tools, weapons and musical instruments, Oriental porcelain and cannon captured from the French in Canada. Open from April to September at various times.

SPORTS AND LEISURE
WESTGATE AND BIRCHINGTON GOLF CLUB (0843 31115) has an 18-hole course in Domneva Road, Westgate. Visitors from other clubs are welcome on weekdays and after 11am on Saturdays and noon on Sundays.

ACCOMMODATION
WOODCHURCH FARMHOUSE, Woodchurch, Birchington CT7 0HE (0843 62502). Basic, inexpensive and convenient for exploring Kent's 'leisure coast'.

BISHOPSBOURNE

Just south of *Canterbury along an avenue of pines off Watling Street (A2), this peaceful, pretty little place has associations with two very different literary figures. Joseph Conrad, born in the Ukraine of Polish parents, came here in 1920 to spend his last years after a long seafaring career and phenomenal success as a novelist in middle age. He is buried at Canterbury and his last home, one of several in Kent, was a former rectory of the Georgian period now called OSWALDS. It shelters behind an old yew hedge and on the other side of it, in an earlier rectory, Richard Hooker wrote his monumental Tudor work *Ecclesiastical Polity* at the same time that Shakespeare was producing *Richard II*, *A Midsummer Night's Dream* and *The Merchant of Venice*. The Reverend Hooker was offered the living of Bishopsbourne by Queen Elizabeth I in 1595 so that he could devote himself to his writing. Although 'Judicious' Hooker was celebrated far and wide in his own time, he was extremely modest and retiring and suffered a nagging wife. A bust in the 13th-century church of St Mary shows him in a black gown and square cap, gloriously illuminated by the light through the stained glass, some of it dating from the 14th century with glowing angels, Dutch and Flemish designs of the 17th century and a good example of the pre-Raphaelite Burne-Jones and William Morris style in the west window. Bishopsbourne is an altogether fascinating village flanked by two stately parks – Bourne, surrounding a Queen Anne mansion, and Charlton, whose grand salon was built for George III.

BOUGH BEECH

A little to the north of *Chiddingstone, a valley of 280 acres was flooded to create a reservoir. Two fine old Wealden houses which would have been lost beneath the water were dismantled timber by timber and taken to the Downland Open Air Museum at Singleton near Chichester where they have been reassembled as exhibits. Part of the reservoir is a nature reserve where many wintering birds gather. It is also home to breeding waders such as green-shank, godwit and sandpiper and breeding tufted duck, heron and grebes. Permits for trout fishing, fly only, can be obtained from the East Surrey Water Company, London Road, Redhill RH1 1LJ (0737 765933). A sailing club also uses the reservoir, which is scenically attractive and can be viewed from HANGING BANK and BROCKHOULT MOUNT, a wooded ridge just east of *Ide Hill of the B2042, where there is space for parking.

BOUGHTON STREET

The 'Street' from which this village takes its title was trodden by Chaucer's pilgrims on the last few weary miles of their journey to *Canterbury. It runs between Tudor façades and ancient timber barns, less in danger of being shaken to pieces now that the Channel ports traffic by-passes the village on a trunk-road section of the A2. It used to be called Boughton-under-Blean from the forest that existed in Chaucer's time and survives today, along with the 13th-century church. A mile on towards Canterbury, with views of 'Bell Harry', the cathedral tower, across the meadow brings us to the hamlet of DUNKIRK. Jack Cornwell, who joined the Navy as a boy in 1915 and won a posthumous Victoria Cross for his conduct on board HMS *Chester* at the Battle of Jutland, went to school here, walking every day from his home at HARBLEDOWN, a last halting place for pilgrims on the way to Canterbury and the site of the Black Prince's Well. The prince is said to have drunk a flask of its waters every day, such was his faith in its healing properties, but it didn't save him from the syphilis which caused his death.

ACCOMODATION
WHITE HORSE, The Street, Boughton ME13 9AX (0227 751343).

Convenient and comfortable small hostelry, moderately priced. Camping site for caravans at the

RED LION CARAVAN PARK, Old London Road, Dunkirk (0227 751904).

BRANDS HATCH

Off the A20 between Swanley and *Wrotham, this is the world-famous venue of the British Grand Prix, the Marlborough Race of Champions and other major events of the Formula One motor racing calendar. It is the scene, too, of Formula Two and Three motor racing, rallycross, go-karting, vintage car rallies and international motorcycle racing. At the school of motor racing here, novices can test their skills on the circuit in their own cars before deciding whether to enrol for a course of tuition (0474 872331).

ACCOMMODATION

BRANDS HATCH PLACE, Fawkham DA3 8NG (0474 872239). A 25-room hotel near the circuit with indoor swimming, squash, tennis and a country garden. Moderately expensive.

THISTLE, Brands Hatch DA3 8PE (0474 854900). Opened in 1988, this hotel has 140 rooms of four-star standard and a range of bars and restaurants. Expensive.

BRASTED

Now that much of the traffic that used to thunder through it on the A25 between *Westerham and *Sevenoaks has been diverted on to the M25 London Orbital Motorway, this village with its pump on the green has regained some of its old rural serenity. It has some rustic cottages and a great house designed by Robert Adam for Dr John Turton, who was physician to King George III. Louis Napoleon lived here in exile with a tame eagle. The hills climb up from the village to BRASTED CHART, at 771ft the highest point in Kent. Nearby

*Ide Hill is known as the Dome of Kent because of its crown of venerable beeches and has the famous *Emmetts Garden on its slopes. Its neighbour *Toys Hill claims Kent's highest pump.

FOOD AND DRINK

WHITE HART, Brasted (0959 62814). A favoured World War II haunt of young fighter pilots stationed at Biggin Hill and their girlfriends. The walls are adorned with nostalgic photographs and Battle of Britain mementoes.

BRENCHLEY

Six miles east of *Tunbridge Wells, amidst acres of hop gardens and orchards, this lovely village, extolled by the poet Siegfried Sassoon in his *Memoirs of a Fox-hunting Man*, has one main street leading into a small square that is shaded by an oak tree much older than the cottages with their oriel windows. The old butcher's shop and other weatherboarded, tile-hung or half-timbered buildings are wonderfully preserved and the early 17th-century OLD WORK-HOUSE is one of the best examples in Kent. All Saints Church, at the southern side of the square, is approached along an avenue of clipped yews, centuries old. Inside, a hammberbeam roof supported by carved angels overhangs a screen dating from 1536. On the outskirts of the village is a cottage where Wat Tyler is said to have lived, looking down the hill to-wards the large Furnace Pond on the road to *Horsmonden. Until the supply of trees to fuel the furnaces was exhausted, iron was made here.

FOOD AND DRINK

BOURNE'S STORES, High Street, Brenchley (0892 723094) is rather more than the usual village 'general', with a list of 150 wines and takeaway pies, pancakes and French and Italian dishes.

THE BULL, High Street, Brenchley (0892 722701). Dates from 1888 and preserves its Victorian decor down to the aspidistra in a brass pot. Bar food includes the Brench-ley 'tradition' of Friday fish and chips.

HOPBINE (0892 722561). In nearby PETTERIDGE, amidst the hop-gardens, serves real ales and bar snacks.

BROADSTAIRS

As far as Charles Dickens was concerned, Broadstairs was the queen of all watering places. It was just a small hamlet with a Norman church and a chapel of Our Lady of Bradstow, much revered by the local fishermen, when he went there with his wife and baby son in 1837 for a long summer break. Dickens was already a successful writer but two years later, while the children were getting 'as brown as berries', he completed *Nicholas Nickleby* in a rented house with a view of the sea and the sands on which he walked at low tide as far as *Ramsgate. *The Old Curiosity Shop* and *Barnaby Rudge* were written in succession at Broadstairs, either at 37 Albion Street (now the Royal Albion Hotel) or Lawn House (now Archway House). Most of *David Copperfield*, the author's own favourite, was written in a fortress-like villa perched on the chalk cliff above Viking Bay, now known as Bleak House.

Broadstairs needs no reminding of its rich literary heritage. Every summer the little town clustered round the harbour and a sheltered sandy beach dresses up in Victorian costume for a festival which includes dramatisations and readings from Dickens, as well as exhibitions and parades. The great novelist tends to overshadow more recent celebrities connected with Broadstairs such as the Prime Minister who took Britain into the European Community in the 1970s, Edward Heath, who was born in the town and often returned to conduct classical concerts. It was here that Alfred Harmsworth, later Lord Northcliffe, planned the first popular newspaper the *Daily Mail* and Thomas Crampton draughted plans for some of the earliest railways.

Yet it remains what it has been since Dickens discovered it – a quiet family resort with donkey rides and Punch & Judy on a clean beach, shops selling buckets and spades, shrimping nets and flippers, colourful parks and gardens, pleasant walks and fishing both from the pier and offshore. There is traditional end-of-the-pier entertainment at the PAVILION THEATRE and an annual WATER GALA. YORK GATE, the 16th-century portcullis arch down by the harbour, was built to defend the village against pirates and smugglers.

The TOURIST INFORMATION CENTRE (0843 68399) is at Pierremont Hall in the High Street.

MUSEUMS
BLEAK HOUSE (0843 62224). Even though it has no connection with that particular novel, it displays Dicken's possessions in the study, dining room and a bedroom to visitors daily from March to November. The kitchen is fitted out in a Victorian style of which even Mrs Beeton would have approved. It also has a collection of items from ships wrecked on the GOODWIN SANDS offshore and a display on smuggling.

DICKENS HOUSE MUSEUM (08433 62853) has more Dickensiana and associations with Betsey Trotwood from *Copperfield*, as it is believed that the author based her on Mary Strong who lived in this pretty white-balustraded house on the seafront. Open in the afternoon from 8 April to 22 October.

CRAMPTON TOWER (0843 64446). Behind the post office near the railway station is a former waterworks building designed by railways pioneer Thomas Crampton, now a museum of his blueprints and drawings as well as a model railway. Inquire for opening times.

ENVIRONS
NORTH FORELAND LIGHTHOUSE is a listed building, nearly 65ft high and painted brilliant white. The first candle-powered lighthouse was erected on this site as early as 1505. The present structure dates from 1790 and is open to visitors daily except Sundays, by appointment with the Principal Keeper (0843 61869).

ACCOMMODATION
CASTLE KEEP, Joss Gap Road, Kingsgate CT10 3PQ (0843 65222). Recommended clifftop hotel with an outdoor swimming pool. Moderately expensive.

CASTLEMERE, Western Esplanade CT10 1TD (0843 61566). With 41 rooms the biggest hotel in town, yet quiet with a pleasant garden overlooking the Channel. Moderate.

BAY TREE, 12 Eastern Esplanade CT10 1DR (0843 62502). Comfort-able and convenient small hotel on the seafront. Inexpensive.

ROYAL ALBION, Albion Street CT10 1LU (0843 68071). Where Dickens stayed, overlooking the harbour and the sands. Moderately expensive.

BROMLEY

There used to be a milestone in the High Street 'London Bridge 10 miles', but no more. Bromley is irretrievably part of Greater London, although its postal address is still Kent. Since the early 1960s when its land value reached a million pounds per acre, the old High Street of family-run emporia has been replaced by modern blocks representing the names of every well-known multiple store. Bromley is a major shopping centre of southeast London and a gateway to the south coast and the Channel ports via British Rail (14 minutes from London Victoria to Bromley South) and the A21 and M25 roads. At its northern end the High Street runs into the Market Place where a rather garish mural pays tribute to Bromley's most famous son, H.G. Wells (1866–1946) focusing on Mr Polly and *The War of the Worlds*. In his later work, Wells predicated with remarkable accuracy the kind of progress which has made Bromley unrecognisable as the Kent country town he grew up in. The few remnants of old Bromley which survive include BROMLEY NORTH RAILWAY STATION and the SWAN AND MITRE pub in the High Street.

ENTERTAINMENT

THE CHURCHILL THEATRE, High Street (01-460 5838). Together with the Fairfield at Croydon, provides an oasis of live professional performance, attracting top names. Restaurant.

BROMLEY LITTLE THEATRE, North Street (01-460 3047). Known to its friends as 'The Little', occupies a converted Victorian bakery and presents a play a month.

ENVIRONS

Bromley hasn't been entirely swamped by urban development, it is still ringed with expanses of green such as Beckenham Place, Sundridge, Petts Wood, Hayes Common on which there are several golf courses. CHISLEHURST retains its triangular common and the prehistoric chalk caves which were used as air raid shelters during World War II. Reached via the A222, they're a tourist attraction, open daily from Easter to October, weekends only at other times, with guides. HAYES, where London ends abruptly and real Kent countryside begins, means 'heath'. It has the remains of 150 neolithic pit dwellings and is the birthplace of the 18th-century Prime Minister

William Pitt, and is where his father, Pitt the Elder, 1st Earl of Chatham, died. KESTON, just to the south is noted for its large ponds, a favourite spot for picnics, angling and sailing model boats. The source is a well round which Caesar's legions camped when they invaded Britain and nearby are the remains of a ROMAN MAUSOLEUM.

FOOD AND DRINK

CAPISANO, 9 Simpsons Road, Bromley (01-460 8036). A good value trattoria.

GIANNINO'S, 6 Commonside, Keston (0689 56410). Excellent cooking in an almost rural setting.

MARIO, 53 Chislehurst Road, Chislehurst (01-467 1341).

BROOKLAND

Tile-hung and weatherboarded cottages cluster round a remarkable 13th-century church in this village on the northern edge of Wallend Marsh which stretches away to *Lydd and the nuclear power stations at *Dungeness. The oddly pagoda-shaped wooden belfry tower of St Augustine's stands aloof from the rest of the church. In its time, it's said, it served as a hiding place for smuggled goods, with the connivance of the parson. The local doctor, who was led blindfolded to treat wounded smugglers, lived at PEAR TREE HOUSE in the main street. In the church, horsebox pews are arrayed beneath the old oak beams and kingposts. The priceless Norman lead font is embellished with the signs of the zodiac and a cavalcade of everyday peasant life.

BURHAM

On the eastern slopes of the Medway valley, on a by-road off the main Rochester–Maidstone road (A229), this forgotten village was pushed into prominence by its situation on the projected route of British Rail's high-speed Channel Tunnel link. A mile from the village, beside a loop in the river, is the site of a ROMAN TEMPLE. It was uncovered during quarrying for lime – an underground chamber, 40ft long and 20ft wide, where the devotees of Mithras worshipped their god of the sun. Remnants of Roman pottery and coins were found. When Christianity prevailed, a church was built on the same site and between the 12th and 15th centuries was embellished with stained glass, a fine chancel and a tower.

CANTERBURY

The early-Gothic Cathedral of Christchurch dominates this ageless city that has been a centre of pilgrimage for 800 years. Although a large area south of Christchurch Gate was devastated in a German air raid in 1942 and has been rebuilt in 20th-century style, Canterbury is unmistakeably medieval, compact and easy to explore within the stretches of Norman town wall which still stand. Many of the old buildings in the High Street escaped the bombs and survive, so that a visitor from a hundred years ago would recognise it at once. Instead of fighting a losing battle against ever-growing motor traffic, Canterbury took the bold step of banishing it entirely from the heart of the city. It may be difficult at peak season to find a space in one of the numerous car parks ringing the centre and the narrow streets may still be packed with visitors on foot but at least the air isn't full of carbon monoxide fumes. An alternative is to take the train to Canterbury East or West stations, either just a short walk from the city centre.

The Archbishop of Canterbury is Primate of All England and the cathedral has been the mother church of England since St Augustine established it in 603, on the site of a former Romano-British church, six years after being sent by Pope Gregory to reclaim the Saxons for Christendom. But Canterbury is even older than that. Three centuries before Christ was born, the invading Belgae tribes set up a fortified camp on the River Stour at this place. The Belgae were still there when the Romans came, managing at first to beat off Caesar's legionnaires but eventually succumbing. It was the Romans who introduced Christianity to Kent centuries before St Augustine arrived, although their churches fell into ruin when they withdrew. Canterbury has seen the Romans, the Saxons and the Normans come and go. As John Twyne, a 16th-century mayor, put it: 'Scarce any City is there in this Kingdom, which for antiquity of origins, or for the dignity of its fortune, can be compared to ours.' The ruins of the abbey that St Augustine built stand without Canterbury's walls, and within, 8ft down, are the mosaics of a Roman villa from the town they called Durovernum. The keep of the Norman castle is the third largest in England, with walls 11ft thick. The gables of the OLD WEAVER'S HOUSE overhang the rustic River Stour as it entwines the heart of the city. In KING'S, in the shadow of the cathedral, Canterbury has an older school than Eton, while the UNIVERSITY OF KENT (one of the country's newest) surveys the city from a hill named for Wat Tyler. Two million people come every year to see Canterbury Cathedral but there are enough places of interest here to keep one occupied for a week, never mind a day.

On 29 December 1170 four knights who had overheard their king

Henry II call out in despair 'Who will deliver me from this turbulent priest?' waylaid Archbishop Thomas Beckett in the cathedral and murdered him. Rome made him St Thomas the Martyr and the pilgrimage to his shrine began. Six centuries after Geoffrey Chaucer wrote 'from every shires end of Engelond, to Caunterbury they wende', they are still coming, but in ever greater numbers and from ever farther afield, even though the influence of Christianity has waned. What they all want to know is 'Where was Becket murdered?' or, more delicately, where 'the tragic event' occurred. A modern metal sculpture, dedicated in 1986, and the one word 'THOMAS' deeply incised into the stone paving beneath it marks the spot in the northwest transept where the knights rushed in from the cloisters to cut him down; although not long afterwards a fire devastated the Norman choir and chapel beneath which Becket's body lay. The spot where he fell is known as The Martyrdom and near it hangs a 15th-century painting of the same name, showing the deed.

After the fire the new TRINITY CHAPEL was built to house the golden tomb of the Martyr Saint. For 300 years this was the mecca of devout Christians, although takings had begun to wane by 1538 when Henry VIII broke with Rome and stemmed the religious tide to Canterbury, denouncing Becket for his 'treason, contumacy and rebellion' and obliterating the shrine. The gold, sapphires, rubies and emeralds removed on the orders of the king filled 26 carts. For some reason, he stopped short of destroying the chapel's richly colourful stained glass windows which became known as the 'Poor Man's Bible', illustrating the Wise Men and the shepherds, Jesus and Herod, Solomon and Noah, the Six Ages of the World and the Six Ages of Man. The worn-down Pilgrims' Steps to Trinity Chapel can still be trodden. Today's pilgrims arrive by the coachload off the motorway and swarm along Burgate towards Christchurch Gate by the old Buttermarket. A short distance away in St Margaret's Street the latest computer and visual technologies are being used to give us a better idea of what it was like to be a pilgrim in 1396.

CANTERBURY PILGRIMS WAY (0227 454888) transports us back in time to the Tabard Inn in Southwark from whence our guide (in the guise of a pilgrim, naturally) leads us down the road rolling through a recreation of medieval Kent, crossing Rochester Bridge at the halfway stage. The journey is enlivened by the Canterbury tales of the 'verray parfit gentil knight', the bawdy miller, the blowsy wife of Bath, the nun's priest and the pardoner. Sound, light and vision and even smell are cleverly used to illustrate their words. Passing through the great West Gate, we find ourselves in the upper gallery of the Chequers of Hope, the inn that stood at the gates of the cathedral in Chaucer's day. A staircase leads from here to a replica of Trinity Chapel, nothing more than a modest sideshow compared to the real thing just down the road although its point is to give some idea of what Becket's gold tomb looked like before it was broken up by Henry VIII. Chaucer is difficult for many adults, let alone children, and this imaginative display, although not as large or as impressive as its Jorvik counterpart at York, is a novel introduction to a masterpiece of English literature and the story of Becket. A teachers' resource pack is available on request.

THE CATHEDRAL

Canterbury Pilgrims Way is a prelude to the real thing, the living heritage of 1,600 years entered through CHRISTCHURCH GATE, built in the Perpendicular style between 1502 and 1519. Every evening at 9pm the carved oak doors are shut following the ringing of the curfew bell, safeguarding the security of the magnificent building, begun in 1070 by the first Norman Archbishop, Lanfranc. It replaced St Augustine's Cathedral which had burned down, yet a hundred years later it too was consumed by flames and had to be recreated by William of Sens from the ashes, using stone from Caen in Normandy shipped to Canterbury by way of the River Stour. When he was crippled after falling from the scaffolding, William the Englishman took over to complete Trinity Chapel. 'Bell Harry', 235ft high and richly ornamented, looms above the four other towers of Canterbury Cathedral and dominates the view, no

matter from which direction you approach the city. A single bell at the top tolls only for the death of a monarch or the primate. When the other bells peal they can be heard for miles around. The first view inside is breathtaking, great columns marching along nave and aisle, light filtering through countless panels of stained glass, a symphony of carved wood, stone, marble and iron and more precious metals. Within a space measuring 500ft from end to end, under a vaulted ceiling soaring to 80ft, there are hundreds of paintings and sculptures distributed among the elaborate screens and small chapels. The works of our forefathers have survived not only time but schism and rebellion, bombs and fire, and the faith that put it all together remains.

Much of the earlier cathedral of Archbishop Lanfranc can be seen in the crypt, cloisters and nave, and that of his successor Anselm in the choir and east transept, but the choir we see today and the Trinity Chapel rising 16 steps from it, is 13th century, the masterpiece of the two Williams, French and English. The 15th century saw major works, including the complete reconstruction of the nave by Henry Yevele, architect of Westminster Hall and the nave of Westminster Abbey, and the building of the 'Bell Harry' tower by John Wastell, master mason of King's College, Cambridge. Its ornate, fan-vaulted ceiling rises 153ft above one's head inside the cathedral. There is so much beautiful stained glass to be seen that it is impossible to give more than a general outline here. The South Window's 12th-century glass depicts 22 patriarchs, including Methuselah chin upon hand, and with four windows in the Southeast Transept as recent as 1960, the work of Hungarian-born Erwin Bossanyi, the sense of continuity is maintained. The West Window is full of medieval kings and patriarchs, with Adam digging, and the 'Miracle Series' of twelve in Trinity Chapel illustrate the life of Becket and the cures he worked. It has been estimated that between 2,000 and 3,000 people are depicted in the windows of Canterbury Cathedral and one small panel often consists of hundreds of pieces. During both World Wars, they were removed from the cathedral for safe-keeping.

The celebrated stone screen or PULPITUM OF THE SIX KINGS runs around the choir. In the niches on one side are the cathedral's founder, King Ethelbert, Richard II and Henry V, and in those on the other side, Edward the Confessor, Henry IV and Henry VI. They survived the assaults of the Puritan soldiers under Colonel Sandys who discharged cannon at the gate and entered the cathedral on 27 May 1642 intent on destroying 'graven images'. Prior Henry of *Eastry, who designed the screen, sleeps beneath the stones a few steps away. Becket's shrine has gone, but near the place where it stood in mosaic-paved Trinity Chapel is the TOMB OF EDWARD, THE BLACK PRINCE, surmounted by a superb brass effigy of the hero of Crecy and Poitiers in full battle armour. Opposite is the only tomb of a king to be found in this cathedral, that of Henry IV beside his wife Joan of Navarre, both in lifelike albaster effigy. It was traditionally held that Henry's body was thrown overboard during a storm on its return from France and the coffin filled with stones, but when both coffins were opened in the 19th century, the remains of the royal couple were found to be almost as well preserved as their effigies. Some 50 Archbishops, as well as deans and cardinals, courtiers and knights are in their company. Surveying the presbytery and choir, the crossing of the nave and transepts under the central tower and the full Perpendicular sweep of the nave is ST AUGUSTINE'S CHAIR. He never sat in it, as it was carved from Purbeck marble in the 13th century, but nevertheless it is used for the enthronement of every new archbishop.

The Norman CRYPT is the largest of its kind in the world, 230ft long and 130ft wide, and much of it is above ground with daylight streaming in on columns which bear the marks and little jokes of the Norman masons who carved them 900 years ago. Animals playing musical instruments, a wyvern fighting a dog, a lion with a cross on its tail, adorn the block capitals of these pillars. It is the oldest part of the cathedral but even older are two columns from a long gone Romano-British church on the Kentish coast at *Reculver.

The GREAT CLOISTER, begun in

1397, was the work of the Kentish master mason, Stephen Lote. In its intricate vaulting is displayed the heraldic shields of more than 800 families, with the addition in 1982 of the emblem of John Paul II, the first Pope in history to be received at Canterbury. The adjoining CHAPTER HOUSE has the second largest wooden roof in England after Westminster Hall, its barrel vault constructed from Irish bog oak. It was here that Prime Minister Margaret Thatcher and the French President François Mitterand signed the treaty which finally set in motion the building of the Channel Tunnel. North of the cloisters, grouped around a large open courtyard, Green Court, are the buildings of the KING'S SCHOOL, founded in 1541 on the site of a monastery. One of its earlier pupils was the dramatist Christopher Marlowe, the son of a Canterbury shoemaker, who benefited from Archbishop Cranmer's desire to bring education to gifted children of humble parents. In more recent times Somerset Maugham attended as a pupil and bequeathed his personal collection of books to his old school in 1961. His ashes were scattered among the roses outside the MAUGHAM LIBRARY and a plaque is set in the wall under the window facing the external NORMAN STAIRCASE in the northwest corner of the court leading to one of the oldest schoolrooms. The school today occupies many mansions in the heart of Canterbury.

Canterbury has a wealth of historic buildings and ancient ruins. EASTBRIDGE HOSPITAL, built around 1175 in honour of Becket the Martyr, consists of a chapel, a refectory and a crypt where poor pilgrims were given free lodging. Churches such as ST MARTIN'S and ST PANCRAS are of Saxon and Roman origin. GREYFRIARS and BLACKFRIARS are missions dating from the 13th century. ST AUGUSTINE'S ABBEY stands just outside the city wall at the top of Lady Wootton's Green. All that remains are ruins except for the Fyndon Gate, built in the early 14th century when the abbey housed one of the richest and most powerful communities of monks in England, and now restored.

The Blitz of World War II failed to destroy this heritage and unwittingly brought to light the remains of even older communities, notably a well preserved ROMAN TESSELLATED PAVEMENT beneath Butchery Lane, now part of the Longmarket shopping precinct. It is a fine example of mosaic and underfloor heating (hypocaust) from a courtyard villa *c.* AD100. It will be closed during 1990 for extensive development, together with a collection of coins, pottery, jewellery and other finds from Roman Canterbury. There is a high-level walk, reached by ramp, along the parapet of the CITY WALLS, originally Roman but extended and further fortified by the Normans. At the southern side, these run round DANE JOHN GARDENS, probably not named after invaders from Scandinavia

The medieval charm of Canterbury

but a corruption of the Norman 'donjon' for CASTLE, the keep of which still stands solidly, overlooking the park with its mound and its charming monument to Christopher Marlowe surrounded by period houses where the latest generation of Canterbury children live and play.

The OLD WEAVER'S HOUSE, a black and white, half-timbered structure overhanging the River Stour, was named for the Protestant weavers who fled from religious persecution on the Continent and settled in Canterbury. The jetty where their raw material was unloaded from barges is now used to embark tourists on sightseeing tours by boat, the guides pointing out the medieval ducking stool which was used to punish nagging wives. The house is part coffee shop, part souvenir store selling local handicrafts.

The city's official guides lead gentle walking tours of the city or the cathedral and city combined, lasting from 75 to 90 minutes (0227 459779). Tours leave from the VISITOR INFORMATION CENTRE in St Margaret's Street (0227 767744), open Monday to Saturday throughout the year and on Sunday from May to September.

MUSEUMS
(Opening times and other details of all museums are available on 0227 766567.)

CANTERBURY HERITAGE in the 13th-century Poor Priests' Hospital in Stour Street uses holograms and computers in a 'time-walk' from Roman times to the Blitz of 1942. Among the treasures on display are silver spoons used by the Romans, the original Canterbury Cross which is a symbol of Christianity throughout the world, a fully threaded loom tended by a model of a Huguenot silk weaver, Joseph Conrad's writing desk and the *Invicta*, the 1830 steam engine which hauled the world's first regular passenger train from Canter-bury to *Whitstable.

ROYAL MUSEUM AND ART GALLERY in the High Street opposite the County Hotel displays, apart from fine paintings (many of local interest), Roman and Anglo-Saxon glass and jewellery, fine porcelain and Victorian toys. It is also the home of the MUSEUM OF THE BUFFS, the Royal East Kent Regiment. First raised in 1572, it took its nickname from the colour of its uniform in Victorian times, which in turn gave rise to the famous cry 'Steady the Buffs!'

WEST GATE, originally one of six built by the Normans was rebuilt in 1380 by Archbishop Sudbury against the rebellious peasants who eventually cut off his head. This is the gate through which Chaucer's pilgrims plodded and Henry V rode, victorious from Agincourt. Until 1829 it was the city jail, but now it is a museum of arms and armour with its 'murder holes' and ports for ancient cannon still intact. Visitors who climb a spiral stair to the battlements are rewarded with a fine view of the city.

ENTERTAINMENT

MARLOWE THEATRE, The Friars (0227 767246) stages a wide programme from opera, battle, serious drama and classical music, to comedy and light entertainment.

GULBENKIAN THEATRE on the University of Kent campus (0227 69075) has an eclectic programme, open to everyone, and a high standard of acoustics and seating comfort.

SHOPPING

People come to shop at Canterbury from many parts of Kent and there are shops for every taste and pocket, from the department stores and famous national chains of the MARLOWE ARCADE, opened in 1875, to the antique, second-hand and junk shops of NORTHGATE or the CHAUCER BOOKSHOP in Beer Cart Lane. The pedestrianised shopping areas are enlivened by the performances of buskers and street musicians. A short stroll down Sun Street and Palace Street bordering the cathedral precincts will take you past (or into) T AND B COUSINS in what was formerly the Sun Hotel dating from 1503 for jewellery and silverware, DEAKINS for fanciful walking sticks, CABLE AND KEAN for unusual French wines, 50 kinds of cheeses, as well as raised pies and farmhouse fudge made at Adisham, NICARO, a ladies' boutique, the CAPTAIN'S CABIN for golf and ski wear, luggage and leather goods. Another old-established store is SAUNDERS, now extended across St Peter's Street from its original premises occupying part of the Three Kings Tavern to the former Dog's Head in the Pot Inn, once owned by medieval monks. It stocks good china and toiletries, framed prints and turn-of-the-century postcards, toys, posters and games. CANTERBURY POTTERY is in the Buttermarket opposite the cathedral gate.

A market is held every Wednesday in Kingsmead Road and antique and collectors' markets take place on Saturdays in the Sidney Cooper Centre, St Peter's Street, and throughout the week at Latimers in Ivy Lane.

SPORT AND LEISURE

ST LAWRENCE GROUND is the home of Kent County Cricket Club. A cricket week is held there in August.

CANTERBURY GOLF CLUB (0227 463586) An 18-hole course at Littlebourne Road. Golfing visitors are welcomed except on Sunday mornings and before 10am on Saturdays.

KINGSMEAD STADIUM is the home of Canterbury City Football Club, where there is also speedway and greyhound racing.

VICTORIA RECREATION GROUND has tennis courts.

KINGSMEAD INDOOR SWIMMING POOL, Kingsmead Road (0227 69817).

CANTERBURY SPORTS CENTRE, Military Road (0227 763723). A variety of ball games and training facilities.

ENVIRONS

BLEAN BIRD PARK (0227 471666). Three miles northwest of Canterbury on the A290 to *Whitstable, an impressive collection of exotic birds such as macaws, cockatoos and toucans. There are also some monkeys and a pets' corner for children with lambs, guinea pigs and rabbits. Open daily from March to November.

HOWLETTS ZOO PARK (0227 721286). Three miles south of Canterbury on the A2 at BEKESBOURNE in the grounds of an 18th-century mansion, 50 exotic species in the wild including tigers, gorillas, rare breeds such as the Asiatic wild dog, the dhole, and striped antelope called bongo. In 1982 the first African elephant to be born in Britain was delivered at Howletts and named Sabi. Open daily, year round. Bekesbourne was the site of a medieval archbishop's palace destroyed by the Roundheads during the Civil War. All that remains is the gatehouse with walls 2ft thick. Archbishop Cranmer, in fear of being put to the stake on the death of King Edward VI, took refuge within. More recently, Ian Fleming found the setting of his novel *Moonraker* and inspiration for his James Bond stories while living at the Old Palace at Bekesbourne and his *Chitty Chitty Bang Bang* drew on a Count Zborowski who lived at nearby BRIDGE and owned a fabulous racing car.

FOOD AND DRINK

Canterbury abounds in taverns and teashops (the TEA POT in Northgate is recommended, as are MORELLI's ice cream parlours).

SEVENTY-FOUR, 74 Wincheap, Canterbury (0227 767411). *Haute cuisine.* Expensive.

WATERFIELD'S, 5a Best Lane, Canterbury (0227 450276). Good. Moderately expensive.

TUO E MIO, 16 The Borough, Canterbury (0227 61471). Welcoming – and busy – Italian restaurant.

ACCOMMODATION

COUNTY HOTEL, High Street CT1 2RX (0227 66266). Most central of positions, enhanced by its excellent restaurant called Sully's.

FALSTAFF HOTEL, 8–12 St Dunstan's Street CT2 8AF (0227 462138). Built in the 15th century, but modernised.

CHAUCER HOTEL, Ivy Lane CT1 1TT (0227 464427). The name, and its Pilgrims Bar, suggests more antiquity than it has but it provides modest comfort at reasonable prices.

UNIVERSITY OF KENT CT2 7NZ (0227 69186). Room for 1,940 guests in January, March–April, June–September and December with excellent facilities and food.

YOUTH HOSTEL, 54 Dover Road CT1 3DT (0227 462911). Inexpensive. Good facilities.

ST MARTIN'S CARAVAN AND CAMP SITE, Bekesbourne Lane CT3 4AB (0227 463216). Good site, 1½ miles east of the city off the A257 and well signposted from the A2 bypass. Open from April to September.

CHARING

This village has no connection with Charing Cross, but like the celebrated London station it is a place that most people seem to rush through, missing gems like moated Wootton Manor and other well preserved Tudor buildings which are hidden away in country lanes within a couple of miles of the busy junction where the A20 to the Channel ports branches to *Canterbury. Charing has been for centuries a staging post on the road from Maidstone to Canterbury and an even older route, the Pilgrims Way, traverses the steep escarpment of the Downs just to the north. In the 19th century the railway came, making Charing 'the last stop before Ashford'. Now the motorway and the Channel Tunnel rail link are passing the same way. For those with time to stand and stare, the old village that nestles in the fork of the two main roads has a timeless charm that resists any amount of traffic rushing by. Tudor houses such as the half-timbered PIERCE HOUSE overhang the long High Street. The village shops, including two family butchers (one of which also bakes bread on the premises) thrive. The remains of the ARCHBISHOPS' PALACE can be seen next to the Elizabethan church of St Peter and St Paul, whose battlemented ragstone tower surveys the red roofs and gables clustered below. It contains magnificent carved oak and a silver chalice. The palace became a farm after Henry VIII called there on his way to the Field of the Cloth of Gold with a retinue of thousands and Archbishop Cranmer made him a gift of it.

FOOD AND DRINK
ROYAL OAK, High Street, Charing (0233 712307). Beers drawn directly by tap and open fires over which chestnuts can be roasted. Fresh country food is served in the dining room, a restored maltings with barbecues on summer weekends in the garden, which includes a floodlit *petanque* pitch.

CHARTWELL

The house among the wooded hills just south of *Westerham off the B2026 would scarcely rate a mention among the galaxy of historic properties in Kent were it not the former and much-loved home of Sir Winston Churchill. When he bought it in 1922 for its bewitching views across the Weald, it was riddled with dry rot and it took two years to rebuild it. Its rooms, left as he knew them together with his books and pictures, documents and personal mementoes, still seem to echo to his much-imitated voice as he dictated his books to relays of secretaries or entertained his family, friends and visitors over the dinner table. The track he wore across the carpet in his study, pacing up and down, is still there. The desk is crowded with family photographs and above the fireplace hangs the flag that was hoisted over Rome by the Allied Army which liberated it in June 1944. Two of the 24 rooms have been adapted as a MEMORIAL MUSEUM by the National Trust, which owns and administers Chartwell, displaying photographs, documents, some of the many gifts that were showered on him and his various hats and uniforms, from the elaborate robes of Lord Warden of the Cinque Ports to the drab 'siren suit' which he habitually wore in his bunker in Whitehall.

So many people flock to Chartwell, especially on summer weekends and bank holidays, that a system of numbered and timed tickets has been introduced for entry to the house and a long wait may be necessary. Provided the weather is suitable, this can be passed pleasantly enough in the 80-acre grounds that delighted Churchill in his lifetime and where he created terraced gardens, the lake with its black swans, a heated outdoor swimming pool and waterfalls and built with his own hands the brick wall round the kitchen garden. Golden roses bloom in a garden specially planted for the Churchills' golden wedding in 1958 and the garden studio where he painted contains many examples of his work.

CHARTWELL (0732 866368) is open from March to November and is well signposted from the M25. It is difficult to get to without private transport. The nearest railway stations are at *Edenbridge, 4 miles away. There is a non-stop direct bus service Green Line 201 from London Victoria in peak summer (01-668 7261 for details). The garden is unsuitable for wheelchairs.

CHATHAM

As long ago as 1724 Daniel Defoe remarked that *Rochester, Strood and Chatham were 'three distinct places but contiguous except the interval of the river between the two first and a very small marsh or vacancy between Rochester and Chatham', and one of Dickens's characters said 'if anybody knows to a nicety where Rochester ends and Chatham begins it is more than I do'. Today these three places, together with GILLINGHAM and RAINHAM, are even more firmly welded together in the vast and unlovely conurbation of the Medway Towns.

Yet like its Siamese twin, Rochester, Chatham is steeped in history and retains a separate identity. From the time of Henry VIII it centred round a naval dockyard which for centuries built the 'wooden walls' on which British seapower depended, from the ships with which Sir Francis Drake outgunned the Spanish Armada to HMS *Victory*, from whose deck Lord Nelson directed the defeat of Napoleon's fleet at Trafalgar. Indeed, Nelson joined his first ship HMS *Raisonnable* at Chatham. In 1667 a Dutch naval force under Admiral de Ruyter attacked Chatham, severly damaging the docks and shipping in the estuary and towing away the flagship *Royal Charles* as a prize. Samuel Pepys was appointed secretary to the Admiralty not long after this humiliation and in his diary writes of Hill House at Chatham 'where they sported well and were late to bed'.

Charles Dickens spent the happiest years of his childhood at No. 2 Ordnance Terrace (now No. 11, marked by a plaque) when his father, a navy pay clerk, was transferred from Portsmouth to Chatham in 1816. Redcoats paraded in Chatham Lines on the hill behind the town, stagecoaches ran to London along the old Roman road and out in the estuary, where the Medway joins the Thames, convicts in chains in the prison hulks awaited transportation to New South Wales. Dickens found on revisiting Ordnance Terrace later in life that the green countryside round about had vanished with the arrival of the railway and the building of Chatham Station opposite his childhood home.

All that is left of Chatham's colourful maritime past is preserved as a museum piece now that it is no longer required for defence. Entering CHATHAM HISTORIC DOCKYARD (0634 812551) through an ornate gate which dates from 1719, visitors can hear and see the detailed story of its 400 years as a naval powerbase up to its closure in 1984. The visitors' centre is in what used to be the GALVANISING SHOP and the former LEAD AND PAINT MILL houses a collection of dockyard relics. But the pride of the dockyard is the covered slipways, where ships were built, and the 1,140ft-long ROPERY, where the traditional craft of making rope, which the young Charles Dickens saw as he went the rounds with his father, is kept alive. It's almost possible to smell the tar and the oak chippings beneath the slipways. HMS *Gannet*, a steam and sail sloop of 1878 is undergoing restoration. The Dockyard is open from Easter to October, Wednesday to Sunday and bank holidays.

The KINGSWEAR CASTLE, Britain's only surviving coal-fired paddlesteamer, carries passengers on Medway cruises from the dockyard and from Strood Pier, with a commentary. It has a vintage saloon selling food, drinks and souvenirs (0634 827648).

ST BARTHOLOMEW'S CHAPEL in the High Street is all that remains of the Norman hospice founded by the builder of the Tower of London, Bishop Gundulf, in 1078 to care for the poor. (Its National Health Service namesake on the original site claims direct descendancy as the oldest hospital in Britain, if not the world.) SIR JOHN HAWKINS' HOSPITAL, opposite, is a group of almshouses round a little square, named for the Elizabethan navigator and inventor of the slave trade. It has steps running down to the river. Founded in the 16th century as a retreat for 'poor, decayed mariners', it was completely rebuilt towards the end of the 18th century and modernised in the late 1950s when the almshouses became flats.

Compared to its glamorous neighbour, GILLINGHAM is left with very little to boast about. Its Football League team, although the only one in Kent, has never hit the top. None the less it is attracting a growing number of visitors, not least from Japan, because of one of its sons of long ago. Will Adams sailed for the East as 'pilot major' of a fleet of five Dutch ships and 22 months later his ship alone arrived off the coast of Japan. He stayed there until his death in 1620, by which time he had achieved Samurai rank, having advised the Shogun, built ships, set up a trading station for England and acquired a Japanese wife and family as well as vast estates. It is not recorded what happened to the wife and family he left behind in Gillingham, where he is commemorated by the imposing CLOCK TOWER MEMORIAL in Sovereign Boulevard. Will Adams was baptised in 1564 at the Norman font in the parish church of St Mary Magdalene at Gillingham Green.

The TOURIST INFORMATION CENTRE (0634 360323) is at Farthing Corner Motorway Services area on the M2, open daily with a 24-hour telephone answering service.

MUSEUMS

MEDWAY HERITAGE CENTRE, Dock Road, Chatham (0634 407116). In St Mary's Church, it tells the history of the Medway from prehistoric times, from the mudflats and creeks between the isles of Grain and Sheppey upriver as far as Allington Lock, *Maidstone, where it ceases to be tidal. Open Wednesday to Saturday and Sunday afternoons; Wednesday and Sunday afternoons only during the winter.

FORT AMHERST, opposite the Heritage Centre (0634 47747). Best example of a Georgian fortress from the Napoleonic era, with its Great Lines begun in 1756 to

Georgian uniforms on parade at Fort Amherst

protect the dockyard. Extensive restoration of the redoubts and 2,500ft of tunnels has been carried out and the 14-acre site includes a picnic area. Open daily in the afternoons from July to September; weekends and Wednesdays at other times of the year.

ROYAL ENGINEERS MUSEUM, Brompton Barracks, direct access from the B2004 (0643 44555). The life, work and sheer inventive genius of soldier engineers from the Romans to World Wars, including the illustrious career of General Gordon of Khartoum. A splendid bronze statue of him mounted on a camel stands within the barracks, opposite a memorial to the general who followed him in the Sudan, Lord Kitchener.

SHOPPING

HEMPSTEAD VALLEY SHOPPING CENTRE, in the green lung of the Medway Towns with easy access from the major roads, is open from 10am to 8pm (9pm on Fridays). SavaCentre and Safeways open at 8am. All toilets have facilities for nursing mothers and there are special facilities for the disabled together with a free wheelchair service. Four 'fast food' outlets operate the PICNIC PARLOUR, seating 200. Centre closed on Sundays but there's a FLEA MARKET on the second Sunday in every month.

SPORT AND LEISURE

CAPSTONE COUNTRY PARK (0634 812196), signposted from Junction 4 on the M2 Motorway, encapsulates the natural flora and fauna of the North Downs, with a picnic area, Visitor Centre and coarse fishing on a lake. It also contains the ALPINE SKI CENTRE (0634 827970), otherwise known as 'the Chatham Alps' for its floodlit 200-metre dry ski slope and nursery slope. There are two ski lifts and equipment can be hired. Restaurant and coffee shop. Open seven days a week.

RIVERSIDE COUNTRY PARK (0634 378987). Sixty acres of unspoiled riverside beside the B2004 at Gillingham for walks along part of the SAXON SHORE WAY, picnics and birdwatching. Visitor Centre with video displays. Free car parking.

BLACK LION SPORTS CENTRE (0634 53784). Near the town centre, has several swimming pools, six squash courts, a projectile range, weights room and a Sports Hall the size of eight badminton courts for the whole range of indoor pursuits. Cafeteria and bar, free parking, special facilities for the disabled. Open daily, year round.

GILLINGHAM MARINA provides extensive berthing facilities for boat owners and access to either upriver or to the estuary beyond Gillingham Reach.

THE ICE BOWL (0634 388477) on the A278 or junction 4 off the M2 is open daily, with skate hire, a licensed bar and a cafeteria. Claims the 'largest video screen in Kent' and has satellite TV.

ACCOMMODATION

CREST, Maidstone Road, Chatham ME5 9SF (0643 687111) is located close to the M2 at Junction 3. It has 105 rooms all with baths and Oliver's restaurant and bar. Moderately expensive.

CHEVENING

Not open to visitors, the great house of the Stanhopes, on the slopes of the North Downs overlooking the M25 between *Westerham and *Sevenoaks, is an impressive if little-visited place. When the last Lord Stanhope died in 1957 it became the official residence of the Foreign Secretary. Among the treasures hidden from prying eyes behind its Inigo Jones battlements are said to be the telescope through which Wellington watched the progress of the Battle of Waterloo, Pitt's despatch box and Byron's manuscripts. There is, however, a public footpath through the great park from the NORTH DOWNS WAY on the hillside above and it's a pleasant walk. The tiny hamlet of Chevening with its Norman church is completely overshadowed by the big house where Lady Hester Stanhope lived before she went to the Lebanon and became leader of the Druses and where the 3rd Earl Charles Stanhope took out patents for steamships and stereotyping, lightning conductors, microscopic lenses and a new way of making cement. He withdrew from political life after finding himself in a 'minority of one' in favour of recognising the French Republic after the Revolution and was referred to as 'Citizen Stanhope'.

CHIDDINGSTONE

The National Trust owns a substantial part of this idyllic village in open countryside between Westerham and Tunbridge Wells, near *Edenbridge: a row of houses dating from the 16th and 17th centuries, the CASTLE INN and the post office and general store in its one street. So perfect is its preservation that it is in demand as a location whenever a film set in Tudor times is being made. St Mary's Church, rebuilt in the 17th century after a fire, has a fine Perpendicular tower and quaint collection of carved stone faces. The iron tomb covers in the floor were made at nearby *Cowden. A public footpath leads to a large sandstone rock, the CHIDING STONE from which the village might have taken its name. It also belongs to the Trust, a gift with the half acre of land on which it stands from Lord Astor of Hever. Nagging wives, it's claimed, were brought here for scolding as a variant of the ducking stool treatment.

CHIDDINGSTONE CASTLE (0892 870347) isn't what, at first sight, it appears to be – a Gothic fortress. Behind its stone castellations and turrets added by a Victorian archi-

tect is the late 17th-century manor house which was the home until 1938 of the Streatfield family, whose fortune was originally founded on the iron industry. It is still privately owned but open to visitors from the last week in March until the end of October. Inside is an oddly assorted collection of ancient Egyptian and Tibetan artefacts, Buddhist paintings, Japanese lacquerwork and relics of the Royal House of Stuart, brought together by a recent former owner of the castle, Denys Eyre Bower who died in 1977. The setting is a broad, rolling park with gardens that are looking in need of love and attention. Day permits are issued for fishing on the lake.

FOOD AND DRINK

THE CASTLE, Chiddingstone (0892 870247). Inn dating from 1420 and maintaining its centuries-old tradition of hospitality with pub food in the bar or garden or full meals in the small restaurant using fresh local produce, with a wide choice of wines. Fairly expensive.

VILLAGE TEA SHOP, Chiddingstone (0892 870326). More than just a teashop, it serves excellent meals (and wines) in a delightful courtyard setting.

CHILHAM

This village built around a square, 6 miles southwest of *Canterbury on the A252, attracts hordes of visitors who feel they are stepping back in time. And apart from the cars and coaches which bring them there, the scene is virtually unaltered from what it would have been four or five centuries ago. The illusion is heightened on Spring Bank Holiday when villagers dressed in medieval costume lay out the stalls for a 'pilgrims' fayre'. On summer weekends knights in armour engage in mock tournaments in the park by the CASTLE (0227 730319), home of the Jousting Association of Great Britain, and falconry demonstrations are given. A ruined keep is all that remains of the octagonal castle built by Henry II for the immense sum of £400 but the title was kept for the Jacobean mansion built by Sir Dudley Digges. Its gables and tall chimneys dominate the 300-acre park, with its terraced lawns and gardens laid out by John Tradescant and views of Canterbury Cathedral in the distance. The mulberry trees which grow here are 500 years old. The house and castle ruins are not open to visitors but the grounds are, from April to October.

The castle gates are at one end of the village square, with the 15th-century flintstone church of St Mary at the other. It has a Perpendicular tower and contains a grandiose marble monument to Lady Digges. The square is lined with Tudor and Jacobean houses, all in a perfect state of preservation and adorned with rambling flowers, a delight to wander round especially during the week or out of season when the crowds have gone.

ENVIRONS

Just to the north is the hamlet with the curious name of OLD WIVES LEES where until this century there was an annual race between two village youths and two maidens for a prize endowed by Sir Dudley Digges. The tradition is no more. PERRY WOOD and SELLING WOOD, 150 acres criss-crossed by paths and tracks with lovely spots for picnics, lie 2 miles northwest of the A252 between SELLING and SHOTTENDEN. On the slopes to the south, on the opposite side of the A28 above the railway level crossing, JULLIBERIE DOWNS takes its name from Julius Laberius who died here fighting for the glory of Rome in 54BC. It is believed that the NEOLITHIC LONG BARROW, which existed thousands of years before then and whose remains survive, was opened to bury the Roman dead.

ACCOMMODATION

WOOLPACK INN, High Street, Chilham CT4 8DL (0227 730208). Oak-beamed bar hung with hop vines, inglenook fireplace. Traditional food and ales are served and there are 17 bedrooms in converted stables and an annexe across the courtyard.

COBHAM

Although the outer suburbia of the Medway towns has been creeping up on it, this village just south of the old Dover road remains a place of pilgrimage to all lovers of Dickens. The author used to go there as a boy on long country rambles with his father and it appeared later in his novels, with vivid descriptions of the LEATHER BOTTLE INN where Mr Tupman retired hurt from his encounters with Miss Wardle. Cobham has further delights for visitors. A cluster of little white Tudor almshouses known as COBHAM COLLEGE is still inhabited by elderly local folk. The church of St Mary Magdalene contains the finest cavalcade in brass to be found anywhere, portraits of some 60 adults and children in the costume of the 14th and 15th centuries. It is in effect a sort of family album of the Cobhams who with the Earls of Darnley had their seat at Cobham Hall, one of Kent's most stately homes. It is of Elizabethan red brick and Caen stone with four domed octagonal towers, a decorative array of chimneys and a colonnaded front. Both Inigo Jones and Robert Adam took a hand in its design and its park was landscaped by Humphrey Repton at the end of the 18th century. Some majestic trees adorn the park including a great chestnut called the Four Sisters and an avenue of limes 1,000 yards long. COBHAM HALL (0474 823371) is now a boarding school for girls but can be visited on some bank holidays and on certain days from late July to early September. The great gallery is 130ft long with a carved marble Tudor chimneypiece and there is a room furnished to receive Queen Elizabeth I, although she never in fact slept in it.

Cobham has two other historic homes: OWLETTS at the west end of the village, a modest red brick house with a staircase and plasterwork dating from the reign of Charles II, and the half-timbered TUDOR YEOMAN'S HOUSE a mile away in the hamlet of Sole Street. Both are owned by the National Trust and administered by tenants who welcome visitors. Owletts is open 2pm–5pm on Wednesdays and Thursdays from 29 March to the end of September. Only the main hall of the Yeoman's House may be visited, on written application.

ENVIRONS

The A2 trunk road bisects the woods that Dickens loved and where he took his last walk before he died on 9 June 1870 at GADSHILL, an ivy-fronted, rose-brick mansion above HIGHAM on the A226 road from Rochester to Gravesend. On this same road Falstaff lay in wait to rob pilgrims on the way to Canterbury. Dickens used a tunnel under it from his house to the garden on the SHORNE side where he worked in a Swiss chalet with views down over the cornfields to the River Medway, busy with shipping. The house isn't open to visitors and the chalet has been moved to the Dickens Centre in *Rochester. Since World War II much of the surrounding countryside has disappeared under new housing estates so we must be grateful for the efforts now being made to preserve some of it at SHORNE COUNTRY PARK, 174 acres of woodland, open heath and wetland, and SHEPHERDS GATE, a 3-acre picnic place in the woods, both adjoining the A2 London–Dover road at the Cobham-Shorne interchange.

FOOD AND DRINK
LEATHER BOTTLE, The Street, Cobham (0474 814327). Straight from the pages of *Pickwick Papers*, this half-timbered tavern continues to dispense ale, food and good cheer. Seven rooms for those who want to tarry.

COOLING

'Pip's village' lies at the heart of a mysterious stretch of marshland and mudflats, criss-crossed by remote creeks, to the south of the Thames Estuary opposite Canvey Island. It is in the Hoo Hundred (an archaic sub-division of a county) and although it is only 40 miles from London this is Kent at its wildest and least visited. Just one major road, the A228 from *Rochester, runs east to west across the wetlands to the Isle of Grain where the Medway and the Thames meet. Cooling is on one of the byroads which meander off the highway and peter out among the reeds. Signposts are few, and one confusingly points in two opposite directions to the village of CLIFFE, once famous as the meeting place of Great Councils of Kent long before the Normans came. Cooling, if you can find it, is a surprising little place with its own castle built by the Cobhams in the 14th century against the possibility of a French invasion. In 1554 it was under siege for just six hours during the revolt of Sir Thomas Wyatt the Younger against Mary Tudor. Until quite recently it was an overgrown ruin but it has been tidied up and the round machicolated towers of the gateway are approached across smooth lawn shaded by weeping willows and other trees, with flowers everywhere. The church of St James's is of the same vintage as the castle, but intact. In the churchyard, near the south door 13 skittle-shaped stones, ten in one row and three in another nearby, mark the graves of children who died of marsh fever 200 years ago. It was this gruesome sight which gave Dickens the dramatic opening of *Great Expectations* where Pip startles Magwitch, the escaped convict from the prison hulk hiding among the graves.

COWDEN

So tucked away is this village in a clearing of the wooded western borders of Kent with Surrey and Sussex that you would never imagine that it was one of the last places in the south of England manufacturing iron before that industry moved north. Such was the demand for cannons that whole forests of mighty oaks had been decimated. Furnace Farm stands by the pond whose waters used to drive the ironmaster's hammers. Now Cowden is an oasis of peace reached by a winding lane off the B2026, which itself is nothing like as straight as the road that the Romans built from London to Lewes and which passed this way.

The village has a 14th-century church with an oak-shingled tower and spire, a schoolhouse with fine Tudor beams, an old inn and several Tudor and Jacobean manor houses round about. The railway station on the London–Uckfield line is almost a mile away across the fields. The SUSSEX BORDER PATH runs beside a stream known as Kent Water to the south of the village.

FOOD AND DRINK
CROWN INN, The Square, Cowden (0342 850477). A cheerful old inn, famed locally for its spit roasts over apple logs.

CRANBROOK

This proud, historic market town of the Weald lies within a circle of wooded hills, just off the A229 road from Maidstone to Hastings and under 50 miles from London but in another world. In the 15th century Flemish weavers migrated here and made it a prosperous centre of cloth manufacture. The vast wealth which these 'Grey Coats of Kent' created over the next two or three centuries is still visible today in the rich architecture of the place. When Queen Elizabeth I was here she trod a full mile of local broadcloth laid from the George Inn to Coursehorn, one of the houses of a prosperous weaver. Whether this predated Sir Walter Raleigh's famous throwing of his cloak over a puddle is uncertain,

but any visitor who cares to retrace her steps without the red carpet can easily visualise the scene as both the inn and the mansion still exist. Queen Elizabeth laid the foundation stone of CRANBROOK SCHOOL, which has long since outgrown this original building, and presented it with a fine table. A year later she granted the school a royal charter bearing her engrossment and seal.

The church of St Dunstan was built in 1291 but adorned so grandly later that it became known as the 'Cathedral of the Weald' and it lives up to its title. It is 150ft long with an octagonal turret and a square tower, 90ft high, with another turret and a gorgeous weather-vane. Above the south porch is a room known as BAKER'S HOLE after

Mary Tudor's Chancellor who used it for torturing protestants before they went to the stake. Sir John Baker used the plunder from his murders to build a castle for himself at *Sissinghurst. Cranbrook's other outstanding sight is the UNION MILL, built in 1814, the sails which gave it the nickname of 'The Peacock' still turning.

In Victorian times a Cranbrook School of Artists flourished and the tradition is continued at the CRAFT CENTRE where the work of local craftsmen and artists is displayed.

The INFORMATION CENTRE at Vestry Hall in Stone Street (0580 712538) handles visitors' inquiries during the summer period only.

MUSEUM

CRANBROOK MUSEUM (0580 714222) concentrates on the vanished cloth and iron industries of the Weald and also has displays of agricultural and domestic items from the past, including toys. It is open on certain days from February to December.

SPORT AND LEISURE

CRANBROOK GOLF CLUB is in Benenden Road (0580 712934).

Visitors are welcome except on competition days.

FOOD AND DRINK

THE GEORGE, Stone Street, Cranbrook (0580 713348). Queen Elizabeth I definitely slept here and a drink or a snack in the low-ceilinged bar is almost obligatory, if you can get in.

WINDMILL, on the edge of the town, up a bank (0580 713119). Over 400 years old. Restaurant serves good English fare. Children's menu.

ACCOMMODATION

KENNEL HOLT, Goudhurst Road TN17 2PT (0580 712032). Elizabethan country house hotel in six acres, 2 miles out of town. Cordon bleu cooking during the week. Traditional roast on Sundays. Comfortable rooms. Moderate.

OLD CLOTH HALL TN17 3NR (0580 712220). A mile along the *Tenterden road, well-preserved example of a prosperous weaver's manor house in its own park, with a swimming pool and tennis court added. Just three bedrooms, unlicensed, dinner for residents only. Moderately expensive.

CROCKHAM HILL

One of the grandest panoramas of the Weald spanning Kent, Surrey and Sussex can be seen from the summit just south of *Westerham on the B2026, a view shared by the old houses of Froghole and Mariners sheltering in lovely gardens on the south facing slopes, just over the hill from Churchill's *Chartwell. A seat has been provided by the National Trust for those who want to pause a while. The gesture is appropriate because Octavia Hill, the founder of the Trust, lies by the altar in Holy Trinity church on the hillside beneath her effigy in grey marble. It is reached by a narrow lane just up the hill from the Royal Oak. The churchyard is a beautiful sunny garden, half wild and sharing the incomparable view. Next to it is the village school, with its own diminutive bell, serving a scattered rural community only 25 miles from London.

ACCOMMODATION

HARMANS ORCHARD, Froghole TN8 6TD (0732 866417). Inexpensive bed and breakfast.
CROCKHAM HILL YOUTH HOSTEL, Crockham Hill, TN8 6RB (0732 866322). Inexpensive beds in a splendid old house, with hot showers. Facilities for camping, also.

DARENTH

Just to the east of the M25 as it approaches the Dartford Tunnel, this hamlet boasts one of the oldest churches in England and the site of a Roman settlement on the banks of the River Darent. The local pride of its inhabitants was demonstrated fiercely in opposition to British Rail's proposals to run the high-speed Channel Tunnel link through the area. The Roman remains include a great villa with a main corridor 12ft wide, courtyards, stables, workshops, water tanks, a 40ft long bath and of course underfloor warm air heating. It had glazed windows, painted walls and tessellated paving. Coins, oyster shells, pottery, bangles and small items such as bronze tweezers from the site are in *Dartford Museum. Flints and tiles from fine buildings that had fallen into ruin were used 1,000 years ago in the building of Darenth Church. The north and west walls of the nave are Saxon. The walls of the sanctuary are immensely thick and above is a small chamber only 12ft square with no access from inside the church, though it has a small round window outside. It may have been a priest's hideout.

ST JOHN'S JERUSALEM GARDEN at *Sutton-at-Hone*, a mile south on the A225 towards FARNINGHAM, is surrounded by a moat beside the river. The Knights Hospitallers church on this site from the time of King John was rebuilt as a private house by Edward Hasted who wrote his monumental *History of Kent* here between 1757 and 1776. A small 13th-century chapel retained for family worship and later converted into a billiards room is open to visitors, together with the garden. Open on Wednesdays only 2pm–6pm from 29 March to the end of October, it is administered and largely maintained for the National Trust by a tenant.

DARTFORD

The name of Dartford is associated mainly with the extremely busy road tunnel beneath the Thames connecting the northern and southern halves of the M25 London Orbital Motorway. It is, however, one of the oldest settlements in Kent. 'Swanscombe Woman', the earliest human remains unearthed so far in Britain, was discovered nearby. Dartford takes its name from the Saxon Darentford, a crossing of the narrow River Darent which flows into the Thames here across the marshes. With the arrival of the Romans, it became a staging post on Watling Street. It played a pioneering role in the Industrial Revolution as the home of steam power. Today's tunnel and tomorrow's bridge to be built across the Thames – both the nearest road crossings to the Estuary – ensure a continuing flow of travellers across Dartford's boundaries. A vista of cement works and freight terminals doesn't encourage tourists but those with the time, inclination and curiosity will find plenty of interest in a town that most pass by, and they'll be treading in the footsteps of Chaucer, Henry VIII, Cardinal Wolsey, Queen Elizabeth I, Samuel Pepys and John Wesley.

Hasted wrote in 1789 'Dartford is at present a handsome and wealthy town, still increasing in size and inhabitants, the principal street of which is the great thoroughfare from London to Dover, on which there are built several good inns.' At least one of those inns, the ROYAL VICTORIA AND BULL with its galleried coachyard, is still in business 200 years later. The River Darent runs under the main street near the church built by Bishop Gundulf, who also built the White Tower of the Tower of London. The church contains a memorial tablet to Richard Trevithick, the Cornishman who built in 1801 a steam-powered road locomotive and in 1804 the first steam engine to run on rails. In his workshop here he adapted steam power to ships, both by paddle and screw, and to agricultural machinery, yet as the tablet says he 'died in poverty and was carried to his grave in the churchyard of St Edmund, king and martyr, by the mechanics of Hall's engineering works, where he was then employed'. John Hall, who also came to Dartford towards the end of the 18th century in search of work, started in a shop the engineering firm which became world famous for its engines. The Dartford and Crayford Ship Canal was built so that vessels could be brought to the workshops to be fitted out, half a century ahead of the Manchester Ship Canal.

Two miles east of Dartford on the A226 to Gravesend, STONE LODGE FARM PARK (03422 343456) recreates a Kentish farm of the past with shire horses, hand milking and spinning. It is open daily from April to September with special craft shows on Sundays.

MUSEUM

DARTFORD MUSEUM in the 1916-vintage Public Library in Market Street (0322 343555) is worth a detour in itself to see a replica of the Swanscombe Skull which is in the British museum and the unique glass Darenth Bowl dating from AD 450, the period of Saxon Christianity a century and a half before St Augustine arrived in Kent. Open Saturdays and weekdays apart from Wednesdays.

ENTERTAINMENT

THE ORCHARD, Home Gardens (0322 343333), a creation of the 1980s seating 900 people, stages plays, opera, ballet and light entertainment and can switch to being a sports arena in between.

SHOPPING

A SATURDAY MARKET still operates in the High Street under a Royal Charter granted by James I. The THURSDAY MARKET, one of the largest of its kind in Kent, is conducted under one vast roof next to the PRIORY CENTRE, a 20th-century shopping mall. Another large complex, THE ORCHARDS, is being developed at the other end of the High Street.

SPORTS AND LEISURE

CENTRAL PARK, 27 acres of open space along the banks of the Darent, is the venue of the annual DARTFORD SHOW in July and nearby is the newly completed WATERWORLD with its swimming pools, chutes, flumes and 'rapids' in the micro-climate of a jungle.

HESKETH PARK maintains a tradition of county cricket going back to 1709.

DARTFORD GOLF CLUB (0322 26409). An 18-hole course where visitors are welcome on weekdays if a member of another club and at weekends with a member. It lies at the edge of 340 acres of open heath where the Dartford Warbler (now found only in Dorset) was discovered in 1773.

THE DARENT VALLEY PATH is a waymarked walk along the riverbank from the Library through Central Park and skirting Brooklands Lake, near which are the remains of an 18th-century Gunpowder Factory.

DEAL

Facing France across the sheltered waters known as the Downs between the shore and the treacherous GOODWIN SANDS, Deal has been a frontier against the Continent for as long as history records. Its shingle beach saw clean-shaven soldiers in armour wading ashore from Caesar's galleys, bronze eagle held aloft, in 55BC. During the reign of Henry VIII in the 16th century three of the great fortresses built to protect England against invaders from the Catholic powers of Europe were on this stretch of coast. DEAL CASTLE, southwest of the town centre (0304 372762) is the largest and most intact example, despite a direct hit by the Germans in World War II.

Six semi-circular bastions fan out from the round central keep, surrounded by a huge moat, a giant's sandcastle turned to stone. It is open all year and a display inside shows how the medieval coastal forts were built. Self-guiding tours on tape are available, players provided, here and at Walmer Castle on the coast to the south, which since the early 18th century has been the official residence of the Lord Warden of the Cinque Ports. It is closed to visitors when the holder of that office (currently, Elizabeth, the Queen Mother) is in residence. The Duke of Wellington was in residence when he died in 1852 and his furnished rooms have been preserved as they were. WALMER CASTLE (0304 364288) contains memorabilia of other Lord Wardens, including Sir Winston Churchill, and is open, together with its gardens and a moat full of flowers, all year.

In the midst of all this antiquity, the town of Deal is almost *parvenu*. Its oldest houses, 18th and 19th century, are crowded into the narrow lanes and alleyways between Middle Street and the High Street. Some of them had access to the beach by secret underground tunnels when smuggling – or 'free-trading' as the fishermen preferred to call it – was a local preoccupation. William Cobbett, passing through on his *Rural Rides* in 1823 found it a villainous place 'full of filthy-looking people'. Present-day Deal is a friendly, unassuming town with none of the excesses of the more developed seaside resorts around the North Foreland. The

beach is steeply sloped and a rescue boat patrols every day in summer. The WALMER LIFEBOAT, a descendant of the first one installed in 1857, stands ready on its ramp on the beach ready to answer any emergency call.

MUSEUMS

TIME BALL TOWER, Victoria Parade (0304 201066). Built on the seafront around 1821 as part of an anti-smuggling campaign to pass semaphore signals to Customs patrols. The timeball came later, connected electrically to Greenwich and dropping at precisely 1pm each day to indicate Greenwich Mean Time to shipping in the Downs. It still does, but for demonstration only, as part of the museum of time and telegraphy, open from Late Spring Bank Holiday to the end of September, except Mondays.

THE TOWN HALL, High Street (0304 369576) contains a museum (open by appointment only) of historical relics including the complete robes of a baron of the Cinque Ports. The TOURIST INFORMATION CENTRE is located here.

THE LIBRARY, Broad Street (0304 374726) houses an Archaeological Collection spanning 5,000 years from the New Stone Age to the Middle Ages. Open Monday to Saturday, closed half day Wednesdays and on public holidays.

MARITIME AND LOCAL HISTORY MUSEUM, 22 St George's Road (0304 362837) includes Deal beach boats which used to carry pilots, passengers and stores to ships anchored in the Downs and the multi-oared galleys sometimes with sails used by smugglers to outrun the Customs cutters. Stern boards from the clipper fleet which included the Cutty Sark (now at Greenwich) are also displayed. Open daily in the afternoons from May to September.

SPORT AND LEISURE

SEA FISHING: The Deal beaches offer excellent cod fishing in winter. The 1,000ft long pier gives good access to cod, whiting, dabs, mackerel, plaice, bass, pout, pollack and garfish all year round, particularly suitable for youngsters. A toll is charged on a daily basis.

ROYAL CINQUE PORTS GOLF CLUB in Golf Road (0304 374007) has 18 championship holes spread over 6,407 yards of coastal links north of Sandown Castle ruins. The last three letters of its phone number give a clue: did James Bond play here in *Goldfinger*? Visitors need a letter of introduction but you can walk the hallowed turf without challenge if you keep to the SAXON SHORE WAY.

ENVIRONS

The celebrated 'white cliffs' start at KINGSDOWN, which lies below RINGWOULD on the A258 just south of Deal. Footpaths run along the foreshore at the end of Undercliffe Road and up on to the cliffs. This area is used as a rifle range by the Royal Marines but a notice board gives firing times and red flags fly when it is in progress.

ACCOMMODATION

Deal has no 'Grand Hotels' but plenty of small, friendly ones of which the following are examples: BLENCATHRA, Kingsdown Hill, Deal CT14 8EA (0304 373725). FINGLESHAM GRANGE, Finglesham, Deal CT14 0NQ (0304 611314). SUTHERLAND HOUSE, 186 London Road, Deal CT14 9PT (0304 362853).

DOVER

Despite the growth of air travel, Dover remains, as it has been for the past 2,000 years, a main gateway to England. Every few minutes a ship, hovercraft or hydrofoil arrives or departs with vehicles and passengers, shuttling back and forth to Continental Europe. The Straits of Dover, a mere ditch of 22 miles, is the M1 of world shipping but it is very easy to 'nip across' in either direction for a day's shopping. The Channel Tunnel, emerging behind the famous white cliffs, is undoubtedly a challenge to Dover's age-old supremacy of the cross-Channel routes but the town has risen to challenges often enough, and survived. It has teamed up with its neighbours *Deal and *Sandwich as 'White Cliffs Country' and in the spring of 1991 will concentrate its tourist attractions into a distinctive brick building with 'a Martello-style tower'. This development, close to the ROMAN PAINTED HOUSE and incorporating Dover's old market hall, will project the history of the port in eleven linked exhibitions and show areas and include the town museum, a cinema, a themed shopping fair and a restaurant. Dover, which was headquarters of the *Classis Britannica*, the northern fleet of Rome, has a lot of history to display. The chalk cliffs were billions of years old when Caesar landed; as soon as he had won the Battle of Hastings in 1066, William the Conqueror hurried round the coast to command them before heading up Watling Street to London; in World War II when Britain stood alone they were a symbol of resistance and of hope of eventual victory. In medieval times Dover was the most powerful of the Cinque Ports and is still dominated by its castle, one of the largest and best preserved in the country. This is the best place to start a tour.

DOVER CASTLE

Beside the steep road that leads up to the castle is a cannon presented by the Dutch and known as 'Queen Elizabeth's Pocket Pistol'. The great keep and the curtain wall around it was built by Henry II in the 12th century for £7,000, a sum comparable to the cost of a Polaris fleet today. Reinforcements and additions continued over the centuries; Henry VIII in particular saw it as the strongest link in his chain of south coast defences. There is not a great deal to see inside the keep apart from a model of the Battle of Waterloo and 'All the Queen's Men', an exhibition tracing the history of the British army. Spiral staircases climb to the top for a rewarding view of Dover and the French coast on a clear day. The Castle (0304 201628) is administered by English Heritage and is open year round. Although the last army units left in 1958, the Royal Artillery fires its 155mm Howitzers in salute on royal anniversaries. The Order of the Black Prince stages medieval combats throughout the summer.

Within the curtain walls is the Saxon church of ST MARY-IN-CASTRO and, immediately beside it, Dover's oldest building, the octagonal PHAROS, or lighthouse, built by the Romans to guide their galleys across from Gaul, stands 40ft high on a green mound. Originally, it was twice that height. Another interesting sight nearby is the LOUIS BLERIOT MEMORIAL, the granite shape of an aeroplane in the turf on the spot where the French aviator touched down in 1909, the first man to cross the Channel by air. Down below on the promenade two statues commemorate other historic crossings – Charles Stewart Rolls (of Rolls-Royce) who flew the Channel both ways in a single flight in 1910 and Captain Matthew Webb, the first man to swim it, in 1875.

On Western Heights, facing the castle across the wide valley of the Dour from which Dover takes its name, is the GRAND SHAFT, a 140ft triple staircase built in 1809 as a short cut to the town and harbour for soldiers based at the large garrison built up during the Napoleonic Wars. It can be explored from 2pm to 5pm between the Spring Bank Holiday and September (0304 201066).

Dover's TOURIST INFORMATION CENTRE is in Townwall Street (0304 205108).

MUSEUMS

ROMAN PAINTED HOUSE (0304 203279) in New Street is a further reminder of the importance and civilisation of Dubris, as the Romans called Dover. The remains of five rooms with underfloor heating can be seen together with illustrations and notes on Roman Dover and other finds. Open from April to September.

DOVER TOWN HALL or Maison Dieu, Ladywell (0304 201066). Originally a hospice for pilgrims founded by the Constable of Dover, Hubert de Burgh, in 1203, it has a beautifully vaulted ceiling, portraits, stained glass and a display of weapons. Open all year, Monday to Saturday.

DOVER TRANSPORT MUSEUM occupies an old pumping station in Connaught Road (inquiries to 33 Alfred Road, Dover CT16 2AD) and tells the story of local transport history by land, sea and air. The exhibits include a Fox-Walker locomotive of 1878 and Folkestone Cliff Lift Car dating from 1890. Open Easter to the end of September on Sundays and Bank Holidays but closed on the last weekend in June.

SHOPPING

Dover's shopping is concentrated in the pedestrianised CHARLTON CENTRE off the High Street.

ENVIRONS

The built-up area stretches inland to Whitfield and TEMPLE EWELL, both of which have ancient churches dating from the Saxons and Normans. The latter was a home of the crusading Knights Templar in the days of King John. On either side of the enclosed ferry docks and jetties is magnificent clifftop walking country. To the west ABBOT'S CLIFF and SHAKESPEARE CLIFF, 300ft high and as dizzying as its description in *King Lear*, are traversed by the NORTH DOWNS WAY, which runs all the way from Farnham in Surrey and forms a wide loop between Canterbury and Dover. There are army firing ranges all along this stretch of coast and warnings are given by red flags.

The clifftop walk east of Dover is part of the long-distance SAXON SHORE WAY, waymarked with a horned Viking helmet. It runs from LANGDON CLIFFS past the white-painted, classic Victorian SOUTH FORELAND LIGHTHOUSE, taken out of commission in 1988 and now in the care of the National Trust. Visitors may see its original machinery, including the 2-ton turntable for the revolving light. Along Lighthouse Road is ST MARGARET'S AT CLIFFE beside secluded St Margaret's Bay, the starting point for Channel swimmers since Captain Webb's day. Noel Coward had a house here, which he sold to Ian Fleming in 1951. The 'Master's' painting of the White Cliffs is now in Dover Museum. The PINES GARDENS, open daily (0304 853229) is imaginative with its larger-than-life Oscar Nemon statue of Sir Winston Churchill, Romany caravan and wishing well in the setting of specimen trees and shrubs, a lake and a waterfall.

ACCOMMODATION

CREST HOTEL, Whitfield, Dover CT16 3LF (0304 821222). A motor hotel on the A2 on the outskirts. All rooms have *en suite* bathrooms and shower and food ranges from coffee shop snacks to a full dinner in Bleriot's Restaurant. Moderately expensive.

WHITE CLIFFS, Waterloo Crescent, Dover CT17 9BP (0304 203633). On the seafront, five minutes from the ferries and Hoverport. Uninterrupted sea and harbour views, moderately expensive. Dogs are welcome, by arrangement.

DOVER MOAT HOUSE, Townwall Street, Dover CT16 1SZ (0304 203270). The town's only four-star hotel, yet moderately priced. It is between the Eastern and Western Docks, close to the railway station. There are family rooms, an indoor swimming pool and facilities for disabled visitors.

CLIFFE COURT, Marine Parade, Dover CT16 1LU (0304 211001). Comfortable, modernised Regency hotel on the seafront with ample parking in the forecourt and facilities for the disabled. Moderately expensive.

CHARLTON HOUSE YOUTH HOSTEL, 306 London Road, Dover CT17 0SY (0304 201314) is the best bargain in town with good facilities, centrally located.

HAWTHORN FARM, Martin Hill, Dover CT15 5LA (0304 852658) has sites for tents and caravans and good facilities, 3 miles northeast of Dover off the A258 road to Deal.

DOWNE

When Charles Darwin was writing his opus *On The Origin of Species by Means of Natural Selection* his 18th-century house was in the depths of the Kent countryside. Today, although Downe is part of the London Borough of *Bromley, it is still surrounded by woods and green fields on a by-road of the A233 south of Keston Ponds. Here Darwin, who had studied medicine and theology and served as a naturalist on the surveying voyage of the southern hemisphere in HMS *Beagle* in the 1830s, settled for 40 years with his wife and raised five daughters and five sons, some of whom became eminent scientists too. It was here that he placed the whole world of living things into a pattern which contradicted literal interpretations of the Book of Genesis and aroused furious controversy in church-dominated Victorian society. DOWN HOUSE (0689 59119) is owned by the Royal College of Surgeons and can be visited. It is closed on Mondays (except bank holidays) and for the whole of February. Darwin's study is as he left it and the grounds where he walked and pondered are preserved as the DARWIN MEMORIAL GARDEN.

Dungeness is known as the 'Cod Mecca'

DUNGENESS

The cooling towers of two nuclear power stations, Dungeness 'A' and 'B' dominate the flat marshland for miles around, but Dungeness, at Kent's most southerly point, should not be missed on their account. The 'A' station (0679 20461) is open to visitors, except children under 14, in the afternoons from June to September. Tickets should be obtained in advance from your nearest Electricity Showroom. Dungeness has a lifeboat station, a variety of lighthouses and the best sea fishing in Kent. It is also a terminus of one of Britain's most unusual steam railways which runs northwards up the coast for 14 miles to *Hythe. The world's shipping passes by on its way up the Channel, divided into 'lanes' to avoid collisions. There was a lighthouse on Dungeness Point from 1615 and the base of its first successor of 1792 is preserved as accommodation for lighthouse keepers. The light of the third model, 1904 vintage, was obscured by the power stations and although the structure still stands it has been replaced by a rather stylish 1961 lighthouse whose powerful Xenon electric arc lamp can be seen for 17 miles out to sea. Striped black and white, it is floodlit at night.

SPORT AND LEISURE

THE POINT around the lighthouse is known as the 'Cod Mecca' and on winter weekends it is thronged with enthusiasts fishing not only for cod but whiting and dab. In summer the catch is pout, bass, dabs, eels and sole. Tides and winds can be difficult and easier fishing can be found behind the power stations, where bass can be caught at low water in summer opposite the outfalls.

A 12,000-acre BIRD RESERVE run by the Royal Society for the Protection of Birds is open on Wednesdays, Thursdays and at weekends. There is an information centre approached along a lane at Boulderwall Farm on the road to *Lydd across Denge Marsh. A colony of terns nests there and Dungeness is the only regular breeding place in Britain of the 'common' gull.

DYMCHURCH

Penned in behind its Redoubt Wall against the Channel, the village is 7½ft below the high water mark. At its back door is the wide expanse of Romney Marsh, once the preserve of sheep and smugglers, now partly converted to arable farming. Dymchurch is still the traditional meeting place of the Lords, Bailiffs and Jurats of Romney Marsh – the 'lords of the Level' whose writ no longer runs. Their court room in NEW HALL ('new' because it replaced a predecessor burned down hundreds of years ago) is the office of the less romantically named Romney Marsh Level Internal Drainage Board and can be visited. Summer visitors come mainly for the pleasant sands and the low-key seaside entertainments of amusement arcades and funfairs, undeterred by the nuclear power stations which loom on the horizon. A ride on the ROMNEY, HYTHE AND DYMCHURCH RAILWAY (0679 62353) behind steam or diesel locomotives scaled down to a third of full size is a popular attraction.

MUSEUM

MARTELLO TOWER (No. 24), High Street (0303 873684) is one of a chain of 74 built between 1805 and 1812, restored in 1966 after long use as a coastguard station. It is now open from March to September with displays giving the background of England's defences against Napoleon.

ACCOMMODATION

Dymchurch abounds in self-catering chalets and caravans. There are a few guest houses, including:
CHANTRY, · Sycamore Gardens TN29 0LA (0303 873137). A well-recommended place with a good beach location, comfortable and moderately priced. Traditional English food.
WATERSIDE, 15 Hythe Road TN29 0LN (0303 872253). Also modestly priced and good value.

EAST FARLEIGH

The Medway here, just above *Maidstone, is crossed by a medieval bridge with five pointed arches, 100 yards long. Across it marched Cromwell's Roundheads under General Fairfax after a bloody battle with the Cavaliers. The VICTORY pub and an old-fashioned country railway station with a level crossing survey a very peaceful scene today. There is a weir and a lock below the bridge, crowded with pleasure boats in summer. In the little church at the top of the hill, between another pub and the post office, a wooden cross made from an aeroplane propellor commemorates a young Royal Flying Corps captain from this village who was killed in action over Ypres. Outside in the churchyard a war memorial remembers all those villagers who did not return, and near it is a simple cross for the victims of a peacetime tragedy – 43 strangers working in the hopfields at the end of summer 1849 who were wiped out by a cholera epidemic. The migratory armies of pickers are no more but East Farleigh is still up to its eyes in hop gardens.

EASTRY

This comfortable village behind *Sandwich, with some good inns and easy access to the coastal golf links, once had a palace of the Kentish kings who divided their realm into 'lathes'. In AD979, Ethelred the Unready gave the manor to the monks of Christ Church, Canterbury. Henry of Eastry, who is buried in *Canterbury Cathedral near his famous screen and for whom the Bell Harry Tower was named, was Prior here. Eastry Court on the site of the royal palace hides its antiquity behind a Georgian façade. Beneath the 66ft-high Norman tower of St Mary's church is the tomb of Captain John Harvey, killed in a battle with the French during the Napoleonic Wars after capturing three ships which are depicted in a marble sculpture. He was one of Nelson's ablest officers and the Admiral with Lady Hamilton was a visitor to Heronden House on the outskirts of the village. Off the lane leading north to WOODNESBOROUGH is a labyrinth of chalk caves, possibly Neolithic, under a private garden.

FOOD AND DRINK
COACH AND HORSES, Lower Street, Eastry (0304 611692). A 300-year-old de-licensed pub cooking fresh local produce accompanied by good wine. Not over-expensive.

EDENBRIDGE

The country charm of Edenbridge, 26 miles from London, has been seriously eroded by a sprawl of featureless estates housing metropolitan overspill, commuters and various light industries. Marlpit Hill is a hodge-podge of additions over the past 20 years, yet the long straight road through the town from the early 19th-century sandstone bridge is spanned by the sign of the 15th-century Crown Inn and remains unspoiled by modern shop and office fronts on either side. This road (B2026) follows the line of the London to Lewes Way paved by the Romans with ragstone 18ft wide and 7 inches thick. The highway crossed the Eden, a tributary of the Medway, at the Pons Edelmi and the town grew along this broad highway approaching the river crossing. In the 18th century Wolfe, father of the victor of Quebec, was employed between campaigns building a military road along the same line. There are some fine old timber-framed houses in and around Edenbridge and glorious gardens and woods.

The playwright John Osborne is the best known of recent residents. The 13th-century sandstone church of St Peter and St Paul has a stained glass window by the pre-Raphaelite Burne-Jones.

MUSEUM

HAXTED WATER MILL, 2 miles east of the town in Haxted Lane (0732 862914) dates from 1580 and has two working wheels on the River Eden. The museum includes working models, a picture gallery and slides with taped commentaries on milling history. The WEALDEN IRON EXHIBITION pinpoints 300 sites where this other vanished industry was carried on. Open year round, with a licensed restaurant and tearoom.

SPORT AND LEISURE

EDENBRIDGE GOLF AND COUNTRY CLUB in Crouch House Road (0732 865097) welcomes visitors but an advance phone call is recommended. Equipment can be hired.

FOOD AND DRINK

YE OLD CROWN, High Street, Edenbridge (0732 862108). An aura of smuggled liquor in the tap room.
HONOURS MILL, High Street, Edenbridge (0732 866757). Restaurant converted from the 18th-century town mill. French cooking. Expensive.

ACCOMMODATION

WHITE HORSE, High Street, Edenbridge TN8 5AJ (0732 862208). Historic inn with six bedrooms, all with colour TV and showers. Restaurant with varied menu. Moderately priced.
BLACK ROBINS FARM, Grants Lane, Edenbridge TN8 6AP (0732 863212). Inexpensive accommodation in three bedrooms on a 150-acre mixed farm.

ELHAM

This village (almost a town) nestles in the valley of that name running north from *Folkestone. Cottages with 18th-century façades of brick and tile cluster round the delightful Market Square, and the High Street is flanked by houses of varying periods, some half-timbered with upper storeys jutting out on carved brackets. It has a royal charter from Prince Edward (later Edward I) granting the right to hold a market every Monday. The grey stone church with its battlemented tower and steeple dates from the 13th century. It contains an alabaster triptych of Thomas Becket, Henry II and the murder in the cathedral. The ABBOTS FIRESIDE in the High Street is a medieval inn with grotesque carvings.

EMMETTS GARDEN

Signposted from A25 at *Sundridge, 5 acres of rare trees and shrubs cover the slopes of *Ide Hill under the natural umbrella of a huge Wellingtonia, whose 100ft high top still stands higher than any other in Kent, despite a battering from freak hurricane winds in October 1987. The rock gardens are being restored. It is open in the afternoon Wednesday to Sunday from 24 March to the end of October and on bank holidays. Spring and autumn visits are highly recommended for beautiful colourings (0892 890651).

EYNSFORD

It is difficult to see where FARNINGHAM ends and Eynsford begins with surburban development spilling over the Greater London boundary into west Kent along the A225. But when you reach the heart of the old village, with its narrow 15th-century stone bridge and ford across the Darent and trim grassy banks ideal for family picnics, all is forgiven. The church of St Martin, eight centuries old, and the flintstone curtain wall, 30ft high and 520ft round, of the castle complement each other and their histories are entwined. The church was freely given to the monks of Christ Church by the lord of the manor who built the castle in the 11th century. When one of his successors, William de Eynesford, rejected a priest appointed by Becket the door of the church was closed to him. Whereupon William enlisted the support of the king against the archbishop. After Becket's murder de Eynesford was so full of remorse that he left his castle for ever and entered a monastery. EYNSFORD CASTLE (0322 862536) is now part of English Heritage and open year round to visitors. The oldest house in this village of Tudor bricks and timber is LITTLE MOTE, built round a solid pillar of Kentish oak. *Lullingstone

Park with its Roman ruins is half a mile to the south.

ACCOMMODATION

FIVE BELLS, High Street, Eynsford DA4 0AA (0322 864878). Historic cottages with three rooms for bed and breakfast. Moderate.

FAVERSHAM

Faversham straddles a creek of the Swale, separating the Isle of Sheppey from the mainland, and in May the orchards inland from the marshy shore are awash with white and pink blossom. The Romans settled here and were followed by the Saxons. Just over a mile west of the town on the A2, the remains of a small medieval church incorporating part of a 4th-century Romano-British pagan mausoleum can be seen. The town achieved a royal charter as early as AD811 and its prosperity continued under the Normans. King Stephen, a grandson of the Conqueror, founded an abbey in 1147 and was buried there with his queen Matilda and their son Eustace. The tomb was sacked during the Dissolution and the abbey left to ruin but the site was excavated in 1964 and a few remnants of a once great church, 360ft long, can be seen in ABBEY STREET. The Tudor and Georgian houses which line this street are evidence of Faversham's heyday as a limb of the Cinque Port of Dover when the creek was busy with shipping and dockyards and its gunpowder mills flourished. The white painted GUILDHALL shelters market stalls beneath its arches. The butcher's shop at 12 MARKET PLACE was the inn to which James II was brought by the fishermen who captured him as he tried to flee to France from William of Orange. On a strip of paper (kept in St Mary's Church vestry) he wrote a list of the Bible chapters he had read to convince them he was not a Papist agitator. The church spire, after Wren, stands out for miles around. From OARE, on the north side of Faversham, a lane ends in a slipway on the Swale from which the Harty ferry used to run. Boats can be launched here still. The SAXON SHORE WAY follows the mud and sand flats round from Faversham Creek through a nature reserve and westward from Harty Ferry along the river wall to CONYER CREEK and on to *Sittingbourne. Eastwards from Faversham the same walking trail skirts the Graveney Marshes and the tiny Norman church of Goodnestone on its way to *Whitstable.

Faversham is a centre for the packaging and distribution of fruit crops from the extensive orchards all around, the 'brewing capital' of Kent and one of the prettiest towns in the county all at the same time. SHEPHERD NEAME BREWERY in Court Street (0795 532206) gives guided tours from Monday to Thursday, showing how traditional ales and modern lagers are produced.

MUSEUMS

FLEUR DE LIS HERITAGE CENTRE, Preston Street ME13 8NS (0795 534542) houses the TOURIST INFORMATION office and an award-winning audio-visual display of 1,000 years of Faversham history in a 15th-century building. It is run by the enterprising Faversham Society.

CHART GUNPOWDER MILLS, off Stonebridge Way opposite the pond, produced powder for the cannons fired at Trafalgar and Waterloo. Restored by the Faversham Society, it is open from Easter to the end of September in the afternoons at weekends and bank holidays.

SPORT AND LEISURE

FAVERSHAM GOLF CLUB (0795 89275). An 18-hole course at Belmont Park. Visitors with a handicap certificate are welcome on weekdays.

ENVIRONS

MOUNT EPHRAIM GARDENS (0227 751496) cover 7 beautiful acres between the A2 and the A299 at the old village of HERNHILL a couple of miles east of Faversham. There is a Japanese rock garden, a small lake and a vineyard with a craft centre and tearoom. Open in the afternoon, Sundays and Bank Holiday Mondays from May to September.

In the churchyard is the graveyard of 'Mad Tom', a Cornishman who came to Kent posing as the Messiah.

ACCOMMODATION

WHITE HORSE, The Street, Faversham ME13 9AX (0227 751343). A traditional inn with 13 bedrooms and a restaurant. Moderate prices.

SYNDALE PARK MOTEL, Ospringe ME13 0RH (0795 532595). New addition to a very old village on Watling Street (A2) at the western edge of Faversham. Thirteen rooms and a swimming pool. Moderate.

BARONS, Sheldwich ME13 0LT (0795 539165). Stands in 16-acre grounds south of Faversham off the A251 to Ashford, overlooking the downs. Twelve bedrooms and French cuisine in a country house atmosphere. Moderately expensive.

HOMESTALL FARM, Homestall Lane, Faversham ME13 8UT (0795 532152). Inexpensive bed and breakfast on a real Kentish farm growing hops and fruit. Also has some rare breeds of animals.

PAINTERS FARM, Painters Forstal, Ospringe ME13 0EG (0795 532995) has sites and facilities for tents, caravans and campervans. Advance booking advisable during peak periods.

FOLKESTONE

After *Dover, Folkestone is the busiest of the Channel ports and is usually passed over (or through) by the crowds arriving and departing on ferries to France and Belgium. Its own tourist attractions are not obvious at first sight. It has no conventional seaside promenade but instead a marvellous, mile-long greensward along the clifftop – THE LEAS. Its wide lawns and flowerbeds fringed by imposing Victorian buildings, with a statue of William Harvey, the 16th-century Folkestone-born physician who discovered the circulation of the blood, look out over the Channel. The METROPOLE ARTS CENTRE on The Leas (0303 55070) organises a varied programme of events and exhibitions and lays claim to being the 'cultural capital of the Kent coast'. Hydraulic power was introduced in 1885 for the lift to clifftop from sea level west of the pier. Thirty years earlier Charles Dickens rented No. 3 ALBION VILLAS and brought his sons over from school in Boulogne for the summer holidays. He interspersed his writing of the opening chapters of *Little Dorrit* with brisk walks on The Leas towards SANDGATE where a later literary figure, H.G. Wells, lived in the early 1900s at the SPADE HOUSE, overlooking the sea. Wells wrote *Kipps* and *The History of Mr Polly* there and entertained contemporaries such as Shaw, Conrad, Kipling and Henry James. The castle and the Martello towers at Sandgate were part of Henry VIII's coastal defences; the beach these days is very popular with windsurfers. Below The Leas an undercliff toll road runs through groves of pines and flowering shrubs. A scale of charges a century out of date is displayed at the Folkestone end: '1d for horse, mule or ass. Hand trucks barrows, bicycles 1d'.

Centuries ago this headland where the 'Wold' met the sea guarded the Saxon shore. Then it faded into obscurity as a fishing village until the railway arrived in the 1840s, bringing visitors and tourists. There is still a small fishing fleet in the harbour, outnumbered by private boats and pleasure craft of all descriptions. It is too small to accommodate the car ferries which load and unload at the massive stone pier running out towards the lighthouse. There are good rail and motorway connections with London, 71 miles away. Just inland at St Martin's Plain, CHERITON, where the northwest fringes of the town meet the open Downs is the EUROTUNNEL EXHIBITION CENTRE, open daily with historical displays, games, videos and models of the newest cross-Channel link scheduled to open on 15 June 1993. The rural landscape traversed by the Pilgrims Way and dotted with tumuli is being churned by excavations for new terminals, roads and railways. The InterCity trains will disppear into the tunnel at Castle Hill and a shuttle train loop for cars and freight skirts NEWINGTON, a village mentioned in the Domesday Book.

Meanwhile Folkestone High Street sloping steeply down to the harbour retains its ancient houses and cobblestones and is reserved for pedestrians only. The old fish market, the STADE, leads to EAST CLIFF SANDS. Parking is limited. High tides drive the summer crowds from the sands up on to the concrete terrace above. Pitch and putt golf is available on the cliff top where three of more than 100

Martello towers built around the coast during the Napoleonic wars can be seen, with panoramic views over the busy shipping lanes out to sea. THE WARREN, reached from the car park above East Cliff Sands, covers 350 acres of chalk terraces and combes nicknamed 'Little Switzerland' and formed by a huge landslip in 1915. Grass and wild flowers, including some rare species, cover fossils and the remains of two Roman villas. The beach below can be reached only on foot and there is camping at EAST WEAR BAY. The NORTH DOWNS WAY runs along the clifftop towards Dover on its loop from *Canterbury and is accompanied for a mile or so by the old Dover road, diverging from the busy A20 at CAPEL-LE-FERNE.

The INFORMATION CENTRE is in Harbour Street (0303 58594).

MUSEUMS
FOLKESTONE MUSEUM AND ART GALLERY, Grace Hill (0303 850123). Displays of local natural and social history and archaeology. Temporary art exhibitions.

SPORTS AND LEISURE
FOLKESTONE SPORTS CENTRE, Radnor Park Avenue (0303 850222). Wide range of facilities including a dry ski slope, 25-metre swimming pool, 9-hole golf course with a slide, a roller skating rink, tennis, squash and badminton. Open daily, year round except Christmas.
FOLKESTONE RACECOURSE (0303 66407) is the only major horse-racing venue in Kent, with some 20 meetings a year, mostly on Mondays and Tuesdays. It is at WESTENHANGER between the A20 and M20.
SENE VALLEY, FOLKESTONE AND HYTHE GOLF CLUB (0303 66726) 18 fine holes on the downs a mile west of Folkestone off the A259. Visitors with a handicap certificate are welcome at any time other than the first and third Thursdays in the month and on competition days.
FOLKESTONE PIER is open to anglers for a small fee paid at local tackle shops. There is good sport from THE WARREN with cod in winter and bass in summer. Charter boat fishing is available (0302 446798).

ENVIRONS
KENT BATTLE OF BRITAIN MUSEUM (0303 893140). On the A260 just north of Folkestone at the former Royal Air Force station at HAWKINGE, a mile along Aerodrome Road, where the old control tower and armoury can be seen together with a Spitfire, Hurricane and Messerschmitt Bf109 used in the film *Battle of Britain*. There is a display of the battle in which Hawkinge played a front-line role, a souvenir shop and picnicking in the grounds where pilots waited to 'scramble' in the summer of 1940.
THE BUTTERFLY CENTRE (0303 83244) at SWINGFIELD MINNIS, a couple of miles further north on the A260, is a butterfly 'safari park', a tropical greenhouse garden with free-flying butterflies from all over the world.

FOOD AND DRINK
PAUL'S, 2a Bouverie Road West,

Folkestone (0303 59657). Bistro-style food in an easy atmosphere. Moderately priced.

EMILIO'S PORTOFINO, 124a Sand-gate Road, Folkestone (0303 55762). Italian cooking and stylish service at reasonable prices.

INDIA, 1 Old High Street, Folkestone (0303 59155). Not just curry, but lobster in white wine and cognac, too, yet authentically ethnic. Moderately expensive.

ACCOMMODATION

BURLINGTON, Earls Avenue, Folkestone CT20 2HR (0303 55301). Situated on The Leas with extensive Channel views. All 57 rooms have private baths. Bay Tree Restaurant. Moderately expensive.

LANGHORNE GARDENS, The Leas, Folkestone CT20 2EA (0303 57233). Less expensive family owned and run hotel with 30 rooms.

BELMONTE, 30 Castle Avenue, Folkestone CT20 2RE (0303 54470). Moderately priced small family hotel with the benefits of good home cooking of fresh local produce.

BLACK HORSE FARM, Canterbury Road, Densole CT18 7BG (0303 892665). North of Folkestone on the A260 at DENSOLE, a pleasant site with 30 pitches for touring caravans and tents. Open all year.

FOLKESTONE RACECOURSE CARAVAN PARK, Westenhanger, Hythe CT21 4HX (0303 68449). Sixty pitches for tents and caravans. Advance booking is necessary at peak periods. Open April to September.

THE WARREN, Wear Bay Road, Folkestone (0303 55093). A picturesque clifftop setting near a Martello Tower, with 82 pitches for tents, open march to September. Unaccompanied children over twelve accepted if they hold a Youth Tenting/Camping Certificate.

FORDWICH

Although it appears to be no more than a hamlet clustered round a hump-backed bridge off the A26 a short drive northeast of *Canterbury, Fordwich has a notable place in the history of that famous city. The River Stour on which it stands is no longer navigable for anything other than small boats, but when the cathedral was being rebuilt in Norman times its quays handled thousands of tons of stone shipped from Caen in Normandy as well as wine and other imported cargoes. In the 13th century the Prior of Christ Church agreed to pay one red rose each year to the Abbot of St Augustine's for land at Fordwich. Recorded as a town in the Domesday Book, Fordwich had a mayor in 1292 and retains its status as a chartered borough and a limb of the Cinque Port of Sandwich to this day. In the *Compleat Angler*, published in the 17th century, Izaak Walton refers to 'Fordwich trout', as large as salmon. The bridge and most of the houses are 18th century but St Mary's, with its churchyard on the river bank, goes back to the Saxons, although the main structure is 13th century. It contains the Fordwich Stone, a single block carved in the shape of a cloister and once believed to be the tomb of St Augustine. There is no documentary evidence of this. The claim that the half-timbered building on the quay near the church is England's smallest and oldest town hall, dating from 1544, is not in dispute.

Fordwich Town Hall (02327 710358) is open to visitors from Easter to September from 11am to 4pm. Amongst the artefacts are drums used by the navy's press gangs, stocks and the ducking stool which was lowered into the river by crane.

ACCOMMODATION

GEORGE AND DRAGON, King Street CT2 0BX (0227 462772). Comfortable riverside inn by the old bridge. Twelve rooms, many with private baths. Moderately priced.

GODMERSHAM

The big house in a deer park running to several hundred acres on the outskirts of this village on the A28 from *Canterbury to *Ashford was the home of Jane Austen's brother and she was a frequent visitor to Godmersham Park. He changed his name to Edward Knight and as such he is remembered in the east window of the Norman church in the village. His old nurse, who went on to nurse all his children, lies under the ancient yews in the churchyard. Godmersham Park, where Jane Austen did some of her writing, isn't open to visitors. It stands in lovely countryside on the banks of the Stour as it winds through woods and over the downs. KINGS WOOD, lies to the west near CHALLOCK, 1,400 acres of hardwood and conifers and sweet chestnut coppice where deer are sometimes seen. There is a car park and a waymarked walk.

GOUDHURST

This high Wealden village, 4 miles northwest of *Cranbrook, surveys mile upon glorious mile of orchards and hopfields. Muscovy ducks paddle in a pond at the bottom of the village street beneath a spreading chestnut tree with the VINE INN across the way. At the top of the hill stands St Mary's, a Grade A listed church whose door is shaded by a yew meticulously clipped in the form of an archway. The building is lovingly cared for, a treasure house of memorials to past generations, including no fewer than 40 of the Kent Culpeper family. Most intriguing are the life-sized wood figures of Sir Alexander Culpeper and his lady, painted in red, green, black and gold, only slightly dimmed by age. He is wearing his armour and sword and on the wall above is a delectable little stone carving of the couple with their numerous offspring. He was an ironmaster, whose foundry at nearby BEDGE-BURY cast some of the cannons that defeated the Spanish Armada. Iron, together with weaving, was the foundation of Goudhurst's prosperity in the Middle Ages. When both declined in the 18th century, smuggling took over. In Goudhurst's main street is a house called SPYWAYS with windows covering both directions. In 1747 the Goudhurst Militia fought a famous battle with the Hawkhurst Gang of smugglers in the church-yard while the villagers took shelter within the stout golden grey sand-stone walls. The ancient yews and gravestones round which the shots rang survive with the same views across the Weald and down the village street flanked by large old houses with recesses for looms. In the basement of the large house opposite the STAR AND EAGLE, William Rootes had a bicycle repair shop, the forerunner of the Rootes Motor Group. Sandstone, brick, white clapboard and black and white timber framing is comple-mented by red and russet tiles on roofs and walls. Among the many historic houses is PATTYNDENE MANOR, dating from 1470 with a timbered banqueting hall, but sadly no longer open to visitors. Weatherboarded Burgess Stores sells just about everything from firewood and nails to liquor and hand-made chocolates, walking sticks and wicker baskets to groc-eries. The coach and car loads of tourists which descend in summer are nothing compared to the annual invasions of hop-pickers which the village experienced from Victorian times up to World War II, when whole families escaped briefly from the smoky, over-crowded terraces of South London and the East End for a working holiday in the fresh air.

ENVIRONS

FINCHCOCKS (0580 211702). A baroque Georgian mansion in its own park 2 miles west of Goud-hurst off the A262 contains pianist Richard Burnett's remarkable collection of antique keyboard instruments, mostly in playing order – a living museum of musi-cal history. Musical tours and recitals are given when the house is open in the afternoon from Easter to 24 September on Sunday and bank holiday Mondays and daily in August except Mondays and Tuesday. Gift shop and licensed restaurant. Teas with home-made cakes 3.30pm–5.30pm.

BEDGEBURY NATIONAL PINETUM (0580 87377) in Bedgebury Forest, 2½ miles south of Goudhurst on the B2079, was started as an off-shoot of Kew Gardens when its own specimen pines fell victim to London's fog and fumes. A Fores-try Commission property, it offers shady walks among scented pines and shrubs around a lake where fishing is available by permit from the VISITOR CENTRE. There is also a listening post trail using tape players. Free parking and toilets with provision for the disabled. Open from 10am to 8pm, or sunset if earlier.

ACCOMMODATION

STAR AND EAGLE, High Street,

Goudhurst TN17 1AL (0580 211512). Former smugglers' inn connected by secret underground passage to the church nearby. Eleven rooms, local variations of old English fare, moderate prices. GREEN CROSS, Goudhurst TN17 1HA (0580 211200). Comfortable, modestly priced inn with a restaurant.

COMBOURNE FARMHOUSE, Goudhurst TN17 1LP (0580 211382). Two double rooms with inexpensive bed and breakfast and evening meal.

GRAVESEND

In Gravesend Reach, where coastal pilots traditionally hand over control of ships to river pilots, the Thames narrows. The headquarters of the Port of London Authority's Thames Navigation Service is here, above the ROYAL TERRACE PIER from which the pilot boats put out. These days the bulk of cargo is going no further upriver than Tilbury on the opposite Essex shore, which can still be reached by the 'Short Ferry' from Gravesend, once the gateway to the world's busiest port. Together with its neighbour NORTHFLEET, it now forms a dense urban and industrial sprawl of cement works and power stations, tower blocks, chimneys and pylons between the A2 and the river which 'just keeps rolling along' regardless. The GORDON PROMENADE along the waterfront, backed by gardens, is a grand place to walk, reflecting on the fact that the Elizabethan explorer navigators assembled their fleets off here and in the 19th century passers-by would have waved Sir John Franklin farewell on his last voyage, in search of the Northwest Passage. Three windows in the mission church of St Andrews commemorate the loss of his ships HMS *Erebus* and *Terror* and all who sailed in them in the Arctic ice. Outside ST GEORGE'S CHURCH, destroyed in the fire of 1727 which devastated most of Gravesend and rebuilt soon afterwards, is the surprising statue of a Red Indian princess. Pocahontas came to England in the early 17th century as the wife of John Rolfe, one of Raleigh's settlers of Virginia, and excited great curiosity at the court of James I. She died of consumption while awaiting a ship home and was buried in St George's churchyard.

The Gordon Promenade marks the northern end of the SAXON SHORE WAY which follows the coast eastwards past Shornmead Fort opposite Coalhouse Fort on the Essex bank and on for another 140 miles round to Rye in Sussex. The esplanade is named for General Gordon, who commanded the Gravesend garrison in the 1860s and superintended the building of the twin forts before becoming the posthumous hero of Khartoum. While here he devoted his spare time and his army pay to charitable work among the slum boys. The fort where he was quartered was demolished in 1944 by a German V2 rocket but the site is preserved with much-needed gardens. The oldest surviving building is MILTON CHANTRY, off the A226 just east of the town centre (0474 321520). It formed part of a leper hospital founded in 1322 and was the gift of the de Valence and Montechais families. It is open to visitors during the summer, when various exhibitions of local arts and crafts are mounted.

The TOURIST INFORMATION CENTRE (0474 337600) is at 10 Parrock Street DA12 1ET.

MUSEUM

GRAVESEND MUSEUM (0474 323159) in the High Street traces the development of the town over the past 2,000 years, back to finds from the Roman temple at SPRINGHEAD. It is closed on Wednesdays, Saturdays and bank holidays.

SHOPPING

Despite the development of 'pre-cincts', Gravesend still has a thriving old-fashioned GENERAL MARKET between High Street and Queen Street, Monday to Saturday from 9am to 5pm.

SPORT AND LEISURE

CASCADE LEISURE CENTRE (0474 337472) 3 miles west of Gravesend has facilities for most indoor and outdoor ball games, plus a BMX bike track. Open daily, year round.

ACCOMMODATION

INN ON THE LAKE, Shorne DA12 3HB (0474 823333). Set in 12 acres of unspoiled Kentish woodland with two lakes (floodlit at night), this hotel has 78 rooms with *en suite* facilities and a lakeside restaurant serving French and English cuisine. Expensive.

TOLLGATE MOAT, Watling Street, Gravesend DA13 9RA (0474 357655). A moderately priced large motor hotel with 114 rooms.

GROOMBRIDGE

Just south of *Ashurst, the Kent–Sussex boundary divides Groombridge in two but the older part, of tile-hung cottages and a 17th-century brick church clustered round a triangular green, is in Kent. So, too, is the gracious 17th-century manor house, Groombridge Place, which the diarist John Evelyn often visited. It was here that Sir Richard Waller, who was at Agincourt with Henry V, held captive the younger brother of the Duke of Orleans until ransom was paid. The house, with its delightful terraced gardens, isn't open to visitors, but the knight and his French 'guest' are portrayed in the south chancel window of the church. A marble tablet over the door commemorates William Cotton Oswell who accompanied Livingstone on some of his African explorations.

HADLOW

The outstanding feature of this village on the main A26 road through the orchards and hop-fields between Maidstone and *Tonbridge is a 170ft octagonal tower which looks not unlike a fantastic multi-tiered cake. It is known far and wide as 'May's Folly' and it is all that survives apart from a massive gatehouse of a mock-Gothic castle built in the 1830s by Barton May and his son. The tower was the flamboyant finishing touch to a marvellous piece of Victorian eccentricity. The River Shode, which rises on the North Downs near Pilgrims Way, flows through the village of weatherboarded and tile-hung houses before joining the Medway in the fertile valley of the Low Weald where the local agricultural college conducts its field experiments. An ancient church tucked away in a quiet lane off the main road has crosses carved in its door by knights off to the Crusades and contains a chair reputed to have belonged to Miles

Coverdale, Bishop of Exeter, who translated the Bible in the 16th century. In the churchyard the Barton May mausoleum is a suitably florid postscript to his 'Folly'.

FOOD AND DRINK
LA CRÈMAILLÈRE, The Square, Hadlow (0732 851489). French cuisine in a 200-year-old dining room with log fire or a vine-covered conservatory in summer. Closed Sundays.

ACCOMMODATION
LEAVERS MANOR, Goose Green, Hadlow TN11 0JH (0732 851442). Ten bedrooms all with *en suite* facilities. Outdoor swimming pool and tennis in 5-acre grounds. Expensive.
HADLOW COLLEGE OF AGRICULTURE TN11 0AL (0732 850551). 150 single bedrooms with ample facilities, available inexpensively to visitors during parts of March, April, July, September and December.

HARRIETSHAM

Long since sliced in two by the A20 arterial route to the coast, this village between *Maidstone and *Ashford has somehow managed to retain at least some of its rustic charm with a group of ALMS-HOUSES endowed by the Fish-mongers Company in 1642 and rebuilt in 1770. They're on the opposite side of the main road to the parish church which has eight

bells, one of them inscribed 'Thomas Lester made us all/Robert Bottle hanged us all'. There is also the Roman Catholic church of the Good Shepherd, originally built as an Anglican chapel in the 1880s for navvies building a branch line to Ashford from Maidstone. There are good camping sites on the slopes of the North Downs off the road from Harrietsham to WORMS-

HILL and the sort of medieval inn that Chaucer's pilgrims would recognise.

FOOD AND DRINK
RINGLESTONE INN, Ringlestone Road, Harrietsham (0622 859207). Traditional pies and beers and ciders from the cask in a setting of oak beams, brick floors and an inglenook fireplace.

HAWKHURST

This large, straggling, mainly residential Wealden village gives its name to the notorious Hawkhurst Gang which terrorised the countryside and coasts of Kent and Sussex in the 18th century. It lies at the hub of busy roads heading south and east to the coast, west into deepest Sussex, north into the heart of the Weald. Like *Goudhurst and *Cranbrook it did well out of iron and cloth for several centuries before both industries declined and died in the Weald. The older part of the village with its chunky 15th-century sandstone church, old workhouse and weatherboarded Wealden houses faces the Moor, which is really a tree-lined green. The shopping centre with its Regency colonnade is in the newer Highgate.

SPORT AND LEISURE
HAWKHURST GOLF CLUB, High Street (0580 752396). Visitors are welcome to this 9-hole course except on Saturday and Sunday mornings. Equipment can be hired.

ACCOMMODATION
QUEEN'S, Rye Road TN18 5DA (0580 753577). Nine rooms, mostly *en suite*. Ample parking. Moderately priced.
WOODHAM HALL, Rye Road TN18 5DA (0580 753428). Licensed guest house with a garden. Inexpensive.
OCKLEY TN18 4EX (0580 752290). Farmhouse with three bedrooms for guests. Outdoor heated pool. Inexpensive.

HEADCORN

The timber buildings show that this was one of the Wealden villages that prospered in the Middle Ages with the arrival of Flemish weavers. Two CLOTH HALLS and a row of weavers' cottages by the church are the heritage and the church itself, built of ragstone and Bethersden marble in the late 14th century by the local branch of the Culpepers is further evidence. Its roof is of good

Wealden oak and there is a living specimen, perhaps 900 years old, outside which survived the battering of the October storm of 1987. Its roots reach 60ft into the ground. The Headcorn Oak was already old when Queen Elizabeth I saw it and it may be the last survivor of the great forest which the Normans found difficult to penetrate. When the weaving trade died Headcorn slumbered beside the sluggish River Beult and was only reawakened when the railways came in 1842. Nearly 100 years later when they were bringing the boys home from Dunkirk, 100 trains a day stopped at Headcorn just long enough for them to be fed. Beef was roasted on spits beside the line. The Kent and East Sussex Light Railway used to run to *Tenterden but was axed. Headcorn's position on the main line from London to the coast, however, makes it a commuter village with plenty of shops and cars but the old and the new exist easily side by side. The KING'S ARMS in the High Street (with its inevitable legends of smugglers) is a good place to escape the traffic.

HERNE BAY

The 7-mile seafront with Sheppey to the west and *Reculver to the east is dominated by an 80ft clock tower presented to the town in 1837, the year of Queen Victoria's accession. The pier, nearly a mile long, had been opened five years earlier. Passengers came down-river from London and were taken overland to Dover by stage coach for the final sea leg to the Continent. It was supposed to cut travelling time, but the railways soon did that more effectively and in the 1850s brought Herne Bay a new prospect as a fashionable watering place, complete with bathing machines. It rapidly over-shadowed the much older village of HERNE, just inland, and a new pier was built. The Grand Pier Pavilion opened by the Lord Mayor of London in 1910 was gutted by fire in 1970 and all that remains today of the pier (the second longest in the country after Southend's before it was damaged and pulled down in 1979) is the Leisure Centre at the landward end opened by Edward Heath three years earlier.

Along with neighbouring *Whit-stable, Herne Bay suffered severe-ly in the great East Coast floods of 1953. Its long shingly beach with some sand at low tide at the western end is somewhat exposed. There is a water skiing channel offshore and the bay west of a stone jetty called HAMPTON PIER is much used by powerboats. The WINDMILL (0227 363345) dating from 1789 in Mill Lane has been restored to full working condition. It is open to visitors from 24 April to September on Sunday and bank holiday Mon-day afternoons and also on Thurs-days in July and August.

The TOURIST INFORMATION CEN-TRE is in the Bandstand in Central Parade (0227 361911).

MUSEUM
HERNE BAY MUSEUM, Library, 124 High Street (0227 374896) depicts the interesting history of the town with many old prints, paintings and drawings as well as archaeological exhibits and fossils found locally. Closed Sundays and bank holidays and half-day Wednesday.

SPORT AND LEISURE

PIER PAVILION LEISURE CENTRE (0227 366921). Squash, badminton, table tennis and roller skating, with equipment for hire. There is a sundeck, gift shop and bar. Membership carries privileges but facilities are available also to non-members.

HERNE BAY GOLF CLUB, Canterbury Road, Eddington (0227 373964). Visitors are welcome at this 18-hole course on weekdays and after 11am at weekends.

ENVIRONS

WEALDEN WOODLAND WILDLIFE PARK (0227 712379). A preserved area of WEST BLEAN WOOD open to visitors daily from Easter to October with nature trails, a forest adventure play area, children's farm, pony rides and a butterfly centre. There is a teashop, picnic area and facilities for disabled visitors. It is located on the A291 Canterbury Road south of Herne Bay.

FOOD AND DRINK

L'ESCARGOT, 22 High Street, Herne Bay (0227 37286). One of the secrets of Herne Bay – superb French cuisine and wines from the proprietors M. and Mme. Bessemoulin. Moderate prices, too. Open for lunch Tuesday–Friday, dinner Monday–Saturday. Closed Sundays.

HEVER

This once remote hamlet on the banks of the meandering little River Eden between *Edenbridge and *Chiddingstone is today a major stopping place on the tourist trail. The reason is the 13th-century castle, which was the scene of probably the most fateful courtship in English history, where King Henry VIII came, usually unannounced and with a retinue of almost insupportable size, to woo the 18-year-old daughter of Sir Thomas Bullen. He wanted the son that his wife Catherine had been unable to give him and in order to get a divorce and marry Anne Bullen (she changed the spelling to Boleyn herself to sound more dignified), the Catholic king broke with the Pope, established the Church of England with himself at its head and sacked the monasteries. Anne, the second of Henry VIII's six wives, was beheaded on Tower Hill after the 'Thousand Days' of political and religious turmoil and a succession of miscarriages, having produced a daughter (the future Queen Elizabeth) but no male heir. This castle in Kent built of gold and grey sandstone quarried at Ide Hill a few miles away was the cradle of the Reformation. William Waldorf Astor, a rich American of German descent, first saw it in 1901 when it had suffered centuries of gradual decay. He bought it, together with 640 acres, in which he created a Tudor-style village outside the moat, using the same stone from Ide Hill that went into the building of the castle in 1270. He restored

Hever Castle, scene of a fateful courtship

the castle to the last detail while at the same time introducing 20th-century plumbing, electricity and central heating and filled it and the 'village' with paintings and furniture, carpets and tapestries, china, glass and objets d'art. He moved both the River Eden and the road to create formal gardens with a lake from rough meadow.

The original castle consisted of the massive gate house and a walled bailey, surrounded by a moat with a wooden drawbridge and portcullis, both regularly operated today. After two centuries, around 1500, the Bullen family built their manor house inside the protective wall. The ornately panelled and plastered apartments contain priceless furniture and china and portraits of Henry VIII (by Holbein) and Anne Boleyn. The original Great Hall (now the Dining Hall) is often used for 'King Henry VIII banquets'. The little panelled room with a half-domed ceiling which Anne Boleyn occupied contains the prayer book or Book of Hours which she carried to the execution block, inscribed in her own hand. As a travelled young lady she found life here exceedingly boring and was once locked in her room to stop communicating with a courtier with whom she had fallen in love. The room along the corridor was the favourite of Anne of Cleves, Henry VIII's fourth wife —the 'Flanders Mare' whom he divorced after only six months. She was given Hever Castle in 1540 and owned it for 17 years. The 100ft Long Gallery is the setting for an exhibition 'Henry VIII and Anne Boleyn at Hever Castle' which recreates one of the royal visits to a background of Tudor music. Other rooms recreate the family life of 'The Astors of Hever', from tiny bedrooms known affectionately as 'the Dog Kennels' to a great chamber filled with memorabilia of four generations. The Armoury houses the regimental museum of the Kent and Sharpshooters Yeomanry, now a Territorial armoured car regiment, while the Council Chamber, the principal room of the castle before Tudor times, contains a collection of medieval instruments of torture and 'correction'.

The Gardens fringe a 35-acre lake beside which visitors can walk and picnic. Plays by the KENT REPERTORY COMPANY and concerts of chamber music and jazz are performed during the summer under a covered auditorium. There is a walled rose garden, fine topiary work and streams, cascades and fountains everywhere. The ITALIAN GARDEN has sculpture and statuary from the Romans to the Renaissance (a carved marble relief from Emperor Claudius's triumphal arch on the Kent coast at *Richborough has been moved indoors). William Waldorf Astor planted a MAZE of slow-growing yew which is one of the few hedge mazes in the country open to visitors. THE PAVILION is a licensed self-service restaurant and elsewhere in the grounds are gift and garden shops and a children's adventure playground. The original village of Hever at the castle gate consists of not much more than an old inn and the 14th-century church which contains Sir Thomas Bullen's tomb and his brass, one of the finest in England.

HEVER CASTLE (0732 865224) is open daily from April to October – Gardens at 11am, Castle at noon. Last admission 5pm. It lies off the B2026 south of Edenbridge and is clearly signposted from the M25 (junctions 5 or 6) and the M23 (junction 10). Hever Station on the Uckfield line from London is a mile from the village, with no taxis. These are available at *Edenbridge Town Station, 3 miles away. Several coach operators organise visits to the castle.

HOLLINGBOURNE

This village just north of the A20, east of *Maidstone, in the shadow of the North Downs and the ancient Pilgrims Way, has more than its share of decorative period houses and a lovely 15th-century church with Roman and Saxon tiles in its tower. Lady Elizabeth Culpeper, who died in 1638, lies beneath her effigy carved in white marble in a chapel devoted to this ubiquitous Kentish family. Curiously, the rings which she wears on each hand are attached to her wrists by fine cords, a fashion which spread from the court of

James I when he gave one of his own rings to a lady for whom it was too large so she tied it to her wrist. Lady Culpeper's four daughters made the Hollingbourne altar cloth, embroidered in gold thread. When not in use, it is kept, understandably, under lock and key. The redbrick Tudor manor of the Culpepers stands behind the church amidst some new housing and there is a half-timbered Malthouse. The KING'S HEAD INN boasts a fine 18th-century brick façade. EYHORNE MANOR (0627 80514) in the hamlet of EYHORNE STREET, south of the railway, is open to afternoon visitors from Easter to September at weekends and bank holidays and Monday to Friday in August. It dates from 1410 with considerable 17th-century alterations and additions and stands in a garden of herbs and flowers. There is a collection of historic laundry implements.

ACCOMMODATION
GREAT DANES, Ashford Road, Hollingbourne ME17 1RE (0622 30022) has high quality rooms and leisure facilities including an indoor pool and tennis court, a restaurant, a garden café and a pub. Expensive.

HORSMONDEN

In the heart of apple and hop country east of *Tunbridge Wells, the village of half-timbered and weatherboarded buildings clusters round a green called 'the Heath' shaded by large old trees. The white-painted GUN INN, famous for its meat spit-roasted over apple logs in a vast inglenook, was where John Browne, a local ironmaster, designed ordnance for the navies of both sides in the Anglo–Dutch wars of the 17th century. He was a Scot. A path through the woods leads to the wide FURNACE POND which once powered the bellows and the hammers of the ironmakers. Now it's a prettier and more peaceful spot. GIBBET LANE is a reminder of the days when sheep stealers, highwaymen and smugglers were publicly hanged in the village. The parish church is, unusually, at least 2 miles away amidst the hopgardens on the edge of a park. At the gate there is a mounting stone for riders with five steps.

ENVIRONS
SPRIVERS (0892 723553), a National Trust property on the B2162 just outside the village, is noted for its flowering and foliage shrubs, old walls and herbaceous borders, spring and summer bedding. Open Wednesdays from May to the end of September. Parking limited.

FOOD AND DRINK
THE GUN AND SPITROAST INN, The Heath, Horsmonden (0892 7226723). Four centuries old. Serves real ale and spit roasts Wednesdays and Saturdays.

HYTHE

In its heyday as a Cinque Port, Hythe saw fleets of ships laden with cargo and bristling with guns coming and going. Now the ancient quays are half a mile inland from the breakers on the Channel shore because of the building up of shingle. The Royal Military Canal built across the inland edge of Romney Marsh westwards from Hythe to *Appledore and on to Rye in Sussex to keep Napoleon's Grand Army at bay is followed by the SAXON SHORE WAY. It is lined with trees and used only by small boats, which can be hired. Between the canal and the existing shoreline, the seaside resort of Hythe has developed with a promenade running east to Sandgate. The Imperial Hotel's 9-hole golf course lies at one side and the military firing ranges beyond the Martello tower at the other. The beach is shingle and sand between timber and concrete groynes. North of the canal the narrow alleys and streets of the old town, first granted a charter in AD732 by the Saxon King Ethelred, wind upwards to a church big enough to be a cathedral. St Leonard's contains a mosaic pulpit of 20,000 pieces from Venice and a chest said to have come from a wreck of the Spanish Armada. But its most unusual, if somewhat grisly, treasure is in the ambulatory or crypt: a store of some 2,000 skulls and 8,000 thighbones amassed between the 13th and 15th centuries, probably in periodic clear-outs of the graveyard. Just north of the town is SALTWOOD CASTLE from which it is claimed the four knights rode out in 1170 to murder Becket in Canterbury Cathedral and more recently came into the ownership of Sir Kenneth Clark, whose series *Civilisation* made television history.

The terminus of the ROMNEY, HYTHE AND DYMCHURCH RAILWAY is beside the canal near the old town centre. It is described fancifully as 'the world's only mainline in miniature' and remains very popular with visitors. For details of the service and fares telephone the principal station on the 14-mile route at *New Romney (0679 62353).

There is a TOURIST INFORMATION CENTRE in Prospect Road car park (0303 67799).

MUSEUM

LOCAL HISTORY ROOM, Oaklands, Stade Street (0303 66152). Illustrates the fascinating history and civic life of this Cinque Port with prints, paintings, furniture and costume. It is open daily at various times, closed on Sundays and public holidays. Entrance is free and there is access for disabled visitors.

SPORT AND LEISURE

Apart from golf and horseracing nearby (see under FOLKESTONE) good fishing can be had from the pier, especially after dark for bass (0303 66228).

BROCKHILL COUNTRY PARK, half a mile south of SANDLING station on the Saltwood road, is a grassy valley with a lake and woodland and sea views from its trails.

ENVIRONS

LYMPNE CASTLE (0303 67571) west of Hythe and signposted from the A259 and the A20 was owned by the archdeacons of Canterbury for 500 years before falling into disrepair. Earlier this century it was restored. The Great Hall flanked by medieval towers commands fine views of Romney Marsh. It contains an exhibition of toys, dolls and reproduction medieval brasses. Open daily from May to September. PORT LYMPNE ZOO PARK AND GARDENS (0303 26446) off the B2067 3½ miles west of Hythe has spacious paddocks for herds of horses, deer and more exotic species such as African buffalo, antelope, rhino and Indian elephants. Even tigers and timber wolves can be glimpsed in the 'wild' of green, flower-filled Kentish countryside. John Aspinall bought the estate for the overflow of animals from his other zoo park near *Canterbury. Terraced gardens and a mansion designed in the Dutch colonial style by Sir Herbert Baker for local MP Sir Philip Sassoon are also open to visitors daily year round, except Christmas Day. Suitable for the disabled.

ACCOMMODATION

HYTHE IMPERIAL, Princes Parade, Hythe CT21 6AE (0303 67441). Large four-star hotel in a 52-acre estate. All rooms have *en suite* facilities and views of the sea or garden. Indoor heated swimming pool, sauna, solarium, indoor sports complex and children's play area. A 9-hole golf course is part of the sports facilities. Visitors with a handicap certificate are welcome and equipment can be hired. STADE COURT, West Parade, Hythe (CT21 6DT (0303 68263). Good restaurant (noted for local fish) and versatile room arrangements from singles to family suites. Shares sports facilities of sister hotel (Best Western) Imperial. Moderately expensive.

IDE HILL

Known as the Dome of Kent because of its crown of venerable beeches, this village above *Sundridge on the A25 boasts the county's highest clock in its church tower. *Emmetts Garden owned by the National Trust adorns its steep approaches.

IGHTHAM

One of the oldest and prettiest villages in Kent, this delightful little place on the A227 (mercifully bypassed by the A25 from *Sevenoaks) first took its name as the Saxon King Ehta or Ohta's settlement. Nearby Oldbury Hill, rising to 620ft, bears traces of even earlier settlement: the earthworks of an Iron Age hill fort and rock shelters used by Neanderthal hunters with flint spears. Ightham's little square of black and white houses have been there for a mere four or five centuries but they all have a story to tell. Old Stones, built in 1560, was the home of a local grocer Benjamin Harrison, who emulated Gilbert White of Selborne, and became famous as an archaeologist, collecting thousands of the earliest flint tools used by man in the locality. The GEORGE AND DRAGON dates from 1515 and the TOWN HOUSE, now a restaurant, from 1480. The church is mostly 14th and 15th century with horsebox pews and some fine oak panelling. It contains the tombs of many of the families who owned Ightham Mote, one of the finest moated manor houses in England, at IVY HATCH 2½ miles south of the village. The effigy in the church of Sir Thomas Cawne, who built Ightham Mote and lived there from 1340 until his death in 1374, shows him in chain mail and armour with belt, gauntlets and stirrups. It is strikingly similar to the effigy of the Black Prince in Canterbury Cathedral, with whom he must have served in France. The oldest brass in Ightham church, beneath a carpet by the altar, shows Sir Richard Clement (who made many alterations and additions to the Mote in the Tudor period) wearing armour and a surcoat bearing his Arms. Several of the Selbys, who lived at the Mote for 300 years, are buried here including Dame Dorothy Selby to whom James I is said to have shown an anonymous letter warning of a 'terrible blow' about to fall on Parliament. She understood at once its import and urged the king to take it seriously, which led to the uncovering of the Gunpowder Plot. Her tomb depicts in graphic style foul Papish deeds being hatched, the Armada in a gale and Guy Fawkes in the cellars of Parliament.

IGHTHAM MOTE (0732 810378) bequeathed to the National Trust by Charles Henry Robinson, the American businessman who bought it in 1953, is a small gem of various periods, from the original moat, Great Hall, Old Chapel and Crypt in the Decorated style, the Tudor Chapel with painted ceiling (c.1520) to the Jacobean fireplace and frieze, the 18th-century Palladian window and hand-painted Chinese wallpaper. In 1989 the most extensive repairs and alterations since Sir Thomas Colyer-Fergusson rescued the Mote from decay a hundred years ago were begun. Visitors will see this work underway. Ightham Mote is open from Good Friday to the end of October daily except Tuesdays and Saturdays. The garden, courtyard and Great Hall are accessible to disabled visitors and there are baby feeding and changing rooms, also a tea bar.

FOOD AND DRINK

TOWN HOUSE, The Street, Ightham (0732 884578). One of Ightham's finest old timbered buildings makes a very comfortable restaurant with food of a high standard. Dinner only, lunch by arrangement. Closed Monday and Tuesday and at certain holiday times. Expensive.

KNOCKHOLT

This is a commuters' village, between Orpington and *Sevenoaks, which fought to stay in Kent rather than become part of Greater London and won the day in 1969, when it was restored to the county. Its famous beeches stand 770ft above sea level and can be seen for many miles around. The church, built mostly of chalk in the 13th century, is shaded by a yew as old, or perhaps older. The NORTH DOWNS WAY passes close to the south of the village.

KNOLE

One of the largest private houses in England, said to have a room for every day of the year, a staircase for each week and a courtyard for every month, Knole was begun in 1456 and greatly extended in 1603 by Thomas Sackville, first Earl of Dorset. It stands magnificently in a park of massive oaks and beeches whose gentle hillocks or 'knolls' give it its name. Six miles in circumference, with deer roaming free, it stands at the southern edge of *Sevenoaks, approached by an almost suburban drive off the main A225 road. It is like going through a humble church porch to find oneself in a cathedral. The Sackville family still lives in part of the house which, together with the park, is administered by the National Trust. It had been the home of lords and archbishops for a century and a half when Queen Elizabeth I gave it to her cousin, the first poet and scholar of the Sackville family, as well as being a statesman and diplomat. His descendant Vita Sackville-West spent her early years here and her friend Virginia Woolf described Knole in her novel *Orlando* as 'more like a village than a house'. The original manuscript is on display in the great hall. Vita thought the room containing a vast hoard of silver rather vulgar. It and portraits of the Sackvilles painted by Reynolds and Gainsborough can be seen by visitors together with the unique collection of 17th-century furniture which includes the first of the Knole drop-end settees and chairs with their original brocade upholstery. There are also some rare tapestries dating from the 15th and 16th centuries. The *pièce de résistance* is the King's Room with its silver decorated table, mirror and candlesticks.

Knole (0732 450608) is open in the afternoon from Good Friday to the end of October, Wednesday to Sunday and bank holiday Mondays. The garden is open on the first Wednesday in each month from May to September. Entrance to the park is free to pedestrians, who are asked to keep dogs on leads because of the deer. Parking (£5) includes one admission to the house (National Trust members free). The ground floor, park and garden are suitable for disabled people.

92

SPORT AND LEISURE
KNOLE PARK GOLF COURSE, Seal Hollow Road (0732 452150). Visitors are welcomed at this 18-hole course on weekdays only and should have a handicap and golf club membership certificate.

LAMBERHURST

This village among the orchards on the Kent–Sussex border has given its name to a renaissance of the vigneron's art in England, lost for centuries. In 1972 Kenneth McAlpine planted Muller-Thurgau vines on a hillside above the River Teise using methods and equipment from the Rhineland. Now vineyards are flourishing among the hopgardens all over Kent and English wine is being taken seriously. The village is in a deep valley with a bridge over the Teise and an old inn the Chequers beside it. Long ago, Lamberhurst rang to the sound of hammers, its furnaces consuming 200,000 cords of local timber annually to produce armaments and other ironmongery. The Gloucester Forge, named after Queen Anne's short-lived son, cast most of the gates and railings for St Paul's Cathedral costing £11,202 at 6d a pound and sent by river down the Medway and up the Thames. They have been dispersed round the world since but some of them have been returned to their place of origin and are proudly displayed in the High Street. Just upriver from the site of the Gloucester ironworks, 2 miles west of Lamberhurst, is another old furnace lake near which are the most impressive abbey ruins in southern England, rivalling Fountains, Jervaulx or Rievaulx in the north. BAYHAM ABBEY was founded in 1210 by the Premonstratensians from northern France and after the Dissolution passed through various hands. The lancet windows and pointed arches of the long, narrow church stand very tall, open to the sky, and a large part of the gatehouse survives, overlooking the Teise. Another romantic ruin, 1½ miles southeast of Lamberhurst, is 14th-century SCOTNEY CASTLE, surrounded by a moat around which rhododendrons, azaleas, water-lilies and wisteria flower in profusion.

MUSEUM
MR HEAVER'S MODEL MUSEUM AND CRAFT VILLAGE (0892 890711). A converted oast house complex off the A262 north of Lamberhurst with a model fairground and stationary engines in a reconstructed village street. The museum is a quirky blend of history and science fiction. Open daily, year round.

GARDENS
SCOTNEY CASTLE GARDEN (0892 890651) is open from Easter to 12 November on Wednesdays and Fridays, afternoons weekends and bank holidays. Shakespeare and other drama is staged in the open-air theatre.
OWL HOUSE GARDEN (0892 890230). Thirteen acres surrounded a 16th-

century cottage (not open to visitors), named for the wool smugglers who used it and imitated an owl's hoot as a warning signal. Enchanting in spring with masses of flowers and rhododendrons, azaleas and camellias in bloom around an informal water garden. Fine sweep of lawns to woodland walks. Open daily, year round except Christmas and New Year's Day.

VINEYARD
LAMBERHURST VINEYARD, Ridge Farm (0892 890890). Its 50 acres make it England's leading vineyard, with a self-guided trail and guided tours, wine shop and tasting bar and the Vineyard Pantry for light refreshments. Open daily, year round.

SPORT AND LEISURE
LAMBERHURST GOLF CLUB, Church Road (0892 890591). An 18-hole course with visitors welcome on weekdays and weekend afternoons. Handicap certificate and an advance phone call essential.

*BEWL WATER offers the best trout fishing in southern England. Day or season permits can be obtained from the fishing lodge, open daily between April and October. There is a boat for disabled anglers. Good fishing, too, at BAYHAM ABBEY LAKE and BARTLEY MILL STREAM.

FOOD AND DRINK
HORSE AND GROOM, Lamberhurst (0892 890302) maintains old inn traditions of hospitality and good food.

ACCOMMODATION
CHEQUERS, The Broadway, Lamberhurst TN3 8DQ (0892 890260). Tile-hung coaching inn by the bridge. Four rooms all with bath. Moderate.
HOOK GREEN POTTERY, Hook Green, Lamberhurst, TN3 8LR (0892 890504). Inexpensive bed and breakfast.
FURNACE FARM, Furnace Lane, Lamberhurst TN3 8LE (0892 890788). Three rooms with shower or bath on 160-acre fruit farm. Inexpensive.

LEEDS CASTLE

One of the oldest and most romantic stately homes in England overshadows the village of Leeds, a castle rising from an encircling lake with black swans gliding on it. It was built in stone by a Norman baron Robert de Crèvecœur nearly 900 years ago to defend himself and his family against the conquered but still hostile English. But there was a wooden fortress on the two small islands in a large lake formed by the River Len, with a drawbridge over the water, for two centuries before that. The Saxon thane who built it was Ledian or Leed, chief minister of Ethelbert IV, King of Kent. The Norman castle, its defences doubled in strength by Edward I, was for three centuries a dower home of eight medieval queens in succession, beginning with Eleanor of Castile. Henry IV and his queen Joan of

Navarre who are buried in Canterbury Cathedral spent a whole summer at what Froissart called that 'beautiful palace in Kent', escaping a plague that killed 30,000 people in London.

Henry VIII adored Leeds Castle and lavished money on its improvement. After him it was owned in turn by the St Legers, the Culpepers and the Fairfaxes, who all played a part in settling the colonies in the New World. Lord Thomas Culpeper was the first Governor or Virginia in 1680. His son-in-law, the 5th Lord Fairfax whose remains lie in a pauper's grave in the hamlet of BROOMFIELD near Leeds Castle, had appointed his younger brother to control the vast but unsaleable family estates in America. His son emigrated after inheriting the title, became both employer and friend of the youthful George Washington and prospered so greatly that he never returned. When he died, aged 89, Washington referred to him as 'the good old Lord'. The wheel came full circle when in 1926 Lady Baillie, of the fabulously rich American Whitney family, fell in love with what Lord Conway called 'the loveliest castle in the whole world' and bought it. She carried out its first major renovation in 100 years, decorated and refurnished it and created the Wood Garden by the little streams of the River Len where anemones grow in profusion. As her home it was the centre of hospitality between the wars for royalty and ambassadors. During World War II, Allied military commanders directed operations from

here and it was a convalescent home for badly burned airmen who were treated by the famous plastic surgeon Archibald McIndoe at East Grinstead. Lady Baillie left Leeds Castle to the nation and it is regularly used for medical and nursing conferences and research seminars, arts events and on one occasion for a Summit meeting on the Middle East.

Leeds Castle (0622 765400), 4 miles east of *Maidstone at Junction 8 of the M20/A20, is open to visitors daily from 24 March to the end of October and afternoons at weekends during the rest of the year. Disabled people and children under five are admitted free. Rooms filled with medieval tapestries and furnishings, armour and heraldry, statuary and paintings (including the finest collection of Impressionists outside London) make this a highlight of many tour itineraries. One of the many fascinating documents on display is a calf-bound book containing the household accounts of Queen Joan of Navarre for 1422 and in the Gate House there's a remarkable collection of ornamental dog collars dating back to the Middle Ages. Five hundred acres of parkland surround the castle and lake and outdoor attractions include the WOOD GARDEN, the CULPEPER GARDEN of box-bordered roses, flowering shrubs and herbaceous plants, a DUCKERY AND AVIARY housing such exotic species as the Roseate cockatoo, Brown's parakeet and the tiny Diamond dove, and a newly planted MAZE with an underground grotto. There is a gift shop in the Stable Yard and a high quality restaurant in the FAIR-FAX HALL, a 17th-century tithe barn where traditional Sunday roasts are served in winter. 'Kentish' evenings are held every Saturday. A 9-hole golf course with the castle as its backdrop is open daily to visitors (separate access of the A20) with changing rooms and equipment provided.

VINEYARD

KENT GARDEN VINEYARD, Yew Tree House, Upper Street, Leeds (0622 861638). Reviving the wine-making skills of the medieval canons, the vineyard and winery is open to visitors. In the house reproduction antique porcelain dolls are made. Open all year Thursday–Sunday and bank holidays.

LENHAM

This village takes its name from the river that rises in the hills to the southwest of Leeds Castle and although it is the home of the huge intercontinental Freightflow lorry depot in Ham Lane off the A20 London–Folkestone road, its main square is still a delight of white weatherboarding and black and white timber framing. The cobbled north side is shaded by a row of fragrant lime trees. There are two old inns, the RED LION and the DOG AND BEAR, the latter with royal arms over the door to commemorate a visit by Queen Anne. The village chemist's shop is called SAXON WARRIORS since the discovery within the building in 1948 of the skeletons of three 6th-century men with their weapons. The mostly 14th-century church with its fine Kentish tower is the last resting place of Mary Honywood who, when she died in 1620 at the age of 92, had witnessed no fewer than 367 descendants spanning four generations. One of these must have been the builder of the half-timbered house called HONY-WOOD in the High Street which bears his initials 'AH' and the date 1621. Like several other villages in Kent, Lenham remembers its 20th-century war dead with a white cross carved out of the chalk in a green hill nearby.

ACCOMMODATION

DOG AND BEAR, The Square, Lenham ME17 2PG (0622 858219). A former coaching inn with 21 rooms, all with *en suite* facilities, and a restaurant. Moderately priced.

LULLINGSTONE

A park of 300 acres by the River Darent just south of *Eynsford off the A225 contains LULLINGSTONE CASTLE (which is really a redbrick Queen Anne mansion), a flint-walled church and (what most visitors come to see) the excavated remains of a ROMAN VILLA (0322 863467), one of the best examples to be found anywhere. During most of 1989 it was closed for a major refurbishment by English Heritage. It dates from around AD100, but the mosaic floor which is its chief glory wasn't laid until two and a half centuries later. Soon afterwards, a Christian chapel was built by an owner who must have been converted at that time. The marble busts which adorned the tiled steps leading up to the splendid country mansion from the river are at the British Museum. The lawns of the park are dotted with lakes and fed by the Darent. John Peche, Sheriff of Kent and later Lord Deputy of Calais, and the Hart Dykes who followed him as owners of the castle and lived there for 400 years into the 20th century, are buried in the church.

The Castle (0322 862114) is open on weekends and bank holidays from April to September, garden and church only on Wednesday, Thursday and Friday afternoons.

SPORT AND LEISURE
Lullingstone Park Public Golf Course (0959 34542) offers 'pay and play' on 18 holes or 9 holes. Equipment can be hired.

LYDD

The 132ft Perpendicular tower of All Saints church sticking up above this large remote village on the heel of Kent, almost surrounded by flat grasslands criss-crossed by dykes, gives a clue to the importance it once enjoyed as a limb of the Cinque port of Romney (now *New Romney). In 1287 both lost access to the sea, their main livelihood, when a great storm dammed the estuary of the River Rother, forcing it southwards from *Appledore to the sea at Rye. Thus ended five centuries of prosperity from trade and taxes for the Saxon Hilda, as Lydd was originally called, and the privileges granted in its first charter from Edward I. It has none the less a few fine 18th-century buildings. The High Street runs down to a shingle shore abandoned to military firing ranges and adjoining the Sussex border and the wide firm Camber Sands.

MUSEUM
Town Museum, Queen's Road (0679 20660). In the old fire station, with an 1890s engine on view, together with a 1908 horse bus and other memorabilia. Open afternoons during the summer and on bank holiday Mondays.

MAIDSTONE

The County Town of Kent is a busy place, situated where the Medway broadens on its journey to meet the Thames Estuary, and a centre not only of administration but of commerce and agriculture. The imposing headquarters of the County Council looms over Maidstone East railway station and conceals from view the prison behind it. Such towns are not usually primarily concerned with tourism, but Maidstone has many historical attractions as well as being a convenient base for exploring either the Weald, the Downs or the Medway valley. It has good rail and road links (via the M20). Despite modern office development, multi-storey car parks and the inevitable tide of traffic, it still has something of the atmosphere of a country market town and now that the tan-sailed barges which used to carry cargoes of paper and timber and the 'stumpies' – special narrow boats used by the brick kilns – are no more, the river is given over to leisure. A short walk along the riverside path from central Maidstone towards Allington brings one within a few minutes to a scene of tranquility away from urban noise, where anglers line the banks under the trees and the only disturbance is the occasional pleasure boat or cruiser puttering past.

The origin of the name 'Meddestane' in the Domesday Book is obscure. According to different authorities it derives from Saxon words meaning Maiden's Town, Mighty Stone Town or Medway's Town – 'Medwegstan'. Nearby Penenden Heath was the ancient meeting place of the shire and the scene of public executions up to the middle of the 19th century. From the establishment of an Archbishop's palace in Norman times, Maidstone was owned and run by the Church until the Reformation. John Ball, the 'mad priest' who led the Peasants' Revolt of 1381 with

Wat Tyler, was imprisoned in the palace dungeons and later hanged. A bridge over the Medway, then tidal up to *East Farleigh, gave the town transport links with the capital by road and water and it grew rapidly in the later Middle Ages. During the Civil War it was the scene of fierce battles before the Royalists, supported by the Men of Kent, were decimated by Cromwell's army. In the strongly Puritan period which followed, six witches (five from Cranbrook, one from Lenham) were sent to the scaffold after a celebrated trial at Maidstone. Samuel Pepys watched flax being dressed in the street in 1669 and Daniel Defoe, 55 years later noted that from here London 'was supplied with more particulars than from any single market town in England' including timber, corn, hops, fruit, sand and stone. It was Kentish rag from Maidstone that paved the streets of the capital and rebuilt St Paul's Cathedral after the Great Fire. Later it became a brewing town (and still is) as well as the producer of brand products such as custard powder and Sharp's Toffee. Two Victorian railway companies, the South Eastern and the London, Chatham and District, fought over Maidstone – the latter claiming a 75-minute run from Maidstone East to Victoria in 1874. Maidstone was also a garrison town, the home of the Royal West Kent Regiment.

Maidstone's oldest group of buildings from Norman times, the Archbishop's Palace, the College of Priests and All Saints Church (both established in 1395), are built from the local ragstone and beautifully sited amidst gardens and waterfalls where the River Len plunges into the Medway. The TOURIST INFORMATION CENTRE, Old Palace Gardens, Mill Street ME15 6YE (0622 673581) occupies the gatehouse overhanging the River Len which is thought to have been a 13th- or 14th-century mill.

MUSEUMS
TYRWHITT-DRAKE MUSEUM OF CARRIAGES, Mill Street (0622 54497). Fascinating collection of horsedrawn carriages, private, official and State (some on loan from the Royal Mews) in the medieval stables of the Archbishop's Palace. Open Monday to Saturday, year round, and also on Sunday afternoons from April to September.

MAIDSTONE MUSEUM AND ART GALLERY, St Faith's Street (0622 56405) occupies the beautifully restored 16th-century Chillington Manor House, to which has been added the Elizabethan timber west wing of Court Lodge at East Farleigh. Apart from many fine paintings, its collections range from local industries such as papermaking and brewing to a brilliantly concise gallery of 20th-century costume. The QUEEN'S OWN ROYAL WEST KENT REGIMENTAL MUSEUM in the same building includes the superb Sutlej gun and limber, all polished brass and copper, wood and solid iron, captured by the regiment during the Sikh Wars of 1845. Open daily, year round, and Sunday afternoons.

MUSEUM OF KENT RURAL LIFE (0622 63936) is on a 27-acre site beside the Medway, signposted from the roundabout at the junction of the M20 and the A229. It can also be reached along the river path. Displays inside the Oast and hoppers' huts and around the farm courtyard portray the history of local agriculture and the countryside including traditional hoppicking by hand, drying over coal fires, hop tokens and the tally man. Open from April to October weekdays (except Wednesdays) and weekend afternoons.

ENTERTAINMENT
HAZLITT THEATRE, Corn Exchange, Earl Street ME14 1PL (0622 602179) takes its name from one of Maidstone's most famous sons, the Georgian writer and critic William Hazlitt noted for invective and scathing irony whose last words in 1830 were 'Well, I've had a happy life'. His eponymous theatre tackles everything from drama (professional and local amateur) to opera, jazz, films and light entertainment.

SHOPPING
Although the old market 'barrows' and John Bradford, fishmonger, with its yellow oilskin-clad effigy outside, survive in Earl Street, most of Maidstone's shopping is concentrated in pedestrianised precincts such as CHEQUERS and BROADWAY to the west of the town with its Safeways and W.H. Smith Do It All. Boots' Photo Lab Express occupies a pretty 1680 building in King Street, its pastel shaded plaster façade decorated with

cornucopia. The newest and poshest development is the ROYAL STAR ARCADE where Hatchards Bookshop retains the oak staircase, fireplace and ceiling of a period building. Traditional markets are still held on Lockmeadow by the river on Tuesdays and Saturdays, with furniture and bric-a-brac on Thursdays, livestock on Mondays and produce on Fridays.

SPORT AND LEISURE

KENT COUNTY SHOW has a permanent site on the slopes of the North Downs at DETLING with panoramic views of the Weald. The show, agricultural and horticultural, has 400 stands and is attended by royalty.

MOTE PARK. Over 450 acres of open country close to the town centre, the setting for the annual 'Cricket Week' when the streets are lined with bunting. A large lake for sailing, fishing and birdwatching, a nature trail and a pitch and putt course. Fishing permits from Southern Water (0643 830655) or Maidstone Victory Angling and Preservation Society (0622 29047). Rod and line licences for fishing in the Len and Medway can be obtained from most tackle shops in town.

MOTE SWIMMING BATHS, Mote Park (0622 764631). Sauna, solarium and a rifle range in the basement for .22 smallbores.

TOVIL BRIDGE BOATYARD, Wharf Road, Tovil (0622 686341) Cruisers for hire from two to five days and rowing boats and powered dinghies by the hour. HIRE CRUISERS, Undercliffe Boat House,

Bishops Way, Maidstone (0622 53740) runs hour-long cruises between Easter and October in the 100-seat Kentish Lady II, calling at Allington Lock.

COBTREE MANOR PARK, Sandling (0622 718728) covers 270 acres of natural downland on the northern outskirts of the town with bridleways, nature trails and picnic sites. The 'pay and play' municipal golf course (18 holes) has equipment for hire (0622 53276). Other courses in the vicinity are at BEARSTED GOLF CLUB, Ware Street (0622 38024), TUDOR PARK GOLF AND COUNTRY CLUB, Ashford Road, Bearsted (0622 35891) and LEEDS CASTLE 'pay and play' (0627 80467).

RECORD TENNIS CENTRE, Mill Meadow, St Peter's Street (0622 681987) has all-weather courts.

ENVIRONS

ALLINGTON CASTLE (0622 54080) lies amidst the trees near ALLINGTON LOCK just off the M20 (follow signs to the A20) or a 2-mile walk along the river towpath from central Maidstone. The lock was built as long ago as 1792 but the electric sluice gates beside it were installed in the 1930s and mark the tidal limit of the Medway. One of the seven chief castles of Kent, Allington was built in 1282 by Sir Stephen de Penchester, the founder of *Penshurst. It has a romantic history. Sir Henry Wyatt, who restored it in Tudor times, was imprisoned in the Tower for challenging the unscrupulous Richard III and was saved from starvation by a cat bringing pigeons to his cell

Maidstone's oldest building, the Archbishop's Palace

window and sleeping on his chest at night to keep him warm. His son, Sir Thomas Wyatt, wrote the first English sonnets a generation before Shakespeare was born. He had been employed on diplomatic missions by Henry VIII but was thrown in the Tower for a time on suspicion of being Anne Boleyn's lover. She is believed to have sent him a jewel by his sister Mary when she was about to go to the executioner's block. It wasn't until 15 years after his death that 31 of his sonnets were published along with work of the Earl of Surrey, who received joint credit for introducing them to the language. Tennyson sets a scene at 'Castle Adamant' (modelled on Allington) where the bells of Maidstone are heard ringing to rouse the population against the marriage of Mary to Phillip of Spain. Thomas Wyatt the Younger, who is plotting with the father of Lady Jane Grey to put her on the throne, sends for the casket containing his father's sonnets to string them 'like losely scattered jewels, in fair order'. He is dragged from this 'woman's work' to occupy Rochester, assume command of the royal ships in the Medway before pressing towards the capital. But the uprising was defeated and the poet's son ended up on the scaffold at Tower Hill. In this century Lord Conway and his American wife bought the ruin of the castle and restored the gatehouse and tiltyard, laying out lawns and lavender walks. In 1951 it was acquired by the Carmelites of *Aylesford and is now a conference and retreat centre open daily in the afternoons to visitors, year round. Guided tours are given from Easter to October.

BOXLEY, a mile or two to the east in the shelter of the North Downs, boasts the remains of the only Cistercian Abbey in Kent, dating from 1146, and Boxley House which was given by Henry VIII to the Wyatts along with the abbey. It features as the home of Admiral Hornblower in C. Northcote Parkinson's *Life and Times of Horatio Hornblower*. Other literary associations are with Alfred Lord Tennyson, who lived at Park House, and whose poem *The Brook* was inspired by the one that flows here towards the Medway. All Saints Church has monuments to Tennyson's beloved sister Cecilia, who was married here, and to Sir Henry Wyatt 'God sent a cat to both feed and warm him'.

BEARSTED has become an eastern suburb of Maidstone but its village green remains inviolate as one of Kent's oldest cricket fields. Apart from 250 years of cricket it has witnessed skirmishes between Cromwell's Roundheads and the Cavaliers and Wat Tyler's peasant army versus the gentry. Like all proper village greens it is over-looked by a good pub, the WHITE HORSE, with seats and benches outside. The Norman church with its high timbered roof and great buttressed tower decorated with three fearsome beasts stands at the end of a lane hedged with holly.

STONEACRE (0622 861861) at Otham, amidst the orchards to the south of Bearsted, is an exquisite 15th-century half-timbered manor house restored in the 1920s, with a very pretty garden and herb garden, now owned by the National Trust. Open from April to September on Wednesday and Saturday afternoons.

BOUGHTON MONCHELSEA PLACE (0622 743120) on the B2163 4 miles south of Maidstone was built in Elizabeth's reign from the rag-stone quarried locally since Saxon times and used in the building of Westminster Abbey. It was re-stored and renovated in the early years of the 19th century so Eliza-bethan gabled dormer windows blend with Regency battlements. The surrounding Wealden land-scape of orchards, hop gardens and oast houses beyond the land-scaped park remains untouched by time. Inside there are many beauti-ful things, furniture and tapestry as well as formal collections of costume and haberdashery. There are collections of carriages and pre-mechanisation farm implements. Still lived in, it is open on weekend afternoons from Easter to early October and bank holidays, as well as on Wednesdays in July and August.

LOOSE, 2 miles south of Maidstone off the A229, once had 13 water-mills driven by two streams flowing into the Medway. The grave of Richard Boys, who was Napoleon's chaplain in exile, is in the church-yard under a yew 1,000 years old. The WOOL HOUSE, a Tudor timbered building in which fleeces were washed, is owned by the National Trust and open to visitors from April to September by written application only.

FOOD AND DRINK

TRADING POST, 22 High Street, Maidstone (0622 53041). All-American steaks, ribs and burgers. Variety of beers.

ATILLA, 16 Gabriel's Hill, Maidstone (0622 56211). Authentic Turkish, with takeaways until 2am.

SIR THOMAS WYATT, London Road, Allington (0622 52515). A 'Roast Inn' catering for families with 'Postman Pat' meals for the children. Inexpensive.

DRAKE'S CRAB AND OYSTER HOUSE, Fairmeadow, Maidstone (0622 52531) Specialises, naturally, in seafood but also does steaks, barbecued chicken and lunchtime snacks.

OLD HOUSE AT HOME, Pudding Lane, Maidstone (0622 52363). Welcoming hostelry in the heart of town, with hanging baskets of flowers outside.

SUEFFLÉ, the Green, Bearsted (0622 37065). Fine cooking with fresh ingredients. Expensive.

ACCOMMODATION

CARVAL, London Road, Maidstone ME16 8QL (0622 62100). Ten comfortable rooms, two with baths *en suite*, in convenient town centre situation. Inexpensive.

BOXLEY HOUSE, Boxley ME14 3DZ (0622 692269). Eighteen rooms all with bath. Historic setting with garden and outdoor pool. Moderately priced.

TANYARD, Wierton Hill, Boughton Monchelsea ME17 4JT (0622 44705). Very comfortable, but expensive. Just five rooms, all with bath.

MARDEN

In the heart of the rich hop and orchard country between Maidstone and the Sussex border, Marden is rich in history, too. The legions camped on the banks of the River Teise near here and a Roman villa stood on the northern edge of the existing village, which appears in the Domesday Book as 'Merdenne'. By then it was important enough to warrant a Court House (its 13th-century timbers survive as a part of a shop). As a Royal Hundred it was for centuries after the Norman Conquest outside the jurisdiction of the county Sheriff, a town of considerable importance

until in the early-17th-century King James I sold it to a local baronet, Sir Henry Brown, who in turn passed it on to the Earls of Pembroke. A vestige of its former glory remains in that the rector of the parish is no less a dignitary than the Archbishop of Canterbury himself. The church, built on 13th-century foundations, has a weatherboarded belfry with a curious wooden structure shaped like a candle-snuffer on top. Lord Chief Justiciar De Luci who lived in the reign of Henry II rests here – his tomb was brought to Marden after being desecrated during the

Reformation. Marden is a stop on the long, straight Wealden railway line which runs from Tonbridge to Ashford.

MARGATE

On the northern shore of the Isle of Thanet, merry Margate continues to reign as the queen of what is now called Kent's 'Leisure Coast'. This means inevitably buckets and spades (Margate's sands won a clean beach award in 1988), funfairs and amusement arcades — fine, if that's what you are looking for, otherwise stay well clear. Margate is no stranger to trippers. It has been attracting them from London in droves since in 1753 Benjamin Beale, a local glovemaker and Quaker, invented the bathing machine to cover the ladies' modesty while they took a dip in the sea. Initially the visitors came down the Thames in fleets of Margate hoys (the sailing boats which gave rise to the nautical cry 'Ahoy!'), until they were superseded first by steamboats and later by the railway. The swimming is very safe for children and lifeguards are on patrol throughout the summer. The LIFEBOAT HOUSE in the harbour, which dries out at low tide, houses the fast inshore rescue boat 'Silver Jubilee' and is open to visitors from May to September, with special rides for the children.

The TOURIST INFORMATION CENTRE (0843 220241) can be found at the centre of the action in Marine Terrace, the main seafront.

MUSEUMS

THE GROTTO (0843 220008) dis-covered in 1835, *may* have been a prehistoric pagan temple. Thousands of shells are embedded in its chalk walls to form an intricate 2,000 sq. ft mosaic. Open weekdays and weekend mornings from Easter to October. Other caves in NORTHDOWN ROAD are open in summer.

TUDOR HOUSE, King Street (0843 225511). Half-timbered building dating from 1525. Collection of local memorabilia and foreign seashells. Open daily from mid-May to September.

LOCAL HISTORY MUSEUM (0843 225511). Two minutes walk from the old Town Hall, open daily except Sunday and Monday from May to September.

SPORT AND LEISURE

BEMBOM BROTHERS THEME PARK (0843 227011) is the trendy name for the funfair known to generations of kids as 'Dreamland'. Its 25 acres of amusements is overshadowed by the Big Wheel, 140ft high.

HARTSDOWN PARK (0843 226221), just behind Margate Railway Station, the sport and leisure centre offers a variety of indoor and outdoor activities and equipment for hire.

AQUARIUM (0843 221951). On the cliffs at Palm Bay, an impressive collection of tropical fish. Open year round.

ENVIRONS

Divided from Margate by a wide greensward with a sunken garden, WESTGATE-ON-SEA is the sedate sister suburb, mostly Victorian and Edwardian redbrick, with beach huts.

ACCOMMODATION

YE OLDE CHARLES INN, Northdown Road, Margate CT9 3PG (0843 221817). Don't be put off by the quaint name – there are six nice rooms (two with showers *en suite*), a garden and a children's play area. Near the old caves and inexpensive.

IVYSIDE, 25 Sea Road, Westgate-on-Sea CT8 8SB (0843 31082). All its 58 rooms have bath or shower and there are heated indoor and outdoor pools, a games room and a children's play area. Moderately priced.

MATFIELD

Birthplace of the World War I poet Siegfried Sassoon, this village east of *Tunbridge Wells on the B2160 is, like its neighbour *Brenchley, delightful to stroll around. The duckpond and cricket pitch on the green are overlooked by the white clapboarded Wheelwrights Arms and some elegant Georgian architecture.

CRITTENDEN HOUSE, about a mile to the north on a quiet lane through orchards, is a 17th-century manor house with immaculate gardens, sometimes illuminated at night. The house itself is not open to visitors but the gardens are at certain times, in aid of environmental charities (0892 283 2254). BADSELL PARK FARM close by is open to visitors to see the various farm animals and pets and to pick fruit in season.

FOOD AND DRINK

CHERRY TREES TEA GALLERY, Matfield Green (0892 722187). Charming tearooms and country garden.

ACCOMMODATION

Matfield Court, Matfield Green TN12 7JX (0892 723515). Four pleasant rooms, two with bath, for inexpensive bed and breakfast. Evening meals if required. The garden has a children's play area.

MEOPHAM

Pronounced 'Meppam', this old village with its long history of cricket is fortunate that postwar plans to turn it into a New Town came to nothing. Records show Meopham playing cricket against Chatham as long ago as 10 July 1778 and matches are still played on the green, by the windmill, both among the best-kept in the county. Meopham hasn't escaped suburbanisation but it has kept its heart, unlike so many other formerly rural parts of Kent. The flintstone church is where John Tradescant, gardener to King Charles I, was married in 1607 and christened his son, also John, the following year. The Tradescants travelled the world collecting exotic species for their many famous gardens and shells, stones, bones and fossils which are in the Ashmolean Museum in Oxford. Among the many trees and shrubs which they introduced to England were the lilac and the acacia. On the B2009 road just north of the village is CAMER COUNTRY PARK, 46 acres of pleasant mature parkland with a small wood.

MEREWORTH

Near a fork in the road where the A26 to Maidstone from Tonbridge sends the A228 northwards to West Malling can be found a fine example of 18th-century Palladian architecture. Reminiscent of Castle Howard in Yorkshire, MEREWORTH CASTLE, a private home still, was built by the Earl of Westmorland, who demolished the best part of the village and its church to make way for it. Surrounded by orchards and one of the largest surviving areas of the ancient forest, MEREWORTH WOODS, the domed building modelled on an Italian palace looks somewhat out of place, as does the 'new' church built by the 7th Earl to replace the one he knocked down. Both buildings are worth stopping to take a look at, if not a special journey.

MINSTER-IN-SHEPPEY

Sheppey is Saxon for 'Sheep Island' and much of it is farmland still. Indeed, unlike Kent's other 'islands', this one is still completely surrounded by water, with the Swale to the south and the Medway and Thames estuaries to the north. Minster stands on a wide beach backed by grassy slopes and low cliffs between the commercial port of *Sheerness and the holiday chalets and caravans of Warden and Leysdown-on-Sea. An abbey was founded at Minster in the 7th century by Queen Sexburga, who became the first abbess of the nunnery here. It was sacked by marauding Danes in the 8th century, rebuilt by the Benedictines in the 12th century and knocked down again in the Reformation of the 16th century. All that survives of this ancient foundation is the GATEHOUSE (0795 872303) which is open in the afternoons, except Thursdays, from Spring Bank Holiday to September. Its displays and photographs of Sheppey's history are quite fascinating. The parish church of St Mary and St Sexburga is really two churches in one – the northern part containing some of the fabric of the original nunnery church. Worth seeing is the monument to Sir Roger de Shurland, Baron of Sheppey and Lord Warden of the Cinque Ports in the 14th century. The horse's head rising from the waves relates to one of R.H. Barham's *Ingoldsby Legends*. Having murdered a monk, Sir

Roger rode his horse into the sea to meet Edward I's ship as it passed by, seeking a pardon. Back on the shore he was met by a witch prophesying that the horse which had saved his life would bring about his death, so he drew his sword and beheaded it. Some time afterwards he came across the skull on the beach and administering a kick, died from the subsequent toe wound! THE LEAS AND CLIFFTOP MINSTER covers 4 acres, perfect for walks and picnics among the sandgrass sloping to the beach. Inland, the village of EASTCHURCH has a memorial to the pioneers of aviation in this century. Rolls, the partner in Rolls-Royce, was killed in a crash nearby with another airman in 1910. Lord Brabazon achieved the first powered flight of a mile and Winston Churchill learned to fly here, where Short Brothers also built the first aeroplane factory in England.

From SHELL NESS to ELMLEY MARSHES along the Swale there are masses of wildfowl and waders, including wigeon, teal, white-fronted geese, redshanks, lapwings and shovelers.

MINSTER-IN-THANET

Like Minster-in-Sheppey, this ancient settlement has its myths and legends including a Saxon version of the little princes murdered in the Tower. Thunor, a Kentish thane, put Egbert I on the throne by murdering the young princes Ethelbert and Ethelred but the place where he hid the bodies was spotlit by two supernatural columns of light. In penitence, Egbert allowed a deer to run free, with the promise that all the land to the east of the course it took should go to the building of an abbey by the dead princes' sister Ermenburga. Although Thunor did his best to keep the animal in the bounds he wanted, the earth 'opened and swallowed him up'. A large hollow at the top of Minster Hill is called Thunorsleap. Ermenburga built Minster Abbey in AD 670 and her daughter Mildred became patron saint of Thanet. The legend of the deer is depicted in stained glass in the parish church at Minster. Like its sister in Sheppey, the abbey at Thanet was raided by the Danes and left in ruins for centuries until the monks of St Augustine's in Canterbury built a grange and a monastic church in Norman times, using Roman bricks as well as stone. Today it is the home of sisters of the Benedictine Order. A little way to the east across Minster Marshes is EBBSFLEET on Pegwell Bay, traditional site of the landing of the Saxons in AD 449 and St Augustine in AD 597. The area abounds in antiquities such as the Boarded Groin, St Augustine's Well and Abbot's Wall along the River Stour.

NETTLESTEAD

On the lovely stretch of the Medway upriver from *Maidstone, Nettlestead is fortunate in being protected from all but selected development. But don't go there looking for Admiral Lord Hornblower's tomb as described in his, quite fictional, biography by C. Northcote Parkinson. It doesn't exist and 'Smallbridge Manor', where Hornblower lived within sight of smoke from locomotives passing on the branch line from Paddock Wood, was conveniently burnt down in 1884. NETTLESTEAD PLACE, the home of Sir Thomas Scott who led 4,000 Men of Kent into battle against the Spanish Armada, *does* exist although converted into flats and not open to visitors. Near the 15th-century gateway to the landscaped grounds is the equally ancient church where some of the Scott family are buried. Their predecessors, the Pympes, filled the windows with glorious glass. Along the Wateringbury road, CHERRY HILL VINEYARD, planted in 1966, has produced several good vintages on the site of an old orchard. It is near one of several vineyards that were planted by the Romans along the Medway valley 1,800 years ago and was the setting in this century for George Orwell's essays on the harsh reality of life 'down on the farm'.

NEWINGTON

Not to be confused with the Newington that finds itself in the very jaws of the Channel Tunnel, this village lies on Watling Street (the A2) in the midst of cherry orchards between the Medway Towns and *Sittingbourne. Near the parish church are two ancient stones that are worth stopping to see because one of them bears the mark of the Devil's footprint, 15 inches long. Local legend has it that Satan couldn't abide the sound of the church bells so he made off with them. Leaping down from the tower he stumbled on the stone, leaving his footprint. The bells rolled out of his sack to vanish in a stream which, ever after, ran 'clear as a bell'.

NEW ROMNEY

Until the great storm of 1287 diverted the course of the River Rother to Rye, this was first among the powerful Cinque Ports above Hastings, *Hythe, *Dover and *Sandwich, charged with providing ships, arms and men for the defence of the medieval realm and receiving in return many trading perks and reductions in tithes and taxes. Today Romney is a quaint backwater, distinguished by the grandiose Norman church built when the town was at the height of its power and influence. William Morris takes most of the credit for preventing well-intentioned Victorian restorers from getting their hands on it. Today New Romney's main claim to fame is as the headquarters of the ROMNEY, HYTHE AND DYMCHURCH RAILWAY (0679 62353) built in 1927 by the eccentric Count Zborowski, who raced the original car which inspired Ian Fleming's *Chitty Chitty Bang Bang*. The coaches are hauled by steam or diesel locos built to one-third of full size.

The TOURIST INFORMATION CENTRE (0679 64044) is in the forecourt of the Light Railway Station and is open from March to October.

OFFHAM

The most unusual feature of this village off the A20 near *West Malling is the tall white post with a swivelling bar at the top which stands on the green. 'Tilting' at the quintain with a lance on horseback and dodging the weight hung at the opposite end of the crossbar as it swings round was once a common sport on village greens. The tilting pole at Offham is the last surviving example in England and is only used annually at the May Day celebration to demonstrate how it works. Cricket is more popular than tilting on the green these days and Offham with its old inn and cottages built from local stone and timber and its handsome 18th-century brick houses provides the perfect setting for it. Offham goes back to Saxon times and gets its name from Offa. In AD832 King Ethelwulf of Kent gave 'Ofne-hamme', as it was called then, to the Church. The existing church is Norman, half a mile down the lane towards ADDINGTON, where, within sight and sound of the M20 motor-way, various mounds and stones mark prehistoric burial grounds. The area is now covered by the fairways and greens of West Malling Golf Club.

OTFORD

Now all but encircled by the London Orbital Motorway (M25) this place was much favoured, like the whole valley of the Darent, by the Romans. Their mosaics and frescoes have been excavated in profusion in this century. Later it was Offa's battlefield against the Men of Kent and Cnut's (Canute) against the Danes. It stands on the Pilgrims Way and Henry VIII camped there with his Queen and 5,000 followers *en route* to the Field of the Cloth of Gold to meet 'dear brother France'. It's said they ate Otford out of house and home, consuming 2,000 sheep in the month that they stayed.

The village clusters round a duckpond overhung by weeping willows and included quaintly among Kent's 'listed buildings'. Not 'listed', but of interest, is the cottage in the High Street (now a restaurant) where D.H. Lawrence came calling on Helen, wife of the soldier poet Edward Thomas, who came from Bearsted. The ruins of the ARCHBISHOP'S PALACE which Henry coveted and eventually got can still be seen, as can BECKET'S WELL, excavated only a few years ago. Becket was unhappy with the purity of Otford's water, so he tapped his crozier on the ground and up bubbled two springs. When a nightingale's song disturbed his prayers, he ordered that none should sing there again. Locals at the BULL INN will tell you in all seriousness that nightingales have never sung in Otford since. The pub has a nice 16th-century fireplace with two roundel portraits on it. At nearby TWITTON the thatched barn of the medieval manor of Sepham is the subject of a memorable painting by Samuel Palmer.

PATRIXBOURNE

Three miles southeast of *Canterbury, this village took the first part of its name from a Norman Lord of the manor, William Patricius. Until the early 1900s a manorial court was held here and a group of cottages, which look Tudor with their overhanging gables and timbers carved with heraldic devices, are in fact Victorian. They were built for the tenants of the 'big house', Bifrons, which they have outlived, its park now used as farmland. The flint and Caen stone Norman church of St Mary survives, too, with its 16th- and 17th-century stained glass imported from Switzerland in the Bifrons Chapel. The NAIL BOURNE stream here flows only when the East Kent chalkbed has soaked up more water than it can hold and then sometimes floods. It can stay dry for years at a time.

PENSHURST

The River Eden flows into the Medway near the ancient stone bridge on the B2176 just to the south of the stately mansion which draws many thousands of visitors to this little village. Sir Philip Sidney, the Elizabethan statesman, soldier and poet who was mortally wounded fighting the Spaniards at the Battle of Zutphen in Holland in 1586, was born at PENSHURST PLACE (0892 870307) and his descendants still live there. It has been in the same family since the boy king Edward VI granted it to his Chamberlain and Chief Steward, Sir William Sidney, in 1552. It is a rich palace tucked away in the country lanes which wind with the two rivers through woods and meadows, approached through a village of half-timbered cottages. The village garage is in what used to be the blacksmith's forge, with hammer and spikes on its gable and a door shaped like a horseshoe.

The bricked court which leads to the churchyard through a timbered archway in a group of cottages is called LEICESTER SQUARE after the Earl of Leicester. Penshurst takes its name from Sir Stephen de Penchester who died in 1299. Entering Penshurst Place through the medieval Garden Tower, the Elizabethan façade of elaborately carved chalk and stone spreads out majestically behind the hedges, paths and beds of its formal gardens. At its heart is the incomparable GREAT HALL built in the 14th century by Sir John de Pulteney, four times Lord Mayor of London. It has a minstrels' gallery and the chestnut beams supporting the roof rise 60ft above the stone-paved floor. Penshurst Place has been added to down the centuries, mirroring various architectural styles, but never losing its entity as a stately home, graceful and a little remote. Not even the steady tramp of visitors' feet through its corridors can diminish the air of nobility about it and there is a sense of melancholy about the portraits of the Sidney family lining the State Dining Room and the Long Gallery where they took their exercise when the weather was inclement. Fine tapestries are displayed in a room reserved for them and another room across the stable courtyard contains a celebrated collection of toys, games, picture books and dolls. Outside in the grounds, an old Sussex barn houses a museum of farm implements, and there's an adventure playground and a nature trail. Dogs are forbidden in the picnic area. Open Tuesday to Saturday in the afternoons from 1 April to 1 October and also on bank holiday Mondays.

VINEYARDS

PENSHURST VINEYARDS (0892 870255). The winery is open year round, except Christmas week, with an opportunity to taste and buy. Wallabies, black swans and rare sheep are extra attractions. Phone beforehand for a guided tour.

FOOD AND DRINK

SPOTTED DOG, Smarts Hill, Penshurst (0892 870253) has great views across the Weald and serves good bar food. There is also a small restaurant, heavily booked especially on Sundays when traditional roast lunches are served.

ACCOMMODATION

LEICESTER ARMS, Penshurst TN11 8BT (0892 870551). The local has seven rooms, all with bath, and serves good food at moderate prices.

SWALE COTTAGE, Old Swaylands Lane, off Ponds Bridge Lane, Penshurst TN11 8AH (0892 870738) has three comfortable rooms, all with bath, and a pleasant garden. Moderately priced.

PLAXTOL

Tucked away in the woods and orchards off the A227 *Tonbridge road beside the River Shode, the village has two pubs with unusual names: the RORTY CRANKLE (which means ingle-nook) and the PAPERMAKER'S ARMS, an indication of the industry which once flourished and still survives along the river bank. OLD SOAR MANOR (0732 810622) in the care of English Heritage, is a mile east. It is a Queen Anne farmhouse with the original solar block of the fortified knight's house built on this site in the late 13th century. It is open daily from Easter to the end of September. Other historic houses in the locality include Fairlawne, which is partly in the neighbouring parish of SHIP-BOURNE. It was the family home of Sir Henry Vane, a Governor of Massachusetts and a member of the Long Parliament who was some-times critical of Cromwell, causing him to cry out one day 'Sir Harry Vane, Sir Harry Vane, the Lord deliver me from Sir Harry Vane!' At the Restoration poor Sir Harry was executed by the Royalists and his headless body returned here where it lies in a lead coffin in the crypt of Shipbourne church. Sir Harry is said to haunt the Wilder-ness Walk at Fairlawne on the anniversary of his execution, carry-ing his head under his arm. A more recent occupier of Fairlawne was the late Major Cazalet's famous racing stable with royal colours.

SPORT AND LEISURE

DENE PARK, Shipbourne, is a 220-acre conifer and hardwood planta-tion off the A227 on a road sign-posted to Plaxtol. A trail from the picnic area leads to interesting viewing points.

ACCOMMODATION

OLD SOAR MANOR, Plaxtol TN15 0QX (0732 810250). Four rooms are provided for inexpensive bed and breakfast.

PLUCKLEY

On a steep hillside in wooded country south of the A20 road to *Ashford, Pluckley commands wide views of the Weald but that doesn't make it remarkable. What does, is its variety of ghosts, making it perhaps the most haunted village in England. The parish church is full of memorials to the Dering family who were the great land-owners hereabouts and had their seat at Surrenden Dering, now gone. The name survives in Dering Wood to the west of the village and in the ghosts – the Red Lady Dering, who searches for a lost child in the churchyard, and the White Lady Dering who looks for the ruins of Surrenden Dering. There are a dozen other spectres, including those of a pipe-smoking gipsy lady and a brickworker who fell to his death in a pit.

ACCOMMODATION

DERING ARMS, Station Road, Pluck-ley (0233 84371). Next to the railway station and not (as far as we know) haunted, the restaurant serves fresh fish and game in season as well as locally brewed ales.

QUEENBOROUGH

This ancient town on the western shore of the Isle of Sheppey, founded by Edward III in the 14th century and named for his Queen Philippa, is today a place of glue works, rolling mills and glass factories. Like many Kentish towns, its appearance belies its fascinating history. As long ago as 1724 Daniel Defoe found it a 'miserable, dirty, decay'd, poor, pitiful, fishing town'. Yet it once boasted a castle commanded by John of Gaunt (somewhere in the vicinity of the railway station, but all vestiges of it removed by Cromwell's men). Here Sir Francis Drake incarcerated the Spanish general Don Cerinimo, whom he took with a treasure-laden galleon and brought to Queenborough. The unfortunate man died in captivity in 1591. Amidst the industrial squalor, Queenborough preserves some handsome 18th-century buildings such as its GUILDHALL and CHURCH HOUSE in the High Street where Lady Hamilton stayed when visiting Lord Nelson. The 19th-century FIG TREE HOUSE actually has a fig tree in its garden. Just across the mouths of the Swale and the Medway on the Isle of Grain are the tanks and towers of the refinery – and the memory of Port Victoria to which Queen Victoria would ride by train to board the royal yacht away from 'vast screaming crowds' as she put it. The South Eastern Railway Company kept a red carpet at the timber-built station on the 400ft-long jetty. Today not a plank of Port Victoria survives among the tanker berths. The last royal person to use it was Kaiser Wilhelm, on his way home to Germany after the Coronation of King George V in 1911.

RAMSGATE

Gathered symmetrically round an almost circular harbour, dubbed 'Royal Harbour' since George IV landed there in 1822, with Georgian terraces at either side, Ramsgate is different again from merry *Margate or bucolic *Broadstairs, the other two resorts of Kent's 'Leisure Coast'. The sands next to the harbour won a clean beach award in 1988 and benefit from a sheltered, south-facing position whenever the sun is shining. The harbour itself is busy with private yachts and pleasure boats and since 1981 Sally Line (0843 595522) has operated cross-Channel ferries to Dunkirk, a trip of 2½ hours. In 1940 an armada of 'little ships' landed 82,000 troops evacuated from the beaches of Dunkirk at Ramsgate Harbour – an event that's commemorated by a stained glass window in St George's Church. Ramsgate seems set to embark on a new phase in the 1990s with its yacht marina, new hotels and cross-Channel traffic. Although the traditional seaside attractions of miniature golf, a bowling green and a boating pool can still be found along ROYAL ESPLANADE, the more sophisticated pleasures of the HARBOURSIDE CASINO are available nightly.

The TOURIST INFORMATION CENTRE (0843 591086) is at the Argyle Centre in Queen Street.

MUSEUMS
RAMSGATE MUSEUM, Library, Guildford Lawn (0843 593532). The civic life and history of the town and its harbour with prints, paintings and displays of local archaeology. Open daily, closed Sundays and bank holidays.
MARITIME MUSEUM, Ramsgate Harbour (0843 587765). Four galleries devoted to the maritime heritage of the area and a restored drydock of 1791, with various vintage vessels including *Sundowner* one of the Dunkirk 'little ships'.
MODEL VILLAGE, West Cliff Promenade (0843 592543). An idealistic reproduction in miniature of the Garden of England, originating from 1953. Open daily from Easter to the end of October.
MOTOR MUSEUM, Westcliff Hall (0843 581948). Over 100 exhibits of all marques from 1900 to 1970. Open daily from Easter throughout the summer. Sundays only in winter.

SPORT AND LEISURE
ROYAL HARBOUR MARINA welcomes visiting yachts. The Harbour Office is in Military Road (0843 592277).
UNDERCLIFF Promenades and jetties offer good fishing for codling, bass, eels, pout and flounders and fishing is free on both piers.
DUMPTON PARK LEISURE CENTRE, Dumpton Park (0843 593333). Greyhound racing on Monday, Wednesday and Saturday evenings and on Fridays from July to September and bank holiday Monday mornings. Also squash, snooker and a gym. Every Friday there's an 'open market' with up to 400 stalls.
ST AUGUSTINE'S GOLF CLUB, Cottingham Road, Cliffs End (0843 590333) 18-hole seaside links near the ancient landing site of St Augustine. Visitors with a handicap certificate are welcome at any time.

ENVIRONS
PEGWELL BAY to the south of the town was the site of the world's first international hoverport in 1968, now abandoned to a replica of one of the Viking dragon-headed longships which invaded in the 5th century. The HUGIN, perched on the slope above the hovercraft depot, was rowed and sailed from Denmark in 1949, the 1,500th anniversary of the landings led by Hengist and Horsa. ST AUGUSTINE'S CROSS is in Foads Lane off the A256 through CLIFFS END.
MANSTON AIRFIELD, a couple of miles inland, was a major Royal Air Force base in World War II and afterwards. Opposite the main gate, a pavilion opened by Dame Vera Lynn in 1988 houses probably the best-preserved Spitfire and Hurricane fighters in the country and examples of postwar jets such as the Canberra bomber

and the Javelin fighter. Open daily (0843 823351, extension 2219).

FOOD AND DRINK

EAGLE CAFÉ at the end of East Pier (0843 592224) with panoramic views of the Marina and the bay, specialises in fish and has a children's menu. Meals served all day at moderate prices.

SUGAR AND SPICE COFFEE SHOP AND OLD POLICE STATION, 18 Queen Street, Ramsgate (0843 585708). A licensed restaurant in unusual surroundings. Traditional set lunch on Sundays. Moderate.

ACCOMMODATION

MARINA RESORT, Harbour Parade, Ramsgate CT11 9DS (0843 588276). Sixty rooms, all *en suite* and mostly with sea views, plus in-house health club with swimming pool, jacuzzi, sauna, solarium and gym. Admirals Restaurant offers à la carte and table d'hote. Expensive.

SAVOY, 43 Grange Road, Ramsgate CT11 9NA (0843 592637). Licensed restaurant and moderately priced bed and breakfast. All rooms have shower and wc.

SPENCER COURT, Spencer Square, Ramsgate CT11 9LD (0843 594582). Licensed family-run hotel in a Regency square overlooking gardens, tennis courts and the sea. Directly above the Sally Ferry Terminal. Inexpensive bed and breakfast.

ABBEYGAIL, 17 Penshurst Road, East Cliff CT11 8EG (0843 594154). Comfortable guest house only 200 yards from the sea. Inexpensive bed and breakfast and evening meal if required.

VIKING, Sandwich Road, Pegwell Bay CT12 5HZ (0843 595823). A motor hotel with 43 bedrooms and chalets, a gym with sauna and solarium, overlooking the bay and the Hugin longboat. Good restaurant, moderate prices.

PEGWELL VILLAGE HOTEL, Pegwell Road, Pegwell CT11 0NJ (0843 586001), in what used to be a smugglers' village now on the southern outskirts of Ramsgate, is handy for the ferry and popular with golfers. Maxina's Restaurant is open seven days a week, for non-residents too.

PRESTON CARAVAN PARKS, Preston Road, Manston (0843 823346). Six pitches with all facilities for towing caravans, tents and campervans. Open March to October.

RECULVER

When the Romans landed, the Isle of Thanet was separated from the mainland by a wide channel at this point on the north coast of Kent, where in the third century they built a fortress called Regulbium to guard the approaches. Massive columns from its original Romano-British church are in the crypt of *Canterbury Cathedral. The twin towers which stand out for miles along the coast and out to sea, are the remains of a 12th-century church built inside the fort. In the 16th century two nuns on a pilgrimage to the shrine of the Virgin at Bradstow were shipwrecked off Reculver. They were twins and the one who survived, Frances St Clare, had spires added to the towers as a memorial and an even more noticeable landmark for mariners. When she died she was buried alongside her sister beneath the twin towers. Today the Wantsum Channel is a mere trickle across the marshes and the spires have long since gone. But the twin towers remain (just off the A299 3 miles east of *Herne Bay) with a few holiday caravans parked around them. Now that Thanet is an isle in name only there is no break in the path that runs for 10 miles along low cliff top and sea wall from Herne Bay to *Margate.

RICHBOROUGH

At the southeastern extremity of the Wantsum Channel, separating the Isle of Thanet from the mainland, the Romans built a twin of Regulbium (*Reculver) which they called Rutupiae. Two almost complete sides and part of a third wall, with the bases of the turrets, survive as RICHBOROUGH CASTLE just north of *Sandwich off the A256 (0304 612013), open all year, with a museum on the site containing pottery, coins and weapons. A ROMAN AMPHITHEATRE and the foundations of the TRIUMPHAL ARCH erected by the Emperor Claudius in AD51 can be seen, too. One of only two other remnants of the latter is at *Hever Castle, the other is in the Louvre in Paris. After centuries of silting, RICHBOROUGH PORT is now some way off across flat fields overshadowed by a power station and the Pfizer drug factory. It may take an effort to imagine the Romans guarding this Saxon Shore against the hordes in winged helmets, but soldiers on guard duty here in World War II when the Mulberry Harbour was being prefabricated for D-Day none the less reported seeing cohorts of ghostly legionnaires marching towards the sea.

ROCHESTER

Anyone who can manage the climb of 150 steps to the top of the massive square keep of Rochester Castle built by the Normans to repel Viking invaders and keep the natives in check will be rewarded (as Dickens and the vertigo-stricken Pepys were) with a view of Kent's chief river rolling down towards the marshes and its union with the Thames off GARRISON POINT. Rochester has been a strategic citadel since the Romans marched inland from *Richborough and took over a Belgae settlement at the river crossing here. Eventually, they built a bridge, downriver from the one which now carries the M2 motorway across the Medway. The town of Durobrivae grew into a walled *civitate*, or district capital, an important staging post on Watling Street, the first great highway across England, and kept that role down the centuries with stagecoaches rattling along the Dover road. The tidal Medway was a highway deep into the Weald long before any roads were built, first bringing out cargoes of stone and timber, later iron and paper, fruit (especially cherries) and hops and returning with butter and cheese from East Anglia, coal from the north, cheese and tiles from Holland, softwood from the Baltic. In the age of steam two railway companies, the London, Chatham and Dover and the South Eastern, vied for supremacy on the route and each built its own bridge at Rochester.

The town exercised a fantastic hold on the imagination of Charles Dickens, who was brought up in neighbouring *Chatham and lived for the latter part of his life at Gads Hill near *Cobham on its western outskirts. Rochester appears again and again in his novels and stories as Cloisterham. A leisurely stroll around the castle and cathedral precincts at the top of the hill and down the pedestrianised High Street brings to life a cavalcade of characters and scenes from his works – Mr Pickwick dining heartily at the Bull, Mr Jingle exploring the castle, Pip entering his apprenticeship at the Guildhall, Mr Grewgious peeping nervously inside the cathedral, Miss Havisham's cobweb-draped house, and many more. Rochester is very proud of its association with the great author. Indeed, he seems to have become a posthumous director of the city's tourism efforts.

The TOURIST INFORMATION CENTRE at Eastgate Cottage in the High Street (0643 43366) will happily supply leaflets, maps and details of guided walking tours, boat trips and even horse-drawn carriage rides.

THE CATHEDRAL, the second oldest in England after Canterbury, was originally Saxon. Bishop Gundulf, who built the White Tower of the Tower of London, began the present structure in the 11th century although most of his work, apart from a section of the beautiful crypt, the nave walls and the bell-tower which bears his name, has been obscured by the masonry of 12th- to 14th-century additions. The modest spire was added as recently as 1904. Although small as cathedrals go, Rochester is imposing with its elaborate recessed west doorway, magnificent nave, down which Simon de Montfort rode on horseback in 1264, and oak roof supported by carved angels. Paulinus, the first Archbishop of York, and Gundulf are both buried at Rochester but it was the tomb of St William, the baker of Perth who gave away every tenth loaf he made and was murdered near here on a pilgrimage at the beginning of the 13th century, who in turn attracted pilgrims. Dickens said he wanted to be buried on the little green just inside the 15th-century cathedral gate beneath an old Catalpa (Red Indian Bean) tree, but they took him to Westminster Abbey. There is a brass memorial to him in the South Transept at Rochester. To the southeast of the choir are the ruins of the Chapter House and the Norman cloister. Self-guided tours

Rochester Cathedral, second oldest in England

on stereo players called 'Sound-alive' are available at the gift stall and there are refreshments and audio-visual displays at the St Andrew's Visitors Cente. Open daily.

THE CASTLE (0634 402276) goes with the adjacent cathedral as a twin and is surrounded by lawns, shrubberies and flowerbeds within the medieval curtain walls. Gundulf built a tower bailey soon after his cathedral in the 1080s but the massive keep that we see today was added in the following century by William de Corbeil, Archbishop of Canterbury. Its walls are 12ft thick and it stands 120ft high. Open daily.

MUSEUMS

CHARLES DICKENS CENTRE, East-gate House, High Street (0634 44176). An Elizabethan house laid out in a series of tableaux of scenes from the lives of Little Nell, Oliver Twist, Fagin and other characters. In the garden with its lily pond and arboured seats is the Swiss chalet in which the author worked in the grounds of his home, Gads Hill. Open daily, closed at Christmas and New Year.

GUILDHALL, High Street (0634 48717). A 17th-century building containing a museum of local history from the Stone Age on, arms and armour, model ships, Victorian toys and dolls and the civic plate and regalia of Rochester, including a splendid mace. Open daily, closed Good Friday, Christmas and New Year.

WATTS CHARITY, High Street (0634 42194) an Elizabethan building with an 18th-century façade, which until 1940 provided overnight accommodation for 'six poor travellers'. Open afternoons, Tuesday to Saturday, from March to October. Tours can be booked.

TEMPLE MANOR, Knight Road, Strood (0634 402276) was originally built by the Knights Templars in the 13th century, with 17th-century additions. Open from April to September.

ENTERTAINMENT

Every summer over 10,000 local people dress in Victorian costume for a four-day DICKENS FESTIVAL which includes a candlelit procession, a Grand Festival Ball and street entertainment. But that isn't Rochester's only festival by any means – the traditional CHIMNEY SWEEPS PROCESSION takes place in May and the river is the scene of 'beating the bounds' and a medieval court held by the Mayor on a barge as Admiral of the Medway. A carnival and a regatta are held in July.

MEDWAY LITTLE THEATRE, High Street, Rochester ME1 1HY (0634 379425) stages both professional and amateur productions.

GARDENS

ESPLANADE riverside gardens in the shadow of the castle offer views up Tower Reach to the bridge. A wall shows three Roman courses with Norman stonework on top.

THE VINES, off Crown Lane leading up from the High Street, is a peaceful park on the site where medieval monks grew great quantities of grapes and produced fine wines.

SPORT AND LEISURE

STROOD SPORTS CENTRE, Watling Street (0634 723888). Comprehensive recreation area for athletics, tennis, swimming, golf, pitch and putt and bowls.

ROCHESTER AND COBHAM PARK GOLF CLUB, Park Pale (0474 823411) 18-hole course in the grounds of historic Cobham Hall. Visitors with a handicap certificate are welcome on weekdays.

ENVIRONS

STROOD, across the Medway bridge from Rochester, once had a number of hospitals to care for pilgrims on their way to Canterbury. Dickens used it as the home of Scrooge and the scene of the pauper funeral in *Oliver Twist*. Many centuries earlier the men of Strood, supporting the King against Becket, allegedly cut off the tail of the archbishop's horse as he rode through the town. Becket retaliated by prophesying that the descendants of those responsible would be born with tails and it's said that they were. Despite having the modern Civic Centre on its side of the river, Strood is a rather dreary place. The paddlesteamer Kingswear Castle plies between here and *Chatham Historic Dockyard.

The HOO PENSINSULA is a spur of land like Plymouth Hoe, forming a wedge between the Thames and Medway estuaries. To the east Yantlet Creek, before it silted up, made a real island of the Isle of Grain and a useful short cut between the two great rivers. It has always been a remote area, as Dickens describes it in the opening of *Great Expectations* in *Cooling churchyard, but in the past 25 years the Rochester conurbation has begun creeping northwards from the Medway. However, large parts of the peninsula are still inhabited only by aquatic birds and the RSPB NATURE RESERVE at Northward Hill, High Halstow, has the largest heronry in Britain. UPNOR CASTLE (0634 402276) was built by Queen Elizabeth on the wide bend of the Medway just north of Rochester and Chatham but it failed to stop the Dutch from attacking the dockyard in 1667. It is open from April to Easter.

South of the Medway there is even more urban sprawl, swallowing a village which gave its name to a reformatory system first put into practice here in 1902. Borstal was a 'closed' institution but it led to 'open' reform camps elsewhere. Today there is a Youth Custody Centre at BORSTAL to the north of the prison and Rochester Airport.

ACCOMMODATION

ROYAL VICTORIA AND BULL HOTEL, High Street, Rochester ME1 1PT (0634 46266) – Mr Pickwick's Bull and the Blue Boar in *Great Expectations* – still serving good English ale and food after 400 years. Only nine of its 31 rooms have private baths, however. Moderate prices.
WHITEFRIARS, Boley Hill, Rochester ME1 1TE (0634 40995). Small, inexpensive guesthouse.

ROLVENDEN

There are two villages, Rolvenden and Rolvenden Layne down the hill, from where in 1758 John Wesley preached. The black and white, gabled WESLEY HALL with its oriel window still bears witness to his eloquence. The 'y' in Layne is just how the locals pronounce it. The weatherboarded buildings of Rolvenden up on its ridge south of *Tenterden are almost all post 17th-century as a result of a fire at that time. Lady Jane Grey, Queen of England for just nine days in July 1554 before she was executed, lived part of her brief life at Halden Place (now a farm) a mile or so

north of the village. At nearby Hole Park, not open to visitors, there is an ancient holy well among the trees, and on the B2086 road to *Benenden skirting the southern edge of the park is a fine post mill, restored to its original condition. To the south on the A28 road to Newenden, GREAT MAYTHAM HALL (0580 84346), designed by Lutyens, is open on Wednesday and Thursday afternoons from May to September. It is now divided into smaller private homes with a communal garden – part of which, curtained off behind its own wall, is said to have given Frances

Hodgson Burnett the idea for her book *The Secret Garden*.

FOOD AND DRINK
STAR INN, 30 High Street, Rolven-

den (0580 241369). A Grade II listed building (originally the village poor house) serving real ales and bar snacks.

SANDHURST

Sandhurst lies a few miles to the southwest of *Rolvenden, above Kent Ditch. It's a charming village of white wooden houses, with a church in a meadow looking out over the Weald to the Channel and several old mills. NEWENDEN, to the east, has an 18th-century red brick bridge across the River Rother which marks the boundary be-

tween Kent and East Sussex.

FOOD AND DRINK
TWO COTTAGES, Back Road, Sandhurst (0580 850486) takes its name from the fact that it is just that – two 18th-century cottages converted to a restaurant serving French-based cuisine. Moderate.

SANDWICH

When an 18th-century Earl of Sandwich, too busy at the gambling table to dine properly, called for a piece of beef between two chunks of bread he gave a new word to the language. But the fame of Sandwich rests on more than that. This was the first Cinque Port, the main port in England, from which the Roman governor Agricola set out at the head of his fleet to discover the boundaries of his domain. He sailed north around Caledonia and back to Sandwich, proving for the first time that Britain was an island. Today, with the sea 2 miles away across the fields and golf links, it takes an effort to imagine it as a port at all, even though the River Stour winds its way northwards from the town to *Richborough Port and Pegwell Bay and is still navigable. Yet the antiquity of Sandwich is evident in

its narrow, winding streets and alleys, its medieval gates and three fine churches. When sand began silting up the harbour in the 15th century Sandwich found renewed prosperity from the wave of Flemish immigrants who brought weaving looms to the town. When that industry moved north, the Scots brought golf links to the sands that had put paid to Sandwich's first career, and with it an indefinable air of exclusivity. Sandwich is one of those happy places which always lands on its feet and even thousands of visitors in their cars and coaches cannot change or spoil it.

The twin turrets of the BARBICAN GATE built by Henry VIII as part of his coastal defences still stand guard over the northern approaches to the town, as if holding back the 20th-century industrialisation beyond the narrow swing bridge over the Stour. The even older FISHER GATE, which overlooks the Quay, was built in 1384 against marauders from across the Channel, but failed to prevent a major French attack in the middle of the next century when the Mayor and several other prominent burghers were killed. To this day mayors of Sandwich wear a black robe in mourning for this event and carry a blackthorn stick as a sign of determination to prevent any repetition. The gardens of THE SALUTATION, designed by Gertrude Jeckyll to complement the early 1900s Lutyens house, are open to visitors during the summer. Strand Street runs along what in olden times was the seafront and is now the riverside. Traffic in the town centre is regulated by a one-way system. Of the three churches, St Clement's, with its beautiful Norman tower supported on four tall, graceful arches, is the most interesting.

The TOURIST INFORMATION CENTRE (0304 369576) is in St Peter's Church in Market Street.

MUSEUMS

GUILDHALL (0304 617197), an Elizabethan building with fine wood panelling, contains many paintings and portraits and the colourful archives of Sandwich, which Charles II made a free town for ever. Other attractions are an exhibition of Victorian photographs and a display of horse brasses. Open for guided tours Tuesday, Wednesday, Thursday and Friday mornings at 11am.

PRECINCT TOY COLLECTION, 38 Harnet Street (0843 62150). A wonderful display dating from 1860 and including all kinds of toys, dolls and their furnished houses, Teddies and Noah's arks. Open from Easter to the end of September daily and on Sunday afternoons, also weekend afternoons in October.

WHITE MILL, Ash Road (0304 612076). Folk museum in the ancillary buildings of an 18th-century smock mill, fully restored with its original machinery. Open in the afternoons on Sundays and bank holidays from Easter to mid-September.

SPORT AND LEISURE

PRINCE'S GOLF CLUB, Prince's Drive (0304 611118) to the northeast of the town between Stonar Cut and the wide sands of Sandwich Flats offers three 9-hole options: Shore, Dunes and 'Himalayas'. Visitors are welcome with advance booking and equipment can be hired.

ROYAL ST GEORGE'S GOLF CLUB (0304 613090). The original holy 18 holes between the town and Sandwich Bay. Visitors are welcome during the week by prior arrangement. Must be members of a golf club.

ROYAL CINQUE PORTS GOLF CLUB, Golf Road, *Deal (0304 374007). The '007' club where a letter of introduction as well as membership of a golf club is required from visitors. Telephone in advance.

SANDWICH BAY NATURE RESERVE, 700 acres of unspoiled sand dunes and saltmarsh administered by the Kent Trust for Nature Conservation, can best be reached by the toll road that runs from Sandwich to the car park by the Prince's Golf Club. The SAXON SHORE WAY runs inland here to follow the Stour from Sandwich to Richborough Port.

ACCOMMODATION
THE BELL, The Quay, Sandwich CT13 9EF (0304 613388). Comfortable rooms all with *en suite* facilities are expensive. Moderately priced restaurant.

FLEUR-DE-LIS, Delf Street, Sandwich CT13 9HD (0304 611131). Mellow red-brick, vaulted old Corn Exchange and oil lamps in one of three bars. Traditional style and moderate prices.

SEVENOAKS

Six of the seven oaks planted here to mark the Coronation of King Edward VII in 1902 were blown down in the Great Storm of October 1987. This was probably the most traumatic event to occur in Sevenoaks this century. It is the sort of place where normally nothing very much happens and that's why hundreds of commuters are prepared to suffer the daily 50-mile roundtrip by rail to London and back just to live there. It occupies a ridge rising from 400ft to 600ft, surveying the Weald of Kent laid out at its feet. One of the most impressive viewpoints is from ONE TREE HILL among the many trees lining the crest above GODDEN GREEN, 2 miles southeast of the town off the A25 road. Sevenoaks feels like a quiet country town despite the spread of housing estates all round it. The A21 trunk road to the south coast from London bypasses the centre. SEVENOAKS SCHOOL was endowed in the 15th century by a foundling who adopted the name of the town and eventually as Sir William Sevenoke became Lord Mayor of London. At the north end of the town is THE VINE, the cricket ground where the first match to be reported nationally – the Gentlemen of Kent *v.* the Gentlemen of Sussex – took place in the 18th century. Cricket is still played there. Most visitors come to Sevenoaks to see *Knole, the stately home of the Sackvilles, which stands in its deer park at the edge of town on the A225 road to *Tonbridge. Knole is by no means the only attraction hereabouts. *Emmetts Garden and *Ide Hill are a short drive away to the west and *Ightham Mote to the east. *Shoreham and *Otford lie just to the north.

The TOURIST INFORMATION CENTRE is in Buckhurst Lane (0732 450305).

MUSEUM
SEVENOAKS MUSEUM in the Library in Buckhurst Lane (0732 452384) has photographs and exhibits of local history. Open daily all year round and on Saturday mornings. Closed Sundays and bank holidays.

SHOPPING
Sevenoaks still has old-established family shops where old-fashioned

courtesies are observed. OUTRAMS store is in a 15th-century building which displays the arms of several Archbishops on its fireplace. DORSET STREET, BANK STREET, WELL COURT are the places in which to browse, as well as the High Street. No livestock has been sold in the Market Place for half a century but the CHEQUERS, which has been there for 300 years, is still a good place to take a break.

ENVIRONS

RIVERHILL HOUSE (0732 452557) is just south of the town, clearly signposted off the A225. It is a lived-in family home with a sheltered hillside garden of roses and rare shrubs. A good time to visit it is in the spring when the bluebells are out in the woods. The gardens are open in the afternoons at weekends and on bank holiday Mondays from Easter to the end of August. The house is open in the afternoon on bank holiday weekends, adults only. Home-made teas are served from 2.30pm. Nearby is the ancient trackway called HAROLD'S ROAD down which the king is said to have rode to meet his end against William the Conqueror at the Battle of Hastings in 1066. Later it became the main Norman route from London to the south coast for the sea crossing to France.

SEVENOAKS WEALD, although only just off the A21 trunk road, is a secretive little place, once the resort of writers and poets. Vita Sackville-West and her husband Harold Nicolson bought the 15th-century LONG BARN, dubiously claimed as

William Caxton's birthplace (see *Tenterden) before they took over *Sissinghurst Castle. In the same way, they extended and developed this property and laid out a garden with the help of Edwin Lutyens. At ELSES FARM in the same village the *Autobiography of a Super-Tramp* was written. Edward Thomas, the poet, loaned a cottage to W.H. Davies, whom he rescued from a dosshouse in Lambeth, and it was here, too, that Davies penned the often quoted lines 'What is this life if full of care/We have no time to stand and stare?'

HOLLANDEN RARE FARM ANIMALS (0732 833858) off the B245, southeast of Sevenoaks is a good place to 'stand and stare' at over 60 breeds, including Portland sheep with spiral horns who are said to be descended from some who swam ashore from the wreckage of Spanish galleons in the Armada, and others with four horns which come from the Isle of Man. There are 'Iron Age' pigs, Erisky ponies and cattle, too, and a display of old farming implements. An adventure playground and pets' corner for the children, shop, refreshments and toilets are part of the amenities. Open daily from May to October.

ACCOMMODATION

ROYAL OAK, Upper High Street, Sevenoaks TN14 5PG (0732 451109). Georgian coaching inn, recently refurbished. Restaurant specialises in French cuisine. Moderately priced.

THE MOORINGS, 97 Hitchen Hatch

Lane, Sevenoaks TN14 3BE (0732 458209). Comfortable, reasonably priced small hotel.

POND COTTAGE, Eggpie Lane, Weald TN14 6WP (0732 463773). Tudor-built with 16th-century and Edwardian additions in spacious grounds with a large pond stocked with fish. Tennis court. Inexpensive.

KEMSING YOUTH HOSTEL, Cleves, Pilgrims Way TN15 64T (0732 61341) offers a choice of inexpensive bed and breakfast, half-board or self-catering.

SHEERNESS

With the success of the Olau Line's vehicle ferries to Vlissingen (a voyage of more than 8 or 9 hours) and the building of deep-water terminals at the junction of the Medway and the Thames new life has returned to this dockyard town dating from the reign of Charles II. Its surveyor was none other than Samuel Pepys. Although it looks somewhat remote on the map, on the northwest tip of the Isle of Sheppey, the A429 trunk route connects it with the M2 motorway (via KINGSFERRY BRIDGE which rises for coastal shipping in the narrow Swale). It is also served by the railway via *Sittingbourne and the Medway Towns. In 1797 the naval forces based here rebelled against the barbarous conditions in which they served. The Nore mutiny, as it was called, was put down ferociously but it drew the attention of the public to inhuman conditions in the Royal Navy and led eventually to some improvement. The body of Nelson was landed at Sheerness from Gibraltar in a barrel of alcohol after the Battle of Trafalgar and sent on to Chatham and Greenwich in a coffin carved from the mainmast of *L'Orient*. The Navy finally withdrew from Sheerness in 1961 but an unexploded US munitions ship which ran aground in 1944 makes a regular and somewhat ominous reappearance at low tide.

SHOREHAM

A great cross shows white in the turf on the chalk hillside above this old village on the banks of the River Darent and the war memorial by the bridge urges us to look up the hill at it. So far, the outward sprawl of the capital stops short 4 or 5 miles away at Orpington and the scent of wild thyme still fills the air on the North Downs high above the traffic fumes of the M25. Shoreham seems to have grown from the chalk. The GEORGE INN is partly built of it, so is the church of St Peter and St Paul, bombed during World War II, but apparently indestructible. Its porch is formed from a great split oak which once grew in the churchyard, its pulpit and organ came from Westminster Abbey and it has a Burne-Jones window in memory of the geologist

Sir Joseph Prestwich, whose home was on the hill above the white cross. Shoreham has known many famous people. William Blake, the composer of *Jerusalem*, often came to stay at the Water House with his young friend Samuel Palmer, whom he influenced greatly and who formed the 'Ancients' group of artists during the late Georgian era. John Wesley, a friend of the vicar, preached at Shoreham every year for 40 years. FILSTON HALL, a Tudor manor house restyled in the 17th century, its moat fed from the Darent, was the home of the Colgates, whose son went to school with Pitt the Younger and emigrated to America in 1795. Who could have predicted that their name would become famous around the world for *toothpaste*?

SISSINGHURST

The BULL INN is one of the many old Kent inns which feature in Jeffrey Farnol's novel *The Broad Highway* but this attractive hamlet, a mile or two east of *Cranbrook on the A262, has become famed far and wide because of a garden. In the 16th century Sir John Baker, a Tudor statesman, built himself a moated manor house northeast of the village. As Queen Mary's Chancellor he became known as 'Bloody Baker' for his eagerness to despatch Protestants to the next world. During the Seven Years War, Sissinghurst Castle became a jail for captured French troops and then gradually fell into ruins. By the time Vita Sackville-West, a descendant of 'Bloody Baker' acquired it in 1930 with her husband, the diplomat and diarist Harold Nicolson, only the gatehouse with its showy octagonal turrets retained the glory of the original mansion. The Nicolsons set about restoring it and transformed the courtyards approached through the soaring gateway into outdoor rooms 'furnished' in various contrasting styles and colours, such as the White Garden with its white roses and silver-leafed pear. In a corner of the garden overlooking a stream and the Wealden landscape is a pavilion erected by Nicolson's sons in his memory. It contains many rare books including Lambarde's *Perambulation* of Kent of 1575, the forerunner of all county guide books. Visitors may climb the gatehouse tower and see Lady Nicolson's first-floor room where she worked with a view of the garden she had created. This room and the library below are richly furnished, with polished oak and Persian carpets, and the original Hogarth press on which T.S. Eliot's *The Wasteland* was printed can be seen. Virginia Woolf set the type and her husband Leonard did the printing. Vita believed that the spiral staircase of the tower was haunted following an incident when her dog raised its hackles and refused to go up for no apparent reason.

SISSINGHURST CASTLE GARDEN (0580 712850), a National Trust property, it is open in the afternoon from Tuesday to Friday between Good Friday and 15 October and from 10am at weekends. It is closed on Mondays, including bank holidays.

FOOD AND DRINK
GRANARY RESTAURANT in Sissinghurst Castle serves coffee, lunches and scrumptious afternoon tea. RANKINS, The Street, Sissinghurst (0580 713964). Pleasant restaurant serving a good dinner, or Sunday lunch, at a moderate price. Closed Monday, Tuesday and Sunday evening.

ACCOMMODATION
SISSINGHURST CASTLE FARM TN17 2AB (0580 712885). Inexpensive bed and breakfast in a comfortable Victorian farmhouse with panoramic views and a pleasant garden at the heart of the working farm of 250 acres round the castle. Evening meals by arrangement.

SITTINGBOURNE

An enterprising place is Sittingbourne, although not as pretty as its sister *Faversham. Straddling the old A2 Roman road west of the Medway towns, it still maintains its connection with the sea in the muddy creek which winds its way northward to the Swale. Today it is the administrative centre of the Isle of Sheppey and a commuter town as well. Fruit and paper production are its staple industries and it has a colourful past on which it has capitalised for tourism. Richard Harris, fruiterer to Henry VIII, planted 105 acres at nearby TEYNHAM with cherry trees imported from Flanders and began a profitable trade which has lasted for centuries. Until quite recent times, barges with red sails carried the cherry crop down Milton Creek to the markets of London and East Anglia, as well as bricks, cement and other cargoes. The spritsail barges have gone (apart from a few), outmoded like the 30-inch gauge railway built to carry paper between the mills and the dock at RIDHAM on the banks of the Swale. Part of it is still used to shuttle visitors in its restored steam trains.

SITTINGBOURNE AND KEMSLEY LIGHT RAILWAY (0795 78221) winds through MILTON REGIS on a concrete viaduct. The Sittingbourne terminus is off Mill Way, a five-minute walk from the BR station, or from the A2 turn on to the B2005. There is a picnic area at KEMSLEY DOWN and light refreshments. Open Easter to mid-October on Sundays and bank holidays and most Saturdays in peak season, also certain weekdays. Talking timetable: 0795 24899.

MUSEUMS
DOLPHIN YARD SAILING BARGE MUSEUM, Crown Quay Lane (0795 24132). A traditional barge building and repair yard on the banks of Milton Creek, the museum occupies the sail loft and forge. Apart from models, paintings, photographs, tools and equipment such as a steam chest which made

timber pliable for working, surviving barges can be seen in the repair and maintenance berths. Open from Easter to mid October on Sundays and bank holidays and some weekdays in peak season. Ample parking, a tea bar and a picnic area.

BRADBURY HOUSE VICTORIANA MUSEUM, 70 High Street, Milton Regis (0795 23762). Extensive collection includes lace, embroidery, mourning jewellery and accessories. Victorian parlour, drawing room and bedroom on display. Open by appointment only. No children.

SPORT AND LEISURE

SITTINGBOURNE LEISURE CENTRE, Central Avenue (0795 20420). The town's newest enterprise includes a swimming pool with a flume, wave machine and beach area, a 'projectile hall' for practising shooting, archery, cricket and golf, as well as the more usual squash courts, sauna, solarium and gym.

SITTINGBOURNE AND MILTON REGIS GOLF CLUB, Wormdale, Newington (0795 842261). Visitors are welcome to this 18-hole course on weekdays, on Saturday by arrangement or on Sunday with a club member.

ACCOMMODATION

CONISTON, 70 London Road, Sittingbourne ME10 1NT (0795 72131). Large hotel, most of its rooms with bath. Expensive.

YEW TREES, 132 London Road, Sittingbourne ME10 1QB (0795 71526). A nice guesthouse with a garden. Parking. Four rooms for inexpensive bed and breakfast.

NEWINGTON MANOR, Callaways Lane, Newington ME9 7LU (0795 842053). A 15th-century mansion in 2-acre grounds, 3 miles west of Sittingbourne off the A2. Comfortable restaurant with log fires. Expensive.

SMALL HYTHE

Once a port for the nearby town of *Tenterden on the north channel of the River Rother, Small Hythe is now an insignificant hamlet on the unromantically named Reading Sewer (which in this neighbourhood of Romney Marsh is simply a watercourse). It lies at the northern edge of the ISLE OF OXNEY, today an island in name only. Tenterden Vineyards are located here, at Spots Farm. Small Hythe has one large claim to fame of its own, however, in that it was the home from 1899 until her death in 1928 of one of England's greatest actresses, Dame Ellen Terry.

MUSEUM

SMALLHYTHE PLACE (0580 62334) is owned by the National Trust and in its grounds is the Barn Theatre. The half-timbered yeoman's house roofed with old red tiles dates from 1480 and was Port House before the channel silted up. The ground floor is a treasure house of theatrical souvenirs, costumes and playbills. Ellen Terry was Henry Irving's leading lady and a friend of George Bernard Shaw. 'No funeral gloom, my dears, when I am gone,' were her last words and her bedroom is kept as she left it. Only 25 people can be admitted at any one time to Smallhythe Place which is open in the afternoons, daily except Thursday and Friday from Good Friday to the end of October.

SMARDEN

North of *Tenterden and west of *Ashford in the depths of the Weald, this almost perfect weatherboarded and black-and-white Kent village is mercifully preserved from motorway, railway or aircraft noise. King Edward III in 1332 granted its original charter to hold a weekly market and an annual fair and Queen Elizabeth I confirmed it in a splendid document kept in the 14th-century church. The church of St Michael, beside the slow, winding River Beult, is reached through an alleyway in a group of old cottages. Kentish rag and Bethersden marble went into its building. It is sometimes called 'the Barn of Kent' because of the great span of its roof—36ft wide without a beam. Gazing up at it, one wonders at the skill of its medieval builders. There are several fine buildings nearby, such as the medieval DRAGON HOUSE, with its weaving shed, and the CLOTH HALL, reflecting the prosperity the Flemish immigrant weavers brought with them, and the 15th-century HARTNUP HOUSE. CHESENDEN HOUSE is a Tudor gem and THATCHED HOUSE by the 15th-century bridge over the Beult is another weaver's house. Smarden is an example of the kind of village that is getting rarer, not a prettified museum piece but a compact centre for the farms dotted around the surrounding hills, not engulfed by housing estates.

ACCOMMODATION

CHEQUERS, The Street, Smarden TN27 0RR (0233 77217). Weatherboarded old pub with very good bar food and inexpensive bed and breakfast.

THE BELL, Bell Road, Smarden TN27 8PW (0233 77283). Inglenook fireplaces, stone floors, beams garlanded with hops. Homely food and inexpensive bed and breakfast.

SPELDHURST

Now almost a suburb of *Tunbridge Wells, this still retains much of the character of the old hill village that it was. St Mary's church at the centre has a series of Burne-Jones windows, beautiful carved oak and a fine Wealden view from its tower. The Arms of Orleans in stone above the porch is in recognition of the fact that the ransom paid for the brother of the Duke of Orleans, captured at Agincourt and held at *Groombridge, went into the building of this church, which was later struck by lightning and is largely rebuilt. The GEORGE

AND DRAGON inn next to the church dates back to Norman times when Sir John de Fereby cleared the forest here for farming. Lower down the Barden Stream which runs into the Medway near *Penshurst, Furnace Farm was the site of one of the Browne family's foundries which cast guns for all sides impartially through the Civil War, the Restoration and the Anglo–Dutch Wars. All that survives is a sluice beside a restored millhouse. East of Speldhurst towards Southborough, off the main A26 road, is DAVID SALOMON'S HOUSE (0892 38614) designed in 1820 by Decimus Burton whose Regency architecture has left its stamp on this whole area of Kent. The furnishings and decor can be viewed on Monday, Wednesday and Friday afternoons but it is closed on bank holidays. David Salomon was the first Jewish Lord Mayor of London and his son of the same name was a noted inventor who organised the first motor show in England. The house is now owned by the National Health Service and used for conferences and seminars.

FOOD AND DRINK
GEORGE AND DRAGON, Speldhurst (0892 863125). Magnificent old beams and real ales. Also a good restaurant.

STAPLEHURST

In total contrast to *Smarden, this village by the River Beult has been swallowed up by suburban development because of its station on the Kent coast line. The old manor house and smaller Elizabethan buildings sit uneasily amidst all the 20th-century red brick. The oak door of the church is remarkable for its iron ornaments of snakes, fishes, dragons and serpents intended to warn off evil spirits. They were made 700 years ago. The churchyard contains an echo of *Upstairs, Downstairs* in the graves of two faithful old servants, Mary Viny's life 'in service' spanned the 18th and 19th centuries and Marian Stammers served one household through the whole of Queen Victoria's reign and up to World War I, having been nanny to twelve children of her employers. She was 96 when she died.

STONE-IN-OXNEY

This hamlet, 2 miles southwest of *Appledore, once stood on the Isle of Oxney before the marshes were drained and it became part of the mainland. But it still has a FERRY INN and a list of fares marked on a wall. The 15th-century church is quite remarkable for it contains not only an altar to the ancient god Mithras but also the fossilised bones of an iguanodon dinosaur.

SUNDRIDGE

Just north of this village on the A25 road west of *Sevenoaks is a fine mansion in 350 acres of parkland. The narrow River Darent flows through it, feeding a lake of 5 acres. In 1815 William Manning, a prosperous City of London merchant, came to live at COOMBE BANK, bringing his seven-year-old son. The little boy from the great house, the future Cardinal Manning, used to play with the two sons of Rector of Sundridge, Reverend Wordsworth, brother of the poet. They grew up to be bishops. Today the M25 motorway slices across the northern edge of the park and Coombe Bank is a school. The old church, up a lane to the south of the A25, stands apparently untouched by time among its yews and cedars. The National Trust's *Emmetts Garden lies just to the south at *Ide Hill.

SPORT AND LEISURE
Fishing is excellent at SUNDRIDGE LAKE where a restricted number of day permits is allowed (01 852 1421) and CHIPSTEAD LAKES, contact the Holmesdale Angling Society (0732 458216).

SUTTON VALENCE

On the A274 road southeast of *Maidstone, this village clings to terraces on a very steep south-facing hillside above the Beult valley, with classical Wealden views of orchards, hopfields and oast houses stretching away to the horizon. It is worth driving that way on a fine day just to see it. The only building of note is that of SUTTON VALENCE SCHOOL, founded in 1576 by a local clothmaker William Lambe, the same who brought fresh water to Holborn as early as 1577 and is remembered for it in the name of Lamb's Conduit Street.

TENTERDEN

Although Tenterden grew rich on the wool trade in the Middle Ages, and still has the fruits of that prosperity in the fine timbered houses lining its impressively broad High Street, the origin of its name goes back to the Saxons of Thanet (Tenet Ware) who cut back the great Wealden forest here for a pig pasture (Den). Much of the woodland hereabouts, on the fringes of treeless expanses of Romney Marsh, survives. When all that was under the sea, Tenterden was a coastal town with its port at *Small Hythe. The handsome church towering over the town is dedicated to St Mildred, the abbess at *Minster-in-Thanet. The 100ft-high tower with its octagonal turrets and pinnacles is similar to that at *Lydd. The story goes that it was built with money that was intended for a sea wall to protect the offshore island of Lomea which belonged to Earl Godwin, so the sea broke through and submerged the island, henceforth known as the Goodwin Sands. In any event, it is a noble tower built of Bethersden marble and from it a beacon in an iron cage was hung to give warning of the approach of the Spanish Armada.

Tenterden lays claim to being the birthplace of William Caxton in 1422. He was sent to London as an apprentice, became a representative of the Merchant Adventurers in Bruges, where he printed the first book in English after learning the art in Germany. Among the hundred or so books that he printed on his return to England was Chaucer's *Canterbury Tales*. Although there is no documentary evidence that Caxton was born in Tenterden it is known that he came from a family of clothmakers in Kent. When the weaving industry moved away and the Rother silted, Tenterden continued to prosper from local agriculture and many of the buildings in the High Street date from this later period of the 18th century. It thrives still as a market town with stylish shops and restaurants, inns such as the WOOLPACK and the EIGHT BELLS, hotels and numerous small businesses.

The TOURIST INFORMATION CENTRE (0580 63572) is in the Georgian town hall in the High Street opposite TUDOR ROSE, a 15th-century hall house now used as a cafe.

KENT AND EAST SUSSEX RAILWAY, Tenterden Town Station (0580 62943) operates full-size steam trains down the Rother Valley 5 miles through unspoiled Wealden countryside. It was opened in 1905 by Lieutenant-Colonel Stephens (see Museum) to connect with the London–Ashford line at *Headcorn and it was axed in 1954. There's a 1930s-style buffet in the restored Edwardian station, a gift shop, a video room and an adventure playground. Parking free. Trains run from 11.30am to 4.30pm daily in August and at weekends and certain other days from Easter to the end of the year.

MUSEUM

TENTERDEN AND DISTRICT MUSEUM, Station Road (0580 64310) illustrates the buildings and history of Tenterden and the Weald and displays the Tenterden tapestry. There's also a collection of material on Britain's first light railway. Open daily in the afternoons from Easter to the end of October, all day in August. There is a public car park next door.

VINEYARD

TENTERDEN VINEYARDS, Spots Farm, Smallhythe (0580 63033). An 18-acre vineyard and winery with the latest processing equipment. Wine tastings. There's a large herb garden and a picnic area. Open daily year round.

SPORT AND LEISURE

TENTERDEN GOLF CLUB, Woodchurch Road (0580 63987). Visitors welcome at 9-hole course except Sunday mornings.
TENTERDEN TROUT WATERS (0580 63201). Rainbow trout in a land-

scaped reservoir. Tuition on theory and casting can be arranged.

ACCOMMODATION

LITTLE SILVER COUNTRY HOTEL, Ashford Road, St Michaels TN30 6SP (0233 85321). Comfortable house with a pleasant garden. All rooms with bath. Expensive. Pre-booking for dinner essential.

FINCHDEN MANOR, Tenterden TN30 7DD (0580 64719). Early 15th-century, Grade II listed building in 4 acres. Panelled rooms and inglenook fireplaces. Inexpensive bed and breakfast.

BRATTLE HOUSE, Cranbrook Road, Tenterden TN30 6UL (0580 63565). Grade II listed Georgian farmhouse. Three rooms for inexpensive bed and breakfast, all with bath.

TESTON

This village on the A26 road from *Maidstone to *Tonbridge was originally called Teeson, but because of an error by a signwriter the nameboard at the station built by the South Eastern Railway Company said 'Teston' and they refused to change it. The railway still runs beside the Medway from Maidstone to Paddock Wood and although the station is no more, the spelling of Teston survives on the map. However, it is still pronounced Teeson! The village stands on a steep hillside overlooking another of those narrow medieval stone bridges which are found along the Medway. This one has six arches and there is a lock nearby set amid 24 acres of water-meadows reserved for picnics, fishing and walking along the tow-path. The church and the not particularly attractive village are clustered at the wrought iron gates of BARHAM COURT, which dates back to Norman times. Randolph Barham was one of the four knights who murdered Archbishop Becket, and he fled to Ireland. Teston church has a well-known 18th-century memorial to a West Indian called Nestor, who was rescued from slavery by James Ramsay when serving as a chaplain in the Royal Navy. Ramsay became Rector of Teston and brought Nestor there as his servant. Horrified by what he'd seen during his service on the West Indies station, the Reverend Ramsay was one of the founders of the movement to abolish slavery after he came to Teston in 1781. Teston today is one of the last bastions of cricket ball manufacture, a craft which used to flourish around Tonbridge.

TONBRIDGE

The atmosphere of an old market and country town still lingers here at the upper end of the navigable Medway. Since the serious floods of 1968 and 1974, Southern Water has constructed a great barrier to contain the upper Medway and its many tributaries in the High Weald and protect the low, fertile plain down to *Yalding. Because the Medway valley flooded so readily on either side of the High Street. Tonbridge hasn't expanded in all directions this century like so many other old towns. Development has tended to spread southwards along the A26 which passes over the Victorian cast-iron bridge in the town centre and northwards along the A227 and the B245 to HILDEN-BOROUGH. Thus the heart of the town is little changed. In Saxon times it was part of the 'lathe' of Elesfort or *Aylesford which extended along most of the Medway valley. In the Domesday Book it appears as Tonebricg. The RIVER WALK from the bridge through the meadows shaded by willows is pleasant and there are rowing boats for hire. The backdrop is the round-towered gatehouse and curtain wall of a 13th-century castle.

TONBRIDGE CASTLE (0732 353241) is open on weekends and bank holidays from late April to late July and then daily until mid-September. The TOURIST INFORM-ATION CENTRE (0732 844522) is in the District Council offices at the castle. Gardens have been planted around what is left of the inner bailey (much of its stone went into housebuilding in the 18th century) and there is a nature trail and a picnic area as well as a small museum. The 65ft-high motte, or mound, on which the Normans erected the first wooden castle is now covered with trees. It was on

their main route to the sea from London, the Rye Road which con-nected with ships sailing to Dieppe or to Paris via the River Seine. But the track through the Wealden clay was impassable in wet weather and by the 18th century the river had become the great highway of 'Tun-bridge' until the railway arrived in 1842. The town then became an important station on the South Eastern Railway route to the Chan-nel ports via the long, straight and level Wealden line to *Ashford. The SER actually started to build a Channel tunnel but it was aban-doned in 1883 because of a scare put up by the military. In the latter half of this century, road traffic to the coast at weekends and holiday times brought the High Street to a standstill until the building of a bypass. From the flyover junction of the A21 and the A26 there is a good view of the town with the river snaking across the Low Weald to the horizon. During World War II German bombers used the river as their guide inland and a plaque at 111 High Street near the town bridge reads: 'Above this roof the Battle of Britain was fought and won, 8 August to 10 October 1940. This plaque is dedicated to the Few.'

Modern Tonbridge has its ANGEL CENTRE, with all the leading shops, and is a commuters' dormi-tory, but several old coaching inns survive including the ROSE AND CROWN, the 16th-century timbered CHEQUERS in the High Street and the 15th-century IVY HOUSE in Bordyke (named from the defensive ditch round the medieval town). TONBRIDGE SCHOOL, founded in 1553 by Sir Andrew Judde of the Skinners' Company and Lord Mayor of London, occupies a Victorian building at the north end of the High Street. The novelist E.M. Forster went to Tonbridge School, which has traditionally produced many Kent cricketers, not least Colin Cowdrey, who went on to captain England.

ENTERTAINMENT
OAST THEATRE, London Road (0732 350261). Small, intimate theatre open to members and non-members.

SPORT AND LEISURE
POULT WOOD GOLF COURSE, Higham Lane (0732 364039). 18-hole municipal 'pay and play' where equipment can be hired and visitors are welcome. Bookings only at weekends.

BARNETTS WOOD is an 8-acre picnic area of grassland and trees next to the coastbound carriageway of the A21 north of Tonbridge. Facilities include toilets for the disabled.

ENVIRONS
TUDELEY church, just east of Tonbridge on the B2017 road to *Beltring, has a rare example of stained glass of the 1960s. The large east window is by the Russian artist Marc Chagall in memory of Sarah d'Avigdor Goldsmid, aged 21, who was drowned while sailing. Her family, active in local and national politics and distinguished in the armed services, own nearby SOMERHILL, a Jacobean house in a fine park with a lake. At CASTLE HILL just to the south, 400ft above the A21 Hastings road, are the remains of an Iron Age fort.

ACCOMMODATION
ROSE AND CROWN, High Street, Tonbridge TN9 1DD (0732 357966). A bedroom wing with *en suite* facilities added to the historic blue and red brick Georgian inn. Expensive.

TOYS HILL

In the hills south of the A25 at *Brasted, Toys Hill claims the highest pump in Kent. Octavia Hill, founder of the National Trust, lived in the neighbourhood and had the well beneath it sunk 96ft. Today part of the 400 acres of heath and woodland hereabouts which is owned by the National Trust is named after Octavia Hill. Some of the woodlands were devastated by the hurricane winds of 16 October 1987, but there has been intensive clearing up and replanting and already nature has covered many of the scars.

FOOD AND DRINK
FOX AND HOUNDS, Toys Hill (0732 75328). Saved by its customers from a proposed 'upgrading' in 1986, it remains a real country pub with even wider Wealden views opened up by the Great Storm.

TROTTISCLIFFE

The old village name is Trottis-cliffe on the map, but it was always pronounced 'Trosley' and the phonetic spelling is used for TROS-LEY COUNTRY PARK, stretching across 160 acres of North Downs 8 miles northwest of *Maidstone off the A227. The visitor centre (0732 823570) open at weekends and bank holidays and daily in August has details of three waymarked paths, one leading to COLDRUM LONG BARROW, a megalithic burial chamber surrounded by standing stones. Early this century 22 skeletons dating from the New Stone Age, 3000BC, were uncovered.

TUNBRIDGE WELLS

Royal Tunbridge Wells, to give it the title bestowed on it in 1909 by King Edward VII (somewhat belatedly since Queen Victoria herself as a young princess had called it '*Dear* Tunbridge Wells'), began with the discovery of an iron impregnated chalybeate spring in the forest south of 'Tunbridge' in 1606 by Lord North. Word soon spread of this equivalent of the Belgian Spa waters. Its remoteness in the depths of Kent meant that the lords and ladies who wished to taste the water had to camp out in the hills with their servants, which led to rumours of other diversions around *les Eaux de Scandale* at Tunbridge Wells. Queen Henrietta-Maria was accommodated in a marquee on the Bishop's Down when she took the waters during her pregnancy in 1629 and gave them the stamp of royal approval. By the end of the 17th century many houses, shops and taverns had been built around the Common and on the surrounding hills, named Mount Ephraim, Mount Sion and Mount Pleasant by the stern Dissenters. This group of settlements formed a new town with the coffee houses, lottery and hazard rooms, apothecaries and bowling greens which seemed to go with the Restoration period, as well as the church of CHARLES THE MARTYR with its white weather-boarded belfry and clock, completed in 1696. In the next two centuries Tunbridge Wells flourished as a centre of fashionable society where people strolled among the Tuscan columns and elms of Queen Anne's Pantiles, laid out where the original spring bubbled forth. Beau Nash arrived from Bath in 1735 as Master of Ceremonies but it was a later architect, Decimus Burton, who really put Tunbridge Wells together in the sunset of the Georgian era, building with the Wealden sandstone blocks quarried at Tonbridge. His style was Greek Revival, with lots of colonnades, pavilions and pilasters, of which the best example can be seen in CALVERLEY PARK CRESCENT. In the Victorian era, with two railways (the South Eastern and the Brighton and South Coast) encouraging prosperous

The Pantiles, historic shopping precinct of Tunbridge Wells

residential development, Tunbridge Wells acquired its starchy Raj reputation ('Disgusted, of Tunbridge Wells') which lingers even today. E.M. Forster, the author of *A Passage to India* was born there. Only now is it coming to terms with the lifestyle of the late 20th century, with new buildings going up everywhere, including a much-needed restoration of The Pantiles which by the mid-1980s was beginning to look almost seedy. Tunbridge Wells is twinned with another spa town, Wiesbaden in Germany. Its natural setting amidst the hills of the High Weald with its massive outcrops of sandstone such as TOAD ROCK and HAPPY VALLEY at Rusthall, HIGH ROCKS and the 250 acres of gorse-covered COMMON close to the compact town centre is attractive as ever.

The CIVIC CENTRE (0892 26121) includes the TOURIST INFORMATION CENTRE in the Town Hall and the MUSEUM AND ART GALLERY in the Library. Open daily, year round, except Sundays this contains some good paintings and interesting local history and archaeology exhibits, dolls and toys. A special room is allocated to 'Tunbridge Ware', a style of inlaid woodwork which made popular souvenirs for 200 years. They are now sought as antiques. In the same town centre complex is the ASSEMBLY HALL, Crescent Road

(0892 30613) which is the major theatre and concert hall for the High Weald, staging everything from hard rock to classical music, as well as ballroom dancing, jazz, musical comedy, plays and pantomime. It not only attracts star names but serves as a venue for KENT OPERA and KENT COUNTY YOUTH ORCHESTRA. Nearby in Church Road, TRINITY ARTS CENTRE (0892 544699) provides a second venue for plays, concerts, dances and exhibitions. It was the town's second church, its foundation stone laid by the Duchess of Kent on her birthday in 1827. At the opposite end of town, THE PANTILES took its name from the square grey tiles which were replaced in 1793, after almost a century, by the large flagstones we see now. In one corner is the original CHALYBEATE SPRING where 'the dipper' is still in use handing out medicinal sips of the water from Easter to September. This original 'pedestrian precinct', including the CORN EXCHANGE, the ASSEMBLY ROOMS which used to be the scene of weekly auctions and the ROYAL VICTORIA inn where Queen Victoria stayed, is undergoing a major facelift and transformation which is intended to preserve the historic façades while providing high quality shopping, entertainment and restaurants. THE BANDSTAND in the Pantiles resounds to military and Kent town bands, such as East Peckham, Cranbrook and Medway, on Sundays and to New Orleans jazz and old time music hall on other evenings.

SHOPPING

CALVERLEY PRECINCT, between Calverley Road and Mount Ephraim at the top of the town, is pedestrianised and contains all the major multiples such as Marks & Spencer, Boots, British Home Stores. MONSON ROAD, the curving, balustraded parade behind it, is the place to go for china, flowers, ornaments and small items of jewellery, fragrant coffee and many varieties of tea at Importers. It runs into CAMDEN ROAD, where there are several interesting antique shops including 'Sawdust and Lace' which sells dolls and dolls' houses, rocking horses, teddy bears and prams. The main north to south thoroughfares of MOUNT PLEASANT ROAD and the HIGH STREET are lined with shops of every description, from Bentalls department store to Breeds the Cutler who sells such arcane items as lobster picks and grape scissors. GREAT HALL has been restored and converted into a glass-roofed arcade with furniture shops, elegant boutiques for men and women and a branch of Hatchard's bookshop. Antiquarian bookshops, art galleries and antique dealers are concentrated in CHAPEL PLACE, NEVILL STREET and THE PANTILES at the bottom of the High Street and there's a variety of other shops, selling saddles and country wear, Italian silk scarves, ties and fine leather bags, and the grandly named Imperial Pharmacy. Todd's Vintry, established in the Pantiles in 1768, has a dazzling array of wines, cheeses and confectionery. No fewer than ten car parks, some multi-storey, serve the immensely varied and busy shops of Tunbridge Wells.

SPORT AND LEISURE

NEVILL CRICKET AND SPORTS GROUND at the southern edge of the town is where two county championship matches are played during Cricket Week. There are two cricket grounds, the Higher and the Lower, on the Common and several other pitches in outlying districts such as RUSTALL and HAWKENBURY.

TUNBRIDGE WELLS GOLF CLUB (0892 23034) with a 9-hole course and NEVILL GOLF CLUB (0892 25818) both welcome visitors by prior arrangement during the week.

CALVERLEY GROUNDS, formerly the garden of Mount Pleasant House, offers hard and grass tennis courts, putting and bowling greens, a children's paddling pool and a refreshment pavilion. There are ten all-weather tennis courts at the Nevill Ground. Inquiries about coaching to 0892 823262.

SPORTS AND 'Y' CENTRE, St John's Road (0892 540744), provides facilities for swimming, diving, squash, badminton, table tennis and trampoline seven days a week from 8am to 10.30pm.

WELLINGTON ROCKS on the Common are a popular playground for children and HIGH ROCKS, 2 miles to the southwest, 40ft high with narrow canyons, are used for serious training by climbers.

BOWLES OUTDOOR CENTRE, 4 miles south off the A26 near ERIDGE GREEN (0892 665665) is a good introduction to the Alps with its artificial ski slope and climbing on Bowles Rocks. The 7-acre site offers a range of facilities including a swimming pool, a lecture hall and accommodation. Run as a non-profit-making educational trust, it offers outdoor pursuits training on a day or residential basis, including canoeing, camping and riding as well as skiing and rock climbing.

FOOD AND DRINK

THACKERAY'S, 85 London Road, Tunbridge Wells (0892 511921). Converted from the kitchens of a staging inn that was formerly the home of William Makepeace Thackeray, serves good English food. Closed Sunday, Monday and Christmas. Advance booking advisable. Expensive.

DUKE OF YORK, 17 The Pantiles, Tunbridge Wells (0892 30482). Converted stables with good lunchtime fare and cask ales.

CHEEVERS, 56 High Street, Tunbridge Wells (0892 545524). High quality food and wine at moderate prices. Closed Sunday and Monday and some holidays.

BINNS, 70 The Pantiles, Tunbridge Wells (0892 27690). Traditionally *the* place for afternoon tea in Tunbridge Wells, now serves full meals as well as snacks, cakes and pastries, and breakfast all day.

BLACK HORSE, High Street, Pembury (0892 822141). One of the oldest buildings (14th century) in a village noted for its green and its woodland walks. Real ales and a full à la carte menu lunchtime and evening. Play area for children and a large garden, with barbecues on fine evenings.

ACCOMMODATION

THE SPA, Mount Ephraim, Tunbridge Wells TN4 8XJ (0892 20331). All 75 rooms *en suite*. Indoor heated pool, children's play area and tennis. Expensive.

ROYAL WELLS INN, Mount Ephraim, Tunbridge Wells TN4 8BE (0892 51118). Family-run hotel near the Common, all rooms with bath. Restaurant in the first floor conservatory serves French and English cuisine. Moderate rates.

LOMBARDS, 16 Birling Park Avenue, Tunbridge Wells TN2 5LQ (0892 21629). Guest house with garden and heated outdoor swimming pool. Inexpensive bed and breakfast. Closed in September.

UPCHURCH

This little village among orchards of cherry and pear, bordering the creeks and mudflats of the estuary is only a couple of miles east of the Medway Towns conurbation. Edmund Drake was vicar of Upchurch from 1560 to 1566, when the eldest of his twelve sons, Francis, was apprenticed to the master of a coasting vessel who left him the ship at his death and launched him on his career as circumnavigator and corsair, culminating in a knighthood and the defeat of the Spanish Armada. The Reverend Drake is buried at Upchurch with another son, Edward, beneath a shingled spire, part square, part octagonal, which guides sailors negotiating the marshes around Slaughterhouse Point and Bishop Ooze. Thirteen centuries before Drake, the Romans knew Upchurch as a place where pottery was made in vast quantities. Hundreds of pots, urns and fragments have been dug out of the mud along this shore.

UPSTREET

Near this unremarkable hamlet on the A28 road from *Canterbury to Thanet is 11 acres of meadowland beside the Great Stour set aside for picnics, walks and fishing (day ticket from the local Bailiff). Just south of the main road a byroad crosses the railway and river by the GROVE FERRY INN and there is a car park and toilets. They used to grow lavender along this pleasant riverside and distil perfume from it.

WESTERHAM

Now that much of the heavy traffic that used to thunder through it on the main A25 road from Kent into Surrey has been bypassed on to the the M25 motorway (from which there is no exit at this point),

Westerham has returned to being something like the slumbering country town, scarcely more than a village, which several famous people knew and loved. When the county town of Maidstone was a considerable journey from this western outpost, courts were held in the old posting inn, the GEORGE AND DRAGON. General James Wolfe, the victor of Quebec against the French, grew up here. William Pitt the Younger spent his summers in a timbered cottage on the outskirts of the town (now a restaurant) and much later another Prime Minister, Winston Churchill, made his home in the high wooded hills to the south at *Chartwell. Northwards, at the top of the steep escarpment of the Downs lies the aerodrome which played a key role in winning the Battle of Britain in 1940, *Biggin Hill. The main street of Westerham, with its old houses, shops, pubs and a restaurant or two, opens out on to a green, more like a town square, which is shared by a copper statue of Wolfe, sword in hand, and an Oscar Nemon statue of Churchill. The Early English church of St Mary, off the square, has a Burne-Jones window in memory of Wolfe and memorials of the Warde family, lords of the manor, with whose sons he and his brother played soldiers as boys. There is also a fine collection of 16th-century brasses. The churchyard overlooks the River Darent, which rises in Squerryes Park and whose valley the M25 follows in an arc to Dartford.

QUEBEC HOUSE (0959 62206) is a 17th-century gabled redbrick house that was already old when James Wolfe was born. It is kept in a good state of preservation by the National Trust, with four rooms as they were when Wolfe senior, a Colonel employed in building military roads, brought his family to live there. The Tudor stable block houses an exhibition of the historic battle fought between Wolfe and the Marquis de Montcalm on the Plains of Abraham in 1759, where the 32-year-old general laid down his life winning Canada for his king. Open daily in the afternoon, except Thursday and Saturday, from Good Friday to the end of October.

SQUERRYES COURT (0959 62345), the ancestral seat of the Wardes where the boy Wolfe received his commission in the army aged 14, is a 17th-century manor house filled with fine paintings, furniture, china and tapestries. Among its curiosities is Mrs Wolfe's 'good water' for the consumption which afflicted her son, written in her recipe book. It includes garden snails, earthworms, beer, milk and a variety of herbs which grow still in the gardens. Landscaped grounds surround a lake and an ornamental dovecote. Open in the afternoons on Wednesdays, weekends and bank holiday Mondays from April to September and Sundays in March. A tearoom is open at weekends.

FOOD AND DRINK
SHAPLA TANDOORI, 20 London Road, Westerham (0959 63397) specialises in chicken tikka, mildly

spiced, and marsala dishes. Moderate.

ACCOMMODATION
KINGS ARMS, Market Square,

Westerham TN16 1AN (0959 62990). All bedrooms with bath, individually designed and named after famous monarchs. Expensive.

WEST MALLING

In its time, West Malling has turned its hand to tanning, brewing, glass-blowing, quarrying and making clocks and straw hats but today it seems content with its role as a dormitory for people who hurry off each morning from the railway station or along the A20 and don't return until evening. West Malling, one feels, deserves more consideration. It has a handsome, wide High Street lined with Georgian and Elizabethan houses, the Bear and the Swan posting inns and three Norman towers. Apart from the lovely old church tower, the tower and gatehouse of a nunnery founded by Bishop Gundulf stand guard over the new buildings of ST MARY'S ABBEY which houses Anglican monks and nuns. The third tower, ST LEONARD'S, dating from just after the Conquest is all that remains of Gundulf's manor house. It is even older than the keep at *Rochester and can be inspected at leisure and without charge. It lies beyond MANOR PARK with its 3-acre lake, nature trails and picnic areas, on the A228 road to *Mereworth. The aerodrome at West Malling was a famous fighter station in the Battle of Britain and is still in use despite building proposals.

SPORT AND LEISURE
WEST MALLING GOLF CLUB, London Road, Addington (0732 844795). Visitors welcome to this 18-hole course during the week and after 11.30am at weekends.

ENVIRONS
LEYBOURNE on the A20 is easily overlooked but the remains of a Norman castle are built into the Grange, once the home of Sir Joseph Hawley whose horses won the Derby four times. The castle was built by the de Leybournes and in the village church is a twin shrine, one part containing the heart of Roger de Leybourne who died on a Crusade to the Holy Land in the 13th century. The other part, intended for his wife's heart, is empty because she married again. *Offam, with its quintain on the green, and ADDINGTON, with its megalithic long barrow and burial chambers, lie to the west.

FOOD AND DRINK
ANGEL, Addington Green (0732 842117). A 14th-century inn facing a well-kept green.

ACCOMMODATION
SWAN, Swan Street, West Malling ME19 6JU (0732 845950). Comfortable rooms and good food in an 18th-century inn.

WHITSTABLE

The name of Whitstable is synonymous with oysters, even though the industry almost died because of pollution and the terrible storm which hit the coasts of Kent and East Anglia in January 1953. The hatchery in the harbour area is flourishing again now and no visit can be considered complete without a tasting of the 'Whitstable Natives', unless, of course, you simply can't stand the things. The Romans introduced them to Kent and they used to be produced in quantity on the Medway but it was Whitstable's that became world famous. An imposing brick building now occupied by a charity still bears the sign 'Royal Native Oyster Stores. By Appointment to HM King George V, also to HM the late Queen Victoria'. There is a salty tang in the air and weatherboarded fishermen's cottages and boatsheds coated in pitch line the harbour wall. The civic authorities are anxious to point out that Whitstable isn't just oysters. Britain's first Sea Cadets were recruited here and some of its earliest council housing built, in 1920. The first steamboat from England to Australia in 1837, the *William IV*, departed from Whitstable. Its harbour, opened in 1832 as the port for *Canterbury, 7 miles inland, was the first to be served by a railway—indeed the *Invicta* (now in the Canterbury Heritage Museum) was the world's first steam locomotive in passenger service. The railway link with the cathedral city was dismantled in 1952 but Whitstable is served by the North Kent coast line (75 minutes from London) and the M2 Motorway via the A299. Its port thrives and it is popular for yachting, water-skiing, fishing. The shingle beach stretches for 7 miles from SEASALTER in the west to SWALECLIFFE in the east and there are wide views across the bay to the Isle of Sheppey. The parish church of All Saints dates from soon after the Norman Conquest when all three manors were the possession of William's half-brother, Odo, Bishop of Bayeux. The quiet resort of TANKERTON, east of a wooded hill surmounted by a ship's mast and a couple of cannon, is dominated by the battlemented TANKERTON TOWER, begun as a 'folly' by Charles Pearson, lord of the manor in 1792. From 1935 to 1974 it was the office of the local council but is now used as a community centre.

The TOURIST INFORMATION CENTRE is at Horsebridge (0227 275482).

SPORT AND LEISURE

LEISURE CENTRE, Beach Walk (0227 274394). Facilities for watersports, including windsurfing and water-skiing, and also squash, table tennis, swimming pool and solarium.

FISHING from the shore is limited to flounders and eels with some bass in spring and summer. Excellent bait digging for lugworm and ragworm with peeler crabs around the groynes from May to July.

WHITSTABLE AND SEASALTER GOLF

CLUB, Collingwood Road (0227 272020). Nine-hole seaside links. Visitors are welcome on weekdays, with a member.

CLOWES WOOD, off the A290 road to Canterbury, has been laid out by the Forestry Commission as a Forest Walk, with a car park and picnic areas.

FOOD AND DRINK

WHEELERS OYSTER BAR, 8 High Street, Whitstable (0227 273311) is *the* place to sample the 'Whitstable Natives'.

GIOVANNIS, 49 Canterbury Road, Whitstable (0227 273034). Lavish displays of fresh raw materials – seafood, meat and vegetables – which go into its English, French, Italian cuisine. Moderate prices.

ACCOMMODATION

DUKE OF CUMBERLAND, High Street, Whitstable CT5 1AP (0227 272031). Comfortable rooms, mostly with shower and wc. Moderate.

WINDY RIDGE, Wraik Hill, Whitstable CT5 2BY (0227 863506). Inexpensive bed and breakfast with sea views. No pets or children under school age.

WICKHAMBREAUX

The 14th-century church of St Andrew in this little village between *Canterbury and *Sandwich contains a rare example of American craftsmanship in an English church, in the east window designed by Arild Rosenkrantz and donated by Count James Gallantin. Its art nouveau style is a foil to the fragment of 13th-century stained glass showing the beheading of John the Baptist. The country around Wickhambreaux is flat and low-lying, leading to the marsh, dykes and lakes of the Great Stour. The village itself is on the banks of the Little Stour with a tall weather-boarded mill whose wheel still turns. Other old buildings include the Bell House from which in Tudor times curfew was rung. An avenue of lime trees runs from the church to the triangular waterside green and the quaintly named Gutter Street, lined with 18th- and 19th-century brick cottages, winds its way out of the village. The HOODEN HORSE INN takes its name from the time-honoured East Kent and Thanet custom of collecting alms through the hinged jaw of a wooden horse's head (see page 4).

WINGHAM

This substantial village on the A257 road west of *Ash welcomed a succession of royal visitors *en route* from Canterbury to the Cinque Port of Sandwich, including King John, Edward I, Edward III, the Black Prince and much later Eliza-beth I on a royal progress around Kent in 1573. Shakespeare refers to 'Best's son, the tanner of Wingham' marching with the rebels under Jack Cade. This rich history is evident in the row of 13th-century half-timbered buildings, including the Dog Inn and the Red Lion, in the shadow of St Mary's Church, whose tall green spire can be seen from a distance along the road from Canterbury. The pillars of its nave are, unusually, of wood because, it's said, a Canterbury brewer ran off with money raised for their building in stone as part of a 16th-century reconstruction. The Old Canonry used to house the canons of Wingham College. Next to it is a lavish redbrick mansion of the 18th century, Delbridge House. With an abrupt left turn,

the main road continues along a handsomely broad High Street with tree-lined grass verges shielding houses of the Tudor and Georgian periods.

Wingham Bird Park (0227 720836) on the A257 road to Sandwich has a variety of species ranging from cockatoos and macaws to owls and lorys in a natural setting. Picnic area, tea room, gift and pet shops. Open every day except Christmas Day.

WROTHAM

Pronounced 'Rootem', this ancient settlement on the slopes of the North Downs bestrides the Pilgrims Way to Canterbury between the converging M20 and M26 motorways. BBC transmitting aerials tower on the hill above the village, with views across the Weald into Sussex and Surrey, dwarfing the church tower below with a clock that's been ticking away for three and a half centuries. The motorways separate Wrotham from neighbouring Wrotham Heath, Wrotham Water and Wrotham Hill Park and from Borough Green, all of which are now reached through a 'spaghetti junction' of bridges and tunnels. Ethelstan, King of Kent, who gave Wrotham

to the monks of Canterbury in AD964 would be utterly perplexed by it. Somehow, though, Wrotham has managed to cling to its village identity. Near the church can be seen the remains of the Archbishop's Palace which was dismantled in the time of Edward III and its stone carted off to build a new one by the river at *Maidstone, where it still stands.

Away from the motorway roar are two areas of countryside protected by the National Trust, Wrotham Water, and beyond Trottiscliffe (always pronounced *Trosley) the 'country park' which contains Coldrum Long Barrow, Kent's miniature Stonehenge.

WYE

This small country town between *Ashford and *Canterbury is best known for its racecourse and its agricultural college. But with its

half-timbered houses and church of St Martin and St Gregory and the priests' college next to it, built by Cardinal Kempe in the 15th century, it's worth visiting without any particular reason. At its western side, the Great Stour flows over a weir and under a medieval bridge with five arches. On one side there is a level crossing of the railway and the station, and on the other a Kentish inn with a riverside garden. The Cardinal was born at OLANTIGH TOWERS, a mile or two upriver where there are two more weirs. His name is remembered in KEMPE'S CORNER, a hamlet nearby. He was close to Henry V and Henry VI and built many fine churches during their reigns. But one of his best was this one in his home town. In the 18th century the priests' college became a boys' grammar school and today it is the home of WYE COLLEGE OF AGRICULTURE, with various other buildings. WITHERSDANE HALL (0233 812401), which is part of the college, has a well-labelled garden incorporating several small, carefully designed sections, flower borders and alpines, spring bulbs, early-flowering shrubs especially suited to chalk and a herb garden. It is open on Sunday afternoons in May, July, August and September, with teas available.

ENVIRONS

WYE DOWNS, noted for their great beauty and views across to the English Channel, are a National Nature Reserve covering 250 acres with woods of ash, hazel and beech and open downland where rare orchids and grasses grow amidst the many wild flowers and herbs. Open all year, with an information centre, toilet facilities, footpaths and a nature trail.

WYE COLLEGE AGRICULTURAL MUSEUM (0233 812401) is at BROOK a little way to the south and houses a comprehensive collection of farm implements and tools from the time when oxen and horses were the main source of power on the land. The displays are set in a faithfully preserved late 14th-century barn and an early 19th-century oast house of unusual internal design. Open from May to September on Wednesday afternoons and also Saturdays in August. Limited parking available.

A stream runs beside the lane through Brook, with little bridges crossing to the houses. St Mary's Church has a remarkable set of 13th-century wall paintings of scenes from the Nativity and the life of Christ which were uncovered in this century.

FOOD AND DRINK

TICKLED TROUT, Wye (0233 812227). Old beams and bare brickwork in the bars and a restaurant overlooking the garden by the river, with outdoor tables. Charming except for the muzak indoors and out.

WIFE OF BATH, Upper Bridge Street, Wye (0233 812540). Fine English and French cuisine with a wine list to match. Moderately expensive.

ACCOMMODATION

NEW FLYING HORSE, Upper Bridge Street, Wye TN25 5AN (0233

812297). Cheerful and inviting inn with well-fitted bedrooms, four with bath. Attractive patio and garden. Moderate prices.
KINGS HEAD, Church Street, Wye TN25 5BN (0233 812412). Comfortable rooms and a good restaurant. Moderate.

WYE COLLEGE TN25 5AH (0233 812401). Inexpensive accommodation in part of March, April, July, August and September. Outdoor swimming pool.

YALDING

From the top of the square tower of the village church of St Peter and St Paul, with its lead-capped cupola and brass weathervane dated 1734, an ageless Kentish landscape stretches away across the fertile Medway plain to the horizon. This was the scene which Yalding's poet Edmund Blunden dreamed of in the trenches of Flanders. It is a patchwork of buff and green dotted with white cowls of the oast houses. There are 86 spiral steps to climb after obtaining the key from the tower captain or one of the charming and friendly ladies who keep the church clean, but it is worth it. Several Kent rivers join with the Medway at this point to carve a course through the Greensand Ridge to *Maidstone. Yalding's medieval stone bridge is the longest in Kent. It has seven arches and runs for 150 yards, spanning two channels and the low-lying meadow between them. Much of Yalding was under water during the floods of 1968 and 1974 but it is hoped that the protection scheme at *Tonbridge will prevent any recurrence of this disaster. The open commonland which fills the triangle between the confluences of the Teise, the Beult and the Med-

way is called YALDING LEAS.

A little way out of the village the B2162 road bridge crosses the Medway over another narrow 15th-century bridge and follows an old canal cut (which avoids the loop in the river) to HAMPSTEAD LOCK, full of people 'messing about in boats', and YALDING STATION. The railway follows the Medway from here all the way to Strood through Maidstone and can be recommended as a way of seeing the many contrasting faces of Kent, rural, urban and suburban, that you won't see from the main roads, let alone the motorways. It's nothing short of miraculous how Yalding's cobbled walks and timbered fronts, thatched roofs and old stone bridges have survived thus far. There is a certain amount of housing development and tarting-up of oast houses going on but much is unchanged. A general smith and farrier still operates in a weatherboarded smithy and an old iron water pump stands at the back of a row of cottages with wisteria and pyracanth climbing their walls.

FOOD AND DRINK
As befits one of the largest hop-growing parishes in England,

Yalding has a plethora of fine old pubs—the WALNUT TREE, the BULL, the GEORGE, the TWO BREWERS, the WOOLPACK and the SWAN, which keeps a cellar under one of the bridge arches. The author cannot claim to have sampled them all, however.

THE COBBLESTONES, Yalding (0622 814326) uses fresh ingredients for its extensive and varied menu which includes a six-course gourmet meal and a special midweek 'Old English' supper (children half price). It is open for lunches from Tuesday to Friday and on Sunday.

4

TOWN WALKS

CANTERBURY

The main places of interest are to be found within a compact area of the city centre. Most of it is barred to motor traffic, so it will be necessary to leave your car at one of the several car parks shown on the map. You can of course start the walking tour at the nearest point to wherever you leave your car. Both East and West Canterbury BR stations and the Bus Station opposite the Fire Station are close to the route, which for our purposes starts at the *Tourist Information Centre in St Margaret's Street.

Going towards the Cathedral, *Canterbury Pilgrims Way exhibition is on your left. Cross the pedestrianised High Street (with

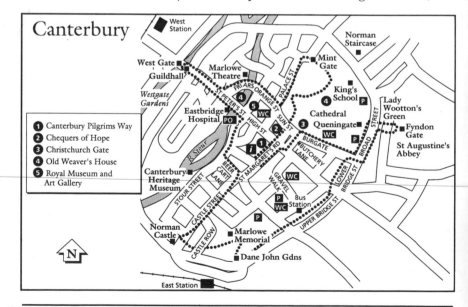

Canterbury

- 1 Canterbury Pilgrims Way
- 2 Chequers of Hope
- 3 Christchurch Gate
- 4 Old Weaver's House
- 5 Royal Museum and Art Gallery

West Station
Norman Staircase
West Gate
Guildhall
Marlowe Theatre
Mint Gate
King's School
Westgate Gardens
Eastbridge Hospital
Cathedral
Lady Wootton's Green
Queningate
Fyndon Gate
St Augustine's Abbey
Canterbury Heritage Museum
Bus Station
Norman Castle
Marlowe Memorial
Dane John Gdns
East Station

Canterbury Cathedral, a splendid prospect

the ancient pilgrims' inn, the Chequers of Hope, to your left) and continue to the elaborate *Christchurch Gate opposite the Buttermarket. Immediately through the gate, a splendid prospect of the *Cathedral dominated by the Bell Harry tower opens up. The main entrance is to your right. If not going inside, keep to the left, passing the west end of the Cathedral and following the path round through the *Cloisters. Turn right after the *Chapter House and left through the Dark Entry, which according to Barham's *Ingoldsby Legends* is haunted by a servant girl who was buried alive beneath the paving stones after discovering her master, a canon, in an illicit affair and poisoning both him and his lover. The Dark Entry leads into Green Court at the heart of the *King's School and the Norman external staircase is in the northwest corner. Continue left through Green Court Gate into Mint Yard.

Mint Yard Gate leads into Palace Street. Turn left and walk down it, taking time to window shop and enjoy the historic buildings. Turn right into Orange Street and continue down The Friars. The *Marlowe Theatre is on your right. Turn right along St Peter's Street past the *Sidney Cooper Centre where antiques markets are held on Saturdays to the 14th-century *West Gate, said to be the finest in England. Next to it is the Guildhall. Retrace your steps along St Peter's Street, continuing on past the junction with The Friars until you come to the unmistakeable black and white *Old Weaver's House beside the Stour River. Immediately opposite is the 12th-century *Eastbridge Hospital.

Turn right into Stour Street opposite the *Royal Museum and Art Gallery, which leads shortly to the *Canterbury Heritage museum in the 13th-century Poor Priests' Hospital. Opposite this building, Beer Cart Lane leads into Castle Street, where you turn right, heading towards the keep of the Norman Castle (ill-used in Victorian times as a coal store but surviving, none the less). A footpath runs from here to Castle Row and on through *Dane John Gardens, where the *Marlowe Memorial can be seen. A ramp leads to the high-level walk along the parapet of the medieval and Roman *City Wall, which runs parallel to Upper and Lower Bridge Street to Broad Street. A short detour across the road will bring you to the ruins of *St Augustine's Abbey, founded in AD602. The imposing gate, built in the 14th century, stands at the top of Lady Wootton's Green.

Retracing your steps to Broad Street, turn left and right into Burgate. A left turn into Butchery Lane leads to the *Roman Pavement (CLOSED during 1990) beneath one of the new shops in the Longmarket precinct. A few steps along the High Street from here bring you to St Margaret's Street on the left, our starting point.

MAIDSTONE

Our walk around Maidstone begins at the original site of the hamlet of 'Mighty Stone', where its oldest buildings are to be found. *All Saints Church, the *College of Priests and the remains of the dungeons where John Ball was incarcerated, together with the *Archbishop's Palace and its stables which house the *Tyrwhitt-Drake

Museum of Carriages, form an attractive group opposite the *Tourist Information Centre in the palace gatehouse. Just behind it, a medieval bridge with two pointed arches spans the River Len. Its mills and eel fisheries are mentioned in the Domesday Book. Pleasant riverside gardens lead down Bishops Way to old Maid-

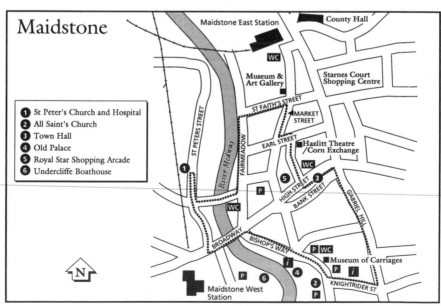

Maidstone

1 St Peter's Church and Hospital
2 All Saint's Church
3 Town Hall
4 Old Palace
5 Royal Star Shopping Arcade
6 Undercliffe Boathouse

stone Bridge and sightseeing river trips can be taken from the Under-cliffe Boathouse, which also hires out craft.

Follow Broadway which crosses the Medway on the Victorian bridge, widened half a century ago (its medieval forerunner was only 11ft wide), and turn right into St Peter's Street, opposite Maidstone West BR Station. St Peter's Church and Hospital was founded in 1260 by Archbishop Boniface as a resting place for Canterbury pilgrims and an almshouse for pensioners. Despite Victorian extensions by Whichcord, the original lancet windows, piscina and sedilla can be seen.

Recross the Medway on St Peter's Bridge, erected beside the old one in 1978 to relieve traffic congestion in the town centre, and turn left into Fairmeadow, given to the townspeople by Edward VI for archery and other 'disportes, pastymes and recreation'. Today's spacious esplanade, with a car park and toilets including facilities for the disabled nearby in the High Street, is still a favourite place for recreation. It was, however, in medieval times the site of a ducking stool and fires for burning witches at the stake. A tablet commem-orates the Maidstone Martyrs of 1557. The ornately decorated hall with a crownpost roof and weather-vane at the corner of Fairmeadow and Earl Street was given to the Corpus Christi Fraternity in 1422 and Henry VI confirms its founda-tion in a letter of 1441. It was a centre of both commerce and

charity in medieval Maidstone but after the Reformation it became a boys' grammar school from 1549 until 1871. It now belongs to Whitbread-Fremlins brewery. Traces of the Old Town Wharf here, once busy with barges and hoys carrying ragstone and Fullers earth down to the estuary and London, have largely disappeared. The river's main activity is now leisure. (Those wanting a longer walk can follow the riverside some 2 miles down to Allington Lock along the towpath which, beyond the railway bridge approaching Maidstone East BR Station, is a scene of rural peace).

Our town walk turns right into St Faith's Street. The Tudor house on the corner was the home of William Weaver, Mayor of Maidstone in 1691. An underground passage from here to the quay is said to have been used by smugglers. Further up St Faith's Street, past the Library and Adult Education Centre is the *Museum and Art Gallery in Chillington Manor, which was rebuilt by Maidstone's first Member of Parliament, Nicho-las Barham, during the reign of Elizabeth I. A 15th-century crown-posted court lodge from East Far-leigh was added in 1874. These beautifully preserved buildings can be seen to even greater advantage from Brenchley Gardens at the rear. Before crossing to Market Street, take a look at the early Tudor cottage on the corner of Station Road. Walk down Market Street into Earl Street, where the remains of Earls Place, birthplace of Archbishop Edward Lee of York in the Middle Ages, can be seen at the corner of Havoc Lane. Opposite is the house of Andrew Broughton, the Roundhead Mayor of Maidstone who, as Clerk of the High Court, read out the death sentence on Charles I. The large silver mace which he provided is still used on civic occasions. Continuing up Earl Street, you come to Market Buildings next to the *Hazlitt Theatre in the Corn Exchange. The market, originally granted by Henry III in 1261, moved here in 1825. The Unitarian Church to the right of the arcade dates from 1736. With its weathervane, freestanding pulpit and gallery, it is the oldest nonconformist church in Maidstone. William Hazlitt's father was minister from 1770 to 1780 and according to the famous essayist was 'much beloved'.

At the opposite side of the market arcade is the High Street, with many new buildings and shopping precincts, but full of historic associations. Opposite the drinking fountain with a figure of Queen Victoria, is one of the first iron-framed buildings in Britain, designed in 1855 by John Whichcord and Arthur Ashpitel. No. 99 (formerly the Chequers Inn) has a medieval crypt or undercroft. At No. 91 the young Disraeli dictated his first electoral address to the editor of the *Maidstone and Kentish Journal*, who persuaded him to leave out the 'foreign' apostrophe in his name. Disraeli entered Parliament as the Member for Maidstone in 1837. The Russian gun on a plinth further along the High Street was captured during the Crimean War.

The Town Hall in Middle Row stands like an island in a broad stream, its clock overhanging the High Street. The building is Georgian and contains the town's regalia, maces and silver as well as two fine tapestries, one depicting the Battle of Aylesford, the other the Battle of Rochester. Above the council chamber's Italianate ceiling are old prison cells with inscriptions carved by those awaiting trial and possible death or deportation.

Bank Street, to the side of Middle Row, has many elegant 17th-century buildings, especially No. 78 with its pargetting of the plumes of Henry Prince of Wales, the son of James I. Look out for another house nearby which displays carvings of four Maidstone 'notables' – Lord Avebury, Lawrence Washington, William Caxton and Archbishop Courtenay.

At the top of the High Street turn right into Gabriel's Hill where a plaque at No. 3 commemorates Samuel Pepys's stay at the Bell Inn which stood here in 1669 ... 'having walked all round the town and found it very pretty ... we to our inne to dinner ...' The Little Bridge referred to in old town documents lies under the road at the bottom of Gabriel's Hill, which was formerly part of the Roman road linking Week Street and Stone Street. Continue along Lower Stone Street and turn right into Knightrider Street. The medieval Mill House on the corner has an ancient corner post with hundreds of nails driven into it, suggesting that it used to be the place for displaying public notices. A plaque on the Queen Anne house further down the street shows that it was the home of William Shipley, founder of the Royal Society of Arts, who died in 1803 and is buried in All Saints churchyard. The Baptist church on the lower corner of Knightrider Street is the site of the former Bluecoat School and also of Maidstone Union Workhouse. The ragstone wall on the other side of the street surrounded the mansion (long since gone) of Lawrence Washington. It's said that the noticeable dent in the wall was deliberate so that the clock on the church tower could be seen from the house. We are now back where our walk began.

ROCHESTER

The Roman's Watling Street, crossing the Medway at Rochester Bridge, midway between London and the Channel ports, is the foundation of the compact city which lies at the heart of the sprawling Medway Towns conurbation. Its 25 municipal charters granted by monarchy stretch back to Richard I in 1190 and in 1446 the chief citizen or Bailiff of Rochester was made Admiral of the Medway from Sheerness to Hawkwood. The High Street, following the line of ancient Watling Street, and well provided these days with car parking space, has been given back largely to pedestrians and restored to its Georgian and Victorian heyday, with traditional gas lamp holders. It is packed with historic interest. Many of the old inns, shops and public buildings, the ancient cathedral and castle, are much as they were when Charles Dickens described them in several of his novels and stories.

Our walk begins at the Esplanade from which there is a good view of the river and its bridges, ancient and modern. A short way above the old bridge to Strood is the *Bridge Chapel dating from 1387 and last restored more than half a century ago. It is still used as the Board Room of the Bridge Wardens who have been responsible for the upkeep of this vital link in the Dover Road for 600 years. A second road bridge beside it was opened in 1970 and upstream a graceful new bridge carrying the M2 motorway can be seen. In the Middle Ages when funds were needed, the church didn't hesitate to use its spiritual influence – in 1489 Archbishop Morton granted indulgences 'remitting from purgatory all manner of Sins for forty days to all persons contributing towards the repair of the Bridge'.

From the Esplanade and the bridge turn right into the High Street. The first notable building on the right is the *Royal Victoria and Bull Hotel which Dickens uses in the *Pickwick Papers* and other books. Opposite stands the *Guildhall of 1687 (with its gorgeous ship weathervane added in 1780). It contains a fascinating museum and a remarkable plaster ceiling, the gift of Sir Cloudesley Shovell, whose treasure-laden fleet floundered off the Scilly Isles in 1707. An even older Guildhall stood on the site, a little further up the High Street, now occupied by the early Georgian Corn Exchange with its overhanging clock. Opposite, a narrow alley leads to the *Castle between a Tudor house and its elegant 18th-century neighbour, No. 42. (The Castle and its gardens can be explored now or at the end of the walk). There are two fine old inns, the George and the King's Head, in this part of the High Street before we come to Chertseys Gate, which appears in Dickens's last unfinished novel *Edwin Drood* as Jasper's Gatehouse. Further along the High Street on the right,

Pilgrims Passage (also known as Blackboy Alley) was used by pilgrims to the shrine of St William of Perth. It leads to the 15th-century Deanery Gate and the north graveyard of the cathedral from which Dickens culled the names of many of his characters. Continuing up the High Street, there are several interesting buildings to look out for. Lloyds Bank occupies the house where James II stayed as the guest of Sir Richard Head before fleeing to France in 1688. The Gordon Hotel (No. 91) has painted panelling and an ornately carved gate. *Watts Charity, open to visitors, was founded in 1579 as accommodation for 'six poor travellers'. Nearby is the Schoolmaster's House dating from 1701, and La Providence Hospital, founded by Huguenot immigrants

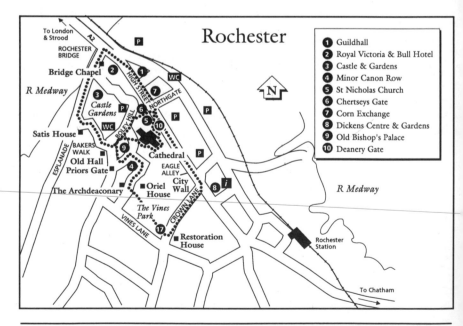

Rochester

N

1 Guildhall
2 Royal Victoria & Bull Hotel
3 Castle & Gardens
4 Minor Canon Row
5 St Nicholas Church
6 Chertseys Gate
7 Corn Exchange
8 Dickens Centre & Gardens
9 Old Bishop's Palace
10 Deanery Gate

in the 18th century and today housing their descendants. Eagle Alley, to the right, leads from the High Street to a well-preserved section of City Wall dating from Roman times.

To the left beyond the junction with Crown Lane is the *Dickens Centre in the Elizabethan Eastgate House (the Nun's House of *Edwin Drood*) and next to it the *Tourist Information Centre in Eastgate Cottage. In the grounds is the Swiss chalet in which Dickens worked in his garden at Gads Hill Place and near the gate a section of the original Watling Street can be seen. The gabled house across the High Street is Uncle Pumblechook's home in *Great Expectations*. (Able-bodied and maritime-minded visitors can continue the walk from here along Eastgate and into the resumed High Street which crosses the imperceptible boundary into *Chatham. An alternative way of returning, and getting a different perspective of the scene, is to board the restored paddlesteamer *Kingswear Castle* at either Chatham Historic Dockyard or Sun Pier and sail to Strood Pier, just across the bridge from our starting point.)

Our walk around Rochester continues up Crown Lane. Restoration House, where Charles II is said to have stayed on his return to England in 1660, is one of a row of houses on the left. This is also the 'Satis House' of *Great Expectations* where old Miss Havisham lived amidst the cobwebs of a wedding breakfast which never took place. The place has jollier memories of Samuel Pepys who records in his diary of 1667 that he 'went into the Cherry Garden and here met a pretty young woman and did kiss her'. As Secretary to the Admiralty, Pepys was here officially to inquire into the humiliating Dutch raid up the Medway. Opposite Restoration House, go into the Vines and walk along the avenue of plane trees planted around 1880 where in medieval times quantities of grapes were grown. At the far side of the Vines stand Oriel House and the 17th-century Archdeaconry. The gate between the two leads to Minor Canon Row, where Dame Sybil Thorndike used to live in one of the delightful Georgian houses. By tradition, No. 7 is the home of the cathedral organist. Continuing round, go through Priors Gate, the best preserved of the three 14th-century monastic gates. To your left, the Diocesan Registrar's Office was built in 1760 on the site of the old Bishop's Prison. The old Bishop's Palace overlooking College Green was where Erasmus stayed as a guest in Tudor times, complaining of the draughts and the cold brick floor in the bishop's library 'as to my own part, I would not live in such a place three hours without being sick'. The *Cathedral faces you (with peaceful Cloister Garth to the right). Evensong is sung each afternoon in the 13th-century Choir within Bishop Gundulf's immense stone walls. The West Door, the only surviving example in England of a Norman column-figure doorway, deserves more than a brief passing glance. On the far side of the cathedral is St Nicholas Church, now used as

Diocesan offices with the nave retained for worship.

Chertseys Gate leads back to the High Street but we go left down Boley Hill between the castle moat and the beautiful western end of the Cathedral precinct. Turning right at the bottom, Old Hall on the left was formerly the east wing of Satis House, a little further along beneath the curtain wall of the castle. Not to be confused with Dickens's 'Satis House' (see earlier), this one takes its name from a visit of Queen Elizabeth I, when she thanked her host, Richard Watts, with the one word 'satis'. A small gate leads into the castle gardens, for perhaps a climb up the spiral staircase within the width of the keep's massive stone walls for a final overview, or one can go down Baker's Walk back to the Esplanade.

ROYAL TUNBRIDGE WELLS

These days almost every town worthy of the name has its new pedestrianised shopping precinct, and Tunbridge Wells is no exception. Only Tunbridge Wells, however, has one laid out in the reign of the Stuarts – The Pantiles. It also has, in Decimus Burton's Calverley Park, the prototype 'garden suburb'. This walk (suitable only for the reasonably fit because of the hilly terrain) combines these two quarters of a town which was a favourite of the royal houses of Stuart and Hanover and whose architecture reflects its privileged past. You will see how, despite some crass 20th-century redevelopment, many of the old buildings survive and signs of a renaissance of its former splendour in some of the latest restoration projects, notably in and around The Pantiles. Another example of this is the *Grand Hall, opposite Central Station at the foot of Mount Pleasant, which is now a fine shopping arcade with a multi-storey car park unobtrusively incorporated at the rear.

From the station (near which is further car parking space), walk down the High Street, taking time to window shop along the way. The variety (see Gazetteer, under Shopping) is remarkable. The High Street leads into Chapel Place and the 17th-century church of *King Charles the Martyr, with the most splendid decorative plaster ceiling of the period in any church outside London. Walk across Nevill Street from the church into *The Pantiles, which opens out into Bath Square, surrounded by timber-boarded and tile-hung buildings. The iron-columned canopy over the chalybeate spring in front of Bath House, built around 1804, was added 40 years later. Tunbridge Wells was born with the discovery of this health-giving spring in 1606. The Bath inside is now underneath Boots the Chemists and a trapdoor may be seen in the floor of the shop, entered at No. 4, The Pantiles. Victoria drank the waters daily during her stay in 1834 and she and her mother, the Duchess of Kent, walked in the Pantiles afterwards. In a corner of Bath Square, at the foot of the steps leading to Fox Brothers, look out for 15 of the original square, hard-baked clay 'pantiles' dating from the early 1700s and preserved amid the later paving slabs. Leading from Bath Square is a colonnaded Upper Walk and a redbrick paved Lower Walk, shaded by a line of lime trees. Opposite the *Bandstand you will see the former *Royal Victoria inn where the young princess stayed with her mother. The coats of arms over the Greek Doric porch are those of the Duke and Duchess of Kent, Victoria's parents. The building next to it, also with a Greek Doric porch, was originally a theatre where Edmund Kean made his debut and Charles Kemble performed. It was later rebuilt as the *Corn Exchange.

The female figure crowning it is Ceres, goddess of the harvest, as is shown by the decorative panel of hops and wheat.

After a leisurely stroll around The Pantiles go through the passageway alongside the Swan Hotel and across Eridge Road to the *Common – switching from an urban to a comparatively rural scene in a few steps. A footpath climbs up through dense woodland, crossing after about 200 yards the Old Race Course, where young Victoria watched the races with her mother from their carriage under a specially erected awning and the Duchess of Kent presented a Gold Cup. It is possible to follow the course, as a grassy track, all the way round. As the path emerges into open common to the right you can see a double avenue of trees originally planted in 1702 on the accession of Queen

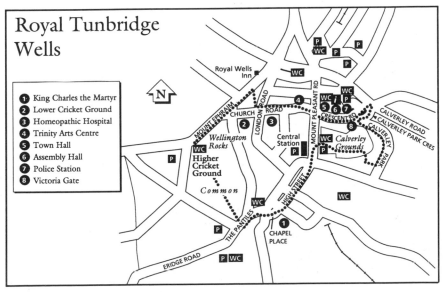

Royal Tunbridge Wells

1. King Charles the Martyr
2. Lower Cricket Ground
3. Homeopathic Hospital
4. Trinity Arts Centre
5. Town Hall
6. Assembly Hall
7. Police Station
8. Victoria Gate

Anne and supplemented in 1835 as the Victoria Grove. To the left a little further on is the *Higher Cricket Ground and to the right *Wellington Rocks. Ahead up the footpath may be seen the ornate Jacobean-style gables and chimney stacks of Mount Ephraim House, where we turn right on reaching the main road. The first large houses in Tunbridge Wells were built on these commanding heights to save royalty and aristocracy from having to 'camp out' on the Common while they took the waters. King Charles II stayed at Mount Ephraim House, which survives, with much later rebuilding and addition, as a WRVS residential club. It and the low-canopied Chalet next to it were for many years used for the manufacture of Tunbridge Ware. Our walk takes us along Mount Ephraim, a busy road lined with large Victorian buildings, some still in use as hotels, alongside other newer office buildings. Down the slope to the right you will see a house nestling against a great sandstone outcrop. The *Royal Wells Inn, built in the 1830s, has a vast coat of arms on its parapet and a glass encased balcony which served as a winter garden. Here is the best overview of Tunbridge Wells, looking across common and town to Mount Sion.

In front of the Royal Wells, turn down the steep footpath that descends across the Common to the junction of London Road and Church Road. Jordan House, on the corner opposite the *Lower Cricket Ground, was once the premises of Messrs Burrows 'Manufacturers of Tunbridge Ware to their Royal Highnesses the Duchess of Kent and the Princess Victoria'. A short walk along Church Road past the Homeopathic Hospital and the Clarence pub is *Trinity Arts Centre, formerly Holy Trinity Church. A Georgian building in the 'Gothick' style, it is now Grade 'A' listed although, almost incredibly, in the late 1970s the Church Commissioners were on the point of demolishing it! Look out especially for the finely carved faces at the dripstone terminations. It was the first building of the 'self-contained landscape village – virtually a new town' which Decimus Burton was commissioned to design in 1828. It was meant as a rival to The Pantiles which had been the fashionable meeting place of Tunbridge Wells since it was founded. Opposite the church stood Calverley Parade, a terrace of three-storey houses of which all that remains is a sandstone wall bearing the town's memorial to the fallen of World War I. Calverley Parade and Calverley Terrace, which linked Burton's landscaped village to the church, were demolished in the 1930s to make way for the Town Hall, Library, Assembly Hall and Police Station complex. But in Crescent Road, just across Mount Pleasant from Church Road, the Calverley Hotel survives. This was the young Victoria's main place of residence in Tunbridge Wells to which she returned as Queen with her consort Prince Albert. Go up Crescent Road past Victoria Gate and the modern St Augustine's Catholic Church next to it to Calverley Road, where there are further examples of Decimus Burton's work, only now being restored after years of disregard. It is more rewarding to double back through *Calverley Park Crescent, which rivals anything in Bloomsbury, Regents Park or Bath. Originally called the Promenade, it was planned as shops and at No. 1 were the Royal Baths 'under the immediate Patronage' of the Duchess of Kent and Princess Victoria, where Mr Seaman offered 'Shampooing, Medicated Vapour, Aromatic, Sulphur, Barege, Nitro-Muriatic-Acid, Tepid, Douche and Shower Baths'. There are two iron posts at the end of the Crescent with St Mary Le Bone embossed on them in white on black. Go through Victoria Gate, with its fluted Doric pillars and Egyptian-style windows, into *Calverley Park. There are 24 Burton-designed villas in a semi-circle around landscaped gardens. They are not large and were meant to be run by a small, for those days, indoor staff of three or four servants. No two houses are the same but their bows, bays, towers and terraces harmonise in proportion and materials.

*Calverley Grounds are now a public park and it is a pleasant walk through them back to Central Station. Near the exit by the car park is a modest stone in a small, lovingly tended garden. It is one of the few memorials to the man who was at the head of Fighter Command throughout the Battle of Britain in 1940, Air Chief Marshal Lord Dowding, who died at Tunbridge Wells in 1970.

This walk was compiled with the assistance of the Royal Tunbridge Wells Civic Society, refounded in 1959 to encourage the conservation and enhancement of the town.

5

DRIVING TOURS

HIGH WEALD COUNTRY TOUR

Weald is the old Saxon word for woodland and much of the countryside covered by this motoring tour was part of the huge forest of Anderida which confronted the Roman legions when they first landed in Britain 2,000 years ago. The first settlements were clearings for swine pastures called 'dens' and in the smaller woods or 'hursts'. The tour guides you through many Wealden towns and villages whose names end in 'den' or 'hurst'. There was more widespread clearance during the Middle Ages when trees were felled to provide charcoal for the iron furnaces which prospered mainly in the armaments trade until coke was found to be a more suitable fuel and the industry moved north. Wealden oak and weatherboarding is much in evidence in the traditional architecture, together with locally quarried ragstone, Bethersden marble, and tiles made from the Wealden clay and hung vertically on façades as well as covering roofs. The High Weald today is a belt of open, rolling landscape, still heavily wooded but much of it used as pasture, orchard and hop-garden, and latterly as vineyard. The tour is signposted in an anti-clockwise direction with the distinctive symbol of the white-cowled conical oasthouse seen so frequently in this region, painted on a brown background. Watch out for this marker and also for other brown and white signs indicating other notable places of interest such as castles, museums, gardens, vineyards, and country parks along the route. The tour can be joined or left at any point. For detailed information on places marked thus * consult the Gazetteer section of this guide.

Southwards from *Tonbridge, an important crossroads and crossing of the Medway with a Norman castle, the tour follows the A26 Eastbourne road before turning sharply right towards Bidborough on the B2176, with fine views from Bidborough Ridge across the Medway valley and back over Tonbridge. Turning right off the

162

Picnic spot at Teston Bridge (see page 165)

B2176, the road descends to cross the plain of the River Medway, where flood level marker poles will be seen. In times of flooding, diversions will be clearly marked. Having crossed the Medway, the route turns left by the Fleur de Lis pub and follows the straight and level Wealden railway for several miles on the B2027 towards Chiddingstone Causeway. (To the right, a sign points to *Bough Beech Reservoir, where there is an Information Centre and an exhibition in a converted oast house, open from April to October on Wednesdays and at weekends.) Passing beneath a low railway bridge on a difficult corner, the tour heads south on a minor road crossing the River Eden to *Chiddingstone, a picturebook period village almost totally owned by the National Trust, with a mock Gothic castle open to visitors. (*Hever Castle is a mile or two to the west on another minor road). From Chiddingstone, the signposted 'Country Tour' follows winding undulating roads through charming unspoilt scenery to *Penshurst. The vineyards are on the right before the minor road joins the B2188, and a visit to Penshurst Place involves a slight detour off the signposted route into the village.

Continuing south from Penshurst on B2188, the tour joins the A264 from East Grinstead and enters *Tunbridge Wells past High Rocks, one of the great outcrops of sandstone which are a feature of the High Weald, a good place for walking, climbing and picnics. The tour leaves Tunbridge Wells on the A267 Eastbourne road, heading south into Sussex and turning on to the B2169 through woodlands for several miles. Bayham Abbey is signposted to the left as the route re-enters Kent at *Lamberhurst, a former iron-making town that is now noted for its major vineyard. From Lamberhurst, the tour follows the A21, with Scotney Castle, *Bewl Water and Bedgebury Pinetum just off the route. Less than a mile beyond the B2079 turn-off to the Pinetum, the tour turns on to the A268 through *Hawkhurst, once notorious as the headquarters of the Hawkhurst gang of smugglers, before turning left and travelling along an old Roman road which joins the B2086 at *Benenden, where daughters of the Royal families, including Princess Anne, were at school. From Benenden the tour heads along the B2086 past a restored windmill (sometimes open to visitors) at Beacon Hill to *Rolvenden, where Frances Hodgson Burnett's *The Secret Garden* was conceived. Via the A28 Hastings road, the tour proceeds to *Tenterden, 'jewel of the Weald', with its handsome main street and fine church. There is ample parking, shopping and accommodation here, as well as numerous tearooms, inns and restaurants. (*Smallhythe, home of Dame Ellen Terry and Tenterden Vineyards, both signposted, is a 2 mile detour).

Continuing from Tenterden on the A28 and then the A262, (Biddenden Vineyards are signposted at Woolpack Corner), the tour takes us to *Biddenden, where the Biddenden Maids are still commemorated after nearly 900 years. Further west along the A262 is *Sissinghurst, with the famous gardens and castle signposted to the right just before the village. (*Cranbrook, 'capital of the Weald', is a short detour off the main road to the west of Sissinghurst). The tour continues along the A262 to *Goudhurst, which as William Cobbett noted on his *Rural Rides* in 1823 'stands upon one of the steepest hills in this part of the Country' 400ft above sea level. You may wish to stretch your legs by leaving your car at the car park near the Village Hall and the Pond where there are toilets and seats and taking a 'walkabout'. The Vine is an old coaching inn and opposite it is the old village smithy with its spreading chestnut tree. Go up the High Street towards the church and the Star and Eagle. The large house opposite has been in turn a Master Weaver's house, barracks for troops during the Napoleonic

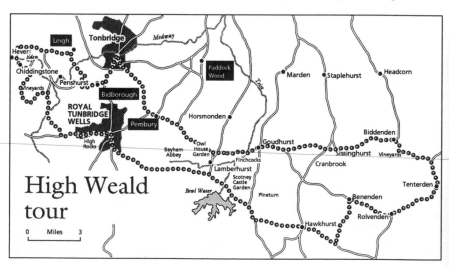

High Weald tour

0   Miles   3

Wars and coffee tavern. Rootes Motor Group had its origins in the basement when William Rootes started a cycle repair shop there at the turn of the century. Down Rope Walk, where ropes were made, there is a Nuttery. Jarvis Lambert perfected the Kentish cob nut at Lamberts by the conical yew in the churchyard. Across the churchyard there are weavers' cottages with long roofspace to house the looms. The church is a gem (see Gazetteer) and the tower may be climbed on Thursdays and Saturdays from May to September

for a view of 68 spires and towers on a clear day. To the south across the hopgardens lies Bedgebury Pinetum. Return to your car via Back Lane, once the main thoroughfare.

The High Weald route continues along the A262 (Finchcocks Living Museum of Music is signposted to the south just before the road crosses the River Teise west of Goudhurst) to join the A21 Hastings road near Lamberhurst, heading to Tonbridge, where the circuit is completed.

HEART OF KENT COUNTRY TOUR

This is a tour of the Garden of England as most people imagine it – orchards buried in pink and white blossom in spring and laden with fruit in autumn, hopgardens, oast houses with their conical roofs and cowls gleaming white in the sun, winding lanes, rippling rivers and villages of thatched and half-timbered houses, weatherboarded inns and tile-hung cottages. There are several farms along the way which welcome visitors and have marked out walking trails. Some have shops selling fresh produce. The motor tour totals some 50 miles and is clearly marked out by the prancing Kent 'Invicta' horse in white on a brown background. Other white on brown signs point the way to places of interest along, or just off, the route. For detailed information on places marked thus * consult the Gazetteer. The country tour is signposted in an anti-clockwise direction, but of course it

can be joined or left at any point. It avoids the larger towns and conurbations but traffic is often quite heavy even on minor roads, so take care. There are so many ravishing views that you will probably want to drive slowly and stop often, anyway.

This guide's chosen starting point for the tour is southwest of *Maidstone on the A26 Tonbridge road at *Teston (pronounced 'Teeson'), where there is a picnic site on the banks of the Medway near the five-arched medieval bridge. Heading west along the A26 through Wateringbury, there is a glimpse through the trees to the left of an 18th-century Palladian castle modelled on the Villa del Capra at Vicenza (not open to visitors, alas) before we get to *Mereworth, built by the Earl of Westmoreland in replacement of the village he knocked down to make way for his castle.

The church dates from 1746. Mereworth lies just off the A228 road which the country tour follows north for a couple of miles before turning left opposite the Startled Saint pub towards Offham, past Manor Park and the Norman St Leonard's Tower. (*West Malling, a pleasant Georgian market town is a short detour northwards). England's last quintain – the target post used by medieval knights to test their jousting skills – can be seen on the green at *Offham, now used only at the annual May Day festivities. From Offham the tour signs direct you towards the confluence of the M20 and M26, bearing left on the A20 and the A25 at the Royal Oak pub before reaching the motorway 'spaghetti junction'. From Platt, the country tour leaves the motorway roar well behind as it skirts beauti-

ful Mereworth Woods, passing typical Kent coppices and oast-houses, with distant views of the wooded Greensand Ridge around *Ightham ahead and the great whaleback of the North Downs to the right. The route fringes *Plaxtol and Old Soar Manor, following Long Mill Lane to Dunks Green, passing the Kentish Rifleman pub before turning left at the crossroads near Puttenden Manor Farm. Shortly afterwards, the wedding cake tower of Hadlow Castle, also known as May's Folly, appears on the skyline. On reaching the A26 Maidstone–Tonbridge road just north of the village of *Hadlow, you turn left. The scenery over the next couple of miles of woods, orchards and hop-gardens with the greensand hills beyond is very attractive. The tower of West Peckham church can

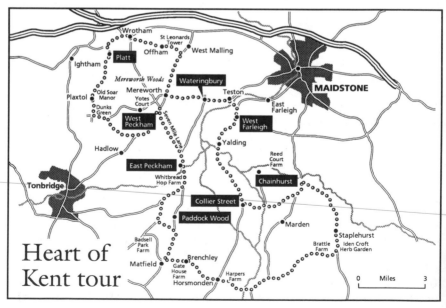

Heart of
Kent tour

be seen among the trees and beyond lies Yotes Court, a 17th-century redbrick mansion, now a hotel and restaurant.

A sharp right turn takes us on to Seven Mile Lane (the B2016, then B2015) towards East Peckham through more fruit and hop country and across the Medway to *Beltring, where the WHITBREAD HOP FARM provides an engaging day out for the whole family. The country tour continues southwards on the B2015, bypassing unlovely Paddock Wood, once a junction of the 'Hop Pickers Line'. Signs point the way to BADSELL PARK FARM, which has two nature trails and is open daily to visitors from April to November. The country tour route turns left on to the B2161 and then climbs gently up the B2160 road towards *Matfield, birthplace of the World War I poet Siegfried Sassoon. (The green, lined with Georgian houses and pleasant inns, lies just off the tour route.) GATE HOUSE FARM, on the edge of *Brenchley, the next village, has a walking route round its 80 acres of orchards with fine views across the Weald. It is open daily from May to October. Alternatively, it is well worth parking in Brenchley and taking a stroll to savour the variety of half-timbered, tile-hung and weatherboarded houses and especially the late 18th-century timber front of Church House, grooved to look like rusticated stone. There is a working forge and the church is particularly lovely.

From Brenchley, the Heart of Kent tour signs guide us along minor roads to *Horsmonden, another centre of the medieval gun-making industry, and beyond across the valley of the River Teise and through several miles of undulating farmland. HARPERS FARM is a typical blend of orchard and hopgarden and a trail around it is open daily from May to August. After following a short section of the B2079, the Heart of Kent route takes to the byroads again. Beyond Curtisden Green, the land is more open, much of it devoted to pasture for sheep. BRATTLE FARM has a museum of agricultural implements going back two centuries, open on Sundays and bank holiday Mondays from April to October. IDEN CROFT HERB GARDEN, with 5 acres of culinary, aromatic and medicinal plants, open year round, is on the outskirts of *Staplehurst, the next large village on the tour route. Staplehurst has several half-timbered Tudor halls and an interesting church. Northwards, the tour follows the A229 along the valley of the slow, winding River Beult towards Stile Bridge but turning abruptly south and then west before reaching it. Ahead, across the river, is a magnificent view of the heavily wooded Greensand Ridge with the white mansion of Linton Park, former home of the Cornwallis family, standing out among the trees. The narrow ridge rising steeply from the flat plain of the Beult and the Teise can be seen to the right of the tour route as it heads towards Collier Street. (Just off the route at Chainhurst is REED COURT FARM, with a choice of two walks round a mixed Wealden farm, open from April to October).

From Collier Street, the tour continues by the B2162 to *Yalding in the midst of mile upon mile of hopgardens, where the Beult and the Teise flow into the Medway. The view from the 13th-century church tower is worth seeing. Continuing northwards on the B2010 via the longest medieval bridge in Kent, the country tour route climbs up through the woods and orchards of the Greensand Ridge to West Farleigh. The village has some good pubs, including the Chequers, and commanding views across the fertile Medway plain to the hills of the High Weald in the distance. A short drive down the steep valley slope on B2163 brings us back to our starting point at Teston bridge.

EAST KENT COUNTRY TOUR

The North Downs south of *Canterbury, with steep, heavily wooded 'scarp' topped by open chalk grasslands where wildlife flourishes undisturbed by traffic, is circled by this 50-mile route, signposted in an anti-clockwise direction by a distinctive white tree symbol on a brown background. Other brown and white signs along the route point the way to historic buildings, vineyards, gardens and various other attractions. The tour takes us through unspoiled countryside to many charming old villages and hamlets. For detailed information on places marked thus * consult the Gazetteer section of this guidebook.

The tour may be joined at any point, but this guide begins at the hilltop village of *Chilham just off the A252 Maidstone road. There are car parks at each approach to the village, which clusters round a square between the church and the gates of CHILHAM CASTLE, where jousting displays are given in summer. The extensive grounds include a heronry and according to legend if the herons haven't returned to Chilham by St Valentine's Day each year, the owner of the estate will suffer a terrible fate. Thus far, they always have! From Chilham the country tour heads northwards off the A252 past the hamlet of *Old Wives Lees and through orchards towards Selling. Half-timbered Rhode Court lies to the left of the road and behind it is PERRY WOOD, a lovely place for walking and picnics. The Pulpit is the local name for a mound which surveys the surrounding countryside. St Mary's Church in Selling is noted for its wall paintings and stained glass. After turning left on to the A251 Ashford road at Sheldwich, just south of *Faversham, the tour heads southwards through open pastures by way of *Badlesmere, crossing the A252 at Challock, and proceeding through KING'S WOOD. This substantial survival of ancient woodland fringing the North Downs scarp is now under the control of the Forestry Commission who have laid out a variety of trails and provided car parking.

Emerging from the woods just north of *Ashford, the tour shadows the stone wall of EASTWELL PARK which Daniel Defoe, on his *Tour through the Whole Island of Great Britain* in 1724, thought the finest he had seen. The manor is now a hotel and the park is private but a slight detour further along the A251 will bring you to its neo-Jacobean gatehouse. (If the detour is continued through narrow country lanes, you will see the ruined Eastwell Church at the edge of a lake and the unnamed tomb of Richard III's illegitimate son, the last of the Plantagenet line, who is said to have ended his days as a workman on this estate.)

The East Kent country tour heads eastwards from Boughton Lees past the Flying Horse Inn on the village green and crossing the A28 Roman road at Kempe's Corner, named thus for Archbishop Kempe who was born in this part of Kent in the 15th century and built the church and college at *Wye, approached by a medieval stone bridge over the Great Stour. There are wide views over the Stour valley and beside the bridge is a mid-Georgian mill house. Wye has many fine old buildings such as the timber-framed Yew Trees in Scotton Street which dates from 1600, attractive shops, tearooms, restaurants and pubs. Continuing east, a white crown can be seen on the hillside to the left. It was carved out of the chalk by the students of the Agricultural College to mark the coronation of King Edward VII in 1902. The road climbs steeply to the nature reserve of WYE DOWNS, where there is limited parking and wonderful views. A few miles further on, the tour route turns south

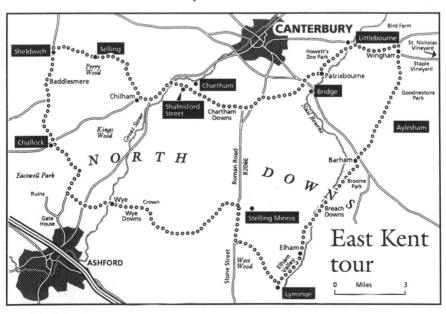

169

on to STONE STREET, the Roman road (B2068) running arrow-straight for most of its length from Canterbury to Lympne. (A slight detour at this point will bring you to Stelling Minnis where there is a smock windmill of tarred weather-boarding that was in use from 1866 to 1970. It is now open to visitors on Sundays and bank holiday Monday afternoons from April to September, but you are advised to leave your car in the village and walk down the rough track to the wind-mill.)

After following Stone Street for 1½ miles or so, the tour turns off to the left through WEST WOOD, where there is a car park and forest walks. North of Lyminge at Yew-tree Cross, the route swings north to follow the beautiful Elham Valley down which flows the Nail Bourne River. *Elham is an historic market town with a church that is worth visiting and several old inns, notably the Abbot's Fireside where there are spit roasts on Wednesday and Friday evenings. The tour passes ELHAM VALLEY VINEYARDS (open to visitors daily between June and October, closed Mondays except bank holidays), before crossing the A2 Dover road near *Barham. The former country estate of Lord Kitchener at BROOME PARK (a short detour towards Dover along the A2) is now a timeshare development with an 18-hole golf course. The country tour continues northwards from the A2 on the B2046 passing close to Aylesham, built in the 1920s for the miners from the now defunct Snowdown Colliery. Betteshanger,

the most southerly coalmine in Britain, was closed in 1989. Signs point the way to GOODNE-STONE PARK, named for Earl Godwin, the father of King Harold. Jane Austen was a visitor here on her circuit of the Georgian 'county set' which she immortalised in her writing. The walled garden with spectacular rose beds is open at various times in spring and summer.

The B2046 carries the tour on to *Wingham, whose green church spire can be seen from afar. It's worth pausing here, leaving the car in the convenient car park and exploring the High Street lined with copper beeches, Spanish chestnuts and other specimen trees. STAPLE VINEYARD is sign-posted from the tour route and lies 1½ miles eastwards. The BIRD FARM and ST NICHOLAS VINEYARD at Ash are along the A257 Sand-wich road. The tour route heads in the opposite direction towards Canterbury through orchards and hopgardens before meeting up with the River Nail Bourne again at Littlebourne. The route turns left off the A257 by a group of oast houses, heading for HOWLETT's ZOO PARK, which has an amazing collection of free-roaming exotic animals and is open every day of the year except Christmas Day. The car park is to the left of the road with the entrance on the other side, so take care when crossing between the two. Continuing through orchard country, under a viaduct carrying the railway between Canterbury and Dover, the country tour turns right at the next mini-roundabout. *Patrix-bourne, with its late Norman church and unusual Swiss glass, is to the left of the roundabout on the old Roman route of Watling Street. Our tour route crosses the main A2 trunk road, bypassing the village of Bridge on a winding country road through wooded hills, orchards and hopgardens dotted with oast-houses and meeting up again with a short stretch of the B2068, before crossing CHARTHAM DOWNS south of Canterbury. The views across the Great Stour valley as we drive down into Shalmsford Street are quite magnificent. Crossing the river and turning left on to the A28, the tour continues along the Stour valley for less than a mile before taking the right-hand fork on the A252 to Chilham, our starting point.

METRIC CONVERSION TABLES

km	miles	km	miles	km	miles
1	0.62	8	4.97	40	24.86
2	1.24	9	5.59	50	31.07
3	1.86	10	6.21	60	37.28
4	2.48	15	9.32	70	43.50
5	3.11	20	12.43	80	49.71
6	3.73	25	15.53	90	55.93
7	4.35	30	18.64	100	62.14

m	ft	m	ft	m	ft
100	328	600	1968	1500	4921
200	656	700	2296	2000	6562
300	984	800	2625	2500	8202
400	1313	900	2953	3000	9842
500	1640	1000	3281	3500	11483

ha	acres	ha	acres	ha	acres
1	2.5	10	25	100	247
2	5	25	62	150	370
5	12	50	124	200	494

kg	lbs	kg	lbs
1	2.2	6	13.2
2	4.4	7	15.4
3	6.6	8	17.6
4	8.8	9	19.8
5	11.0	10	22.0

°C	°F	°C	°F	°C	°F
0	32	12	54	24	75
2	36	14	57	26	79
4	39	16	61	28	82
6	43	18	64	30	86
8	46	20	68	32	90
10	50	22	72	34	93

INDEX